Get the eBook FREE!

(PDF, ePub, Kindle, and liveBook all included)

We believe that once you buy a book from us, you should be able to read it in any format we have available. To get electronic versions of this book at no additional cost to you, purchase and then register this book at the Manning website.

Go to https://www.manning.com/freebook and follow the instructions to complete your eBook registration.

That's it!
Thanks from Manning!

Grokking Data Structures

Grokking

Data Structures

Marcello La Rocca

Foreword by Daniel Zingaro

MANNING
SHELTER ISLAND

Manning Publications Co.
20 Baldwin Road
Shelter Island, NY 11964

Development editor: Marina Michaels
Technical editor: Beau Carnes
Review editor: Dunja Nikitovic
Production editor: Keri Hales
Copy editor: Lana Todorovic-Arndt
Proofreader: Mike Beady
Technical proofreader: German Gonzalez-Morris
Typesetter: Dennis Dalinnik
Cover designer: Leslie Haimes

ISBN: 9781633436992
Printed in the United States of America

Good programmers worry about data structures and their relationships.

—Linus Torvalds

brief contents

contents

foreword

Programmers today can work at higher levels of productivity than ever before, relying on higher-level programming languages, higher-level libraries and tools, and generative AI. And you know what? I love that. It's important that we branch out as a community and make the affordances of programming available to more people. If some super-sophisticated deep-learning Python library can help people who otherwise couldn't use AI responsibly, then I'm all in.

At the same time, though, I still think many people need to know the fundamental data structures and algorithms that have underpinned computing for the past 60 years and will continue to do so for many more. It seemingly doesn't matter what task I'm doing: fundamental questions about how to organize my data for efficiency always seem to crop up. Why is my code so slow here? Should I be using a linked list here instead of an array? Hash tables are supposed to be fast—what the heck's going wrong with mine right now?

The best part is that you can learn this stuff just once (it's not changing any time soon) and then apply it to all your future programming projects or programming interviews.

Learning data structures is as critical as learning algorithms. As Marcello La Rocca demonstrates in chapter 1, data structures and algorithms are so closely entwined that it makes most sense to learn them together. In this book, you'll learn about both the most important data structures and the algorithms that work on them. (If you want a companion book fully dedicated to algorithms, and you're vibing with the Grokking style, I encourage you to check out Aditya Bhargava's *Grokking Algorithms* as well.)

I worked as Marcello's acquisitions editor for the book, and we had many discussions during the book-writing process. I can personally attest to Marcello's deep care and respect for learners and the material he is teaching them. I congratulate Marcello on expertly presenting data structures in the distinctive, example-driven, and graphically rich Grokking style.

I'd also like to highlight Marcello's commitment to *really* teaching these data structures. You'll see in the table of contents that there are three chapters on arrays. You may be wondering, "Seriously, three? Aren't arrays simple?" Well, for a "simple" data structure, there's actually a lot going on under the hood; Marcello has the patience and teaching prowess to be able to carefully present these details in a way accessible to many.

I applaud you for dedicating yourself to learning elements of the bedrock of computing—for taking time away from the latest and greatest "in" thing to equip yourself with knowledge that you'll apply again and again. Happy Grokking!

—Daniel Zingaro, PhD

preface

Back in 2016, I was a regular contributor to tech blogs, mostly writing about JavaScript and its frameworks. I enjoyed it, and it helped me gain an even deeper understanding of the language, which I was using daily in my work at Twitter. But, at some point, I asked myself if that was the topic I really wanted to cover. It was kind of a rhetorical question because, since my sophomore year of college, I knew that the topics that would make me tick were algorithms, data structures, and optimization.

This was the beginning of a five-year journey that led to the publication of my first book, *Advanced Algorithms and Data Structures* (Manning, 2021).

In the spring of 2023, I wasn't planning to write another book anytime soon. Then, the opportunity to work on *Grokking Data Structures* came up when I had more free time than usual—almost serendipitously.

I could see the challenge ahead, but I was enthusiastic to take it on and decided to focus on the draft of *Grokking Data Structures* for the next six months. It was not easy, because this book is profoundly different from *Advanced Algorithms and Data Structures*. While the latter is a deep dive into advanced topics, the goal of every book in the Grokking series is to make concepts, no matter how complex, easy to understand at their root for the widest possible audience. This meant that I had to pivot my approach and focus on different things.

The first challenge was to create a path through the book that would guide readers and keep their interest high. I decided to start by building some core knowledge about arrays and linked lists, spend some time delving into these topics, and then build more complex data structures around them.

What I have tried to do throughout the book is to show each data structure from different angles: its theory, of course, to understand how it works, but also how it can be used in practice, and how it can make your life easier or your code more robust. I also explain why we need each data structure and why we should prefer one over the other if we have a choice between more than one.

The format of the books in the Grokking series is also unique, and I embraced that unique-ness, especially when it came to providing a story for each chapter that readers can relate to and empathize with, and to illustrations, which are used more than in regular books.

Writing a book, like many tasks, is often about finding the right balance between many different aspects. I chose to focus on explaining each data structure properly and clearly, giv-ing you a solid foundation in each structure. I hope this approach will help you familiarize yourself with data structures, or if you are already familiar with this amazing topic, perhaps deepen your understanding and discover something new about them. And, more impor-tantly, I hope this book can inspire you and make you passionate about data structures and algorithms the way I was inspired by some of the classic books on the subject.

acknowledgments

This book is the result of the combined efforts of many people. It was truly a team job, so I have a long list of people I'd like to thank.

First, I'd like to thank Daniel Zingaro, the acquisitions editor. Dan is the reason I wrote this book. He was there every step of the way: helping, guiding, reviewing, and planning. The table of contents and chapter structure are the result of many meetings between the two of us. He was always available when I needed help, going above and beyond his role to make things smoother for me. Working with him was truly inspiring and a pleasure. In short, I couldn't have done this without Dan's help.

Thanks also go to Marina Michaels, my development editor, whose contribution was also huge and essential in improving the manuscript and organizing the whole process. Thank you for your patience and for making this book much better with your guidance and feedback.

Thanks to Beau Carnes, software developer and teacher with freeCodeCamp.org, who is the book's technical editor: your feedback was always great and insightful. And thanks to German Gonzalez-Morris, my technical proofreader, for patiently catching bugs and inconsistencies.

I'd also like to thank all the behind-the-scenes staff at Manning who made the publication of this book possible. In addition, a huge thanks to the reviewers: Ganesh Falak, Ganesh Swaminathan, Jonathan Camara, Jonathan Womack, Kollin Trujillo, Maxim Volgin, Najeeb Arif, Navjot Singh, Pablo Herrera J., Patrick Regan, Poorvi Shetty, Rahul Kavale, Ritobrata Ghosh, Romell Ian De La Cruz, Sally Tsung, Sasha Sankova, Simone De Bonis, Simone Sguazza, Sören Schellhoff, Tam Thanh Nguyen, Tatiana Komaristaia, Weronika Burman, William Jamir Silva, and Yilun Zhang. All your suggestions helped make this a better book.

On a different note, I'd like to thank those who supported me in this adventure. From the beginning, Manning's goal (and mine) was to get this book to the readers within a year, which meant that I had to really focus on working on the manuscript, taking time away from my personal life and my incredibly understanding and supportive loved ones and friends.

As always, I'd like to give special recognition to the people who have allowed me to become the person and scientist I am today. This includes, of course, my college and high school professors: I was lucky to have a good education in the Italian education system, which is based on the right to education, and my alma mater, the University of Catania, which offered a world-class computer science curriculum. My hope is that this educational system will continue to be improved in the future. I hope that education will become fairer and more equitable on a global level to guarantee the best possible education to children, regardless of their nationality and personal means.

Most of all, I would like to thank my mother for supporting me in my studies at the cost of many personal sacrifices, and for always encouraging me to dream big. She shares some of the credit for all the good parts of this book, because without her support, I wouldn't have this career.

Who should read this book?

This book is for beginners: if you're a student, recent graduate, or junior programmer who wants to learn more about data structures, you may find the approach of this book interesting. Topics cover beginner and (some) intermediate data structures; I don't get into mathematical details or proofs—there is almost no math in this book.

The book discusses the core data structures you need to understand before learning advanced algorithms and data structures. We'll see the key ideas behind them and understand how they work and how you can use them in your daily work.

The book may be the perfect choice if these concepts are new to you, if you'd like a refresher on ideas you learned in school, if you want to prepare for a coding interview, or if you just want to improve the quality and performance of your code.

For more advanced or a deeper discussion of this subject (perhaps after reading this book), check out my other book, *Advanced Algorithms and Data Structures* (Manning, 2021).

How this book is organized: A road map

This book is divided into 13 chapters. Most chapters focus on a single data structure. If you are approaching this topic for the first time, or as a complete beginner, read the chapters in order. Each chapter builds on top of the previous ones and, for instance, the deeper understanding of arrays you get in chapters 2 and 3, or the basics of asymptotic analysis in chapter 4, will help you make sense of the more complex data structures in the chapters that follow.

After reading the book for the first time, you can use it as a reference and go straight to the data structure or topic you need to brush up on. The same applies if you are approaching this book as an intermediate or advanced reader—it's still worthwhile to skim through the chapters in their proper order at least once.

Let's go through each chapter in detail:

- Chapter 1 is a gentle introduction to data structures, discussing when, how, and why you can have an advantage by questioning what data structures you use.

- Chapter 2 introduces arrays, showing how they work and the typical operations they support. In this chapter, we focus on statically sized arrays.

- Chapter 3 discusses sorted arrays, how to take advantage of their benefits, and how to deal with their drawbacks. You'll learn about binary search and get an idea for why it works better than linear search.

- Chapter 4 introduces big-O notation and asymptotic analysis and explains how we can use them to compare the performance of arbitrary algorithms on a given problem. We then use these notions to formally show that binary search has a real advantage over linear search.

- Chapter 5 closes the loop on arrays by describing how we can create the illusion of dynamically sized arrays without sacrificing their ability to scale.

- Chapter 6 discusses linked lists, which can be used in place of arrays to store data sequentially. Throughout the chapter, we compare linked lists to arrays and use what we learned in chapter 4 to understand when we have an advantage in using one over the other.

- Chapter 7 clarifies the difference between data structures, abstract data types, and implementations. The theory is then applied to concrete examples. It then introduces the class of containers and the bag, a simple container.

- Chapter 8 presents the stack, a container that implements the LIFO policy. It explains how it works and how it can be implemented. It also shows some practical applications of stacks.

- Chapter 9 presents the queue, a container that implements the FIFO policy, and shows how it differs from stacks. It discusses various implementations with both arrays (linear and circular queues) and linked lists.

- Chapter 10 generalizes the concept of queues with priority queues. It explains the concept of priority, the API of the abstract data type, and then introduces the binary heap, the most common implementation of priority queues.

- Chapter 11 is the first chapter to go beyond containers. It discusses trees, a class of data structures, and focuses on binary search trees, a data structure that can provide a good balance for the performance of all the basic operations (insert, delete, search).

- Chapter 12 introduces the dictionary abstract data type and discusses how it can be implemented with the data structures presented in the previous chapters. It then introduces hash tables, explaining how they work and why they are better suited for implementing dictionaries.

- Chapter 13 concludes this book by introducing a pivotal data structure—graphs. After defining what a graph is and presenting its basic properties, the chapter discusses two possible implementation strategies for graphs and finally examines the BFS and DFS search algorithms.

Most chapters contain exercises for you to solve. Sometimes they ask you to implement a variant of what I have discussed in that chapter; other times, they are more abstract and open-ended questions. Both types of exercises are good opportunities to self-check your understanding of the topic, so I encourage you to spend at least a few minutes trying to solve them. Although you won't find the solutions to the exercises in the book, I've added discussions and hints for the exercises in the book's repo on GitHub.

About the code

The first difficult decision I had to make was the programming language to be used for coding. In my previous book on data structures, I decided to use pseudocode for code snippets and provide accompanying code in several languages. The idea was to avoid tying the book to a single language to emphasize that algorithms are at a higher level than implementations and are independent of programming languages.

This choice had some disadvantages. In particular, testing pseudocode was hard and error prone, and for readers, a pseudocode language might be as much of a hurdle to learn as a new programming language. Or maybe even more.

So for this book, I decided to use Python instead. Why?

Python is one of the most widely used programming languages. It's used to teach students in universities and bootcamps, so the probability that readers, and especially beginners, already know some Python was higher.

In addition, Python is loosely typed and has a simple syntax with minimal redundancy, which makes it more concise than other statically typed languages—an important feature when you have limited space, such as on a book page.

Python is easy to use as both an imperative and an object-oriented language, and it's great for rapid prototyping—a characteristic made even more convenient by great tools such as

Jupyter notebooks. Finally, there is a consolidated and broad ecosystem of libraries available for Python, covering data structures, machine learning, visualization, and many other areas, even quantum computing.

An object-oriented approach

Although Python allows for an imperative approach to programming, with global functions taking the data to be operated on as an argument, I mostly used object-oriented programming (OOP) throughout this book.

While OOP can be less concise and add a bit of complexity compared to the imperative paradigm, there are some key advantages to using OOP:

- *Abstraction*—OOP allows us to abstract complex systems into simpler, more manageable objects.

- *Encapsulation*—OOP hides internal implementation details and exposes only necessary interfaces through encapsulation. This provides a clear separation between the internal workings of an object and its external use.

- *Modularity and reusability*—As a direct result of encapsulating data and behavior within objects, OOP promotes modular design, which enables code reusability by allowing objects to be easily reused in different parts of the program or other projects.

- *Code maintenance and scalability*—Both are improved with OOP.

These are just a few examples of the advantages we get from OOP. OOP is not perfect, and it doesn't solve all our problems. You may prefer or be used to other alternative and successful approaches. Some of them are not mutually exclusive or incompatible with OOP; for example, it's possible to integrate many ideas from functional programming (FP) into OOP. And that's exactly what I do here.

Scala is maybe the best example of a language where these two approaches coexist and complement each other. Python is not a purely FP language, but it supports some FP concepts, and it's versatile enough to allow different programming styles.

Tests, style, and simplifications

Writing a book requires tradeoffs. For starters, readers today have limited time, so authors must choose wisely what to include in their book. But there is more—to explain concepts clearly, an author must sometimes focus on what's important and avoid getting lost in detail, even if that means oversimplifying.

Because I wanted to make the code as clear as possible for the reader, I provided the simplest possible working version of the data structures in this book. I left out details such as performance optimization, memory loitering, or thread safety. These are important details in real applications, of course, but delving into these problems would distract the reader from the key topic—how data structures work.

The code in the book also doesn't have type hints. You can find these instead in the version hosted on GitHub. I did this to reduce code clutter and avoid additional cognitive load for beginners who may not be familiar with type hints in Python.

I can't stress the importance of tests enough. Testing your code is critical for many reasons. Although testing can't guarantee bug-free code, tests with a high coverage ratio definitely help your present and future self. In the present, they help you find existing bugs and double-check the requirements and logic of your program. In the future, they will help you and your team maintain the code, and if you happen to refactor your code, they can alert you if you accidentally break something.

All the code in this book has been thoroughly tested. Tests are often more verbose and longer than code; a 3:1 ratio for the number of lines is not uncommon. Although you won't find tests in the book, they are available in the GitHub repository.

Finally, this book contains many examples of source code both in numbered listings and in line with normal text. In both cases, source code is formatted in a `fixed-width font like this` to separate it from ordinary text.

In many cases, the original source code has been reformatted; we've added line breaks and reworked indentation to accommodate the available page space in the book. In rare cases, even this was not enough, and listings include line-continuation markers (➥). Additionally, comments in the source code have often been removed from the listings when the code is described in the text. Code annotations accompany many of the listings, highlighting important concepts.

You can get executable snippets of code from the liveBook (online) version of this book at https://livebook.manning.com/book/grokking-data-structures. The complete code for the examples in the book is available for download from the Manning website at https://www.manning.com/books/grokking-data-structures, and from GitHub at https://github.com/mlarocca/grokking_data_structures.

liveBook discussion forum

Purchase of *Grokking Data Structures* includes free access to liveBook, Manning's online reading platform. Using liveBook's exclusive discussion features, you can attach comments to the book globally or to specific sections or paragraphs. It's a snap to make notes for yourself, ask and answer technical questions, and receive help from the author and other users. To access the forum, go to https://livebook.manning.com/book/grokking-data-structures/discussion. You can also learn more about Manning's forums and the rules of conduct at https://livebook.manning.com/discussion.

Manning's commitment to our readers is to provide a venue where a meaningful dialogue between individual readers and between readers and the author can take place. It is not a commitment to any specific amount of participation on the part of the author, whose contribution to the forum remains voluntary (and unpaid). We suggest you try asking the author some challenging questions lest his interest stray! The forum and the archives of previous discussions will be accessible from the publisher's website as long as the book is in print.

Other online resources

You can find the full Python code presented in this book and the tests for the code in the book's GitHub repository: https://github.com/mlarocca/grokking_data_structures.

We are also working on adding implementations in other programming languages like C# and Java as well, so check the repo out from time to time.

about the author

Marcello La Rocca is a research scientist and software engineer. As a principal software engineer, he has contributed to the development of large-scale web applications and machine-learning infrastructure at companies such as Twitter, Microsoft, and Apple. Marcello has also worked on applied research in both academia and industry. His work and interests focus on graphs, optimization algorithms, genetic algorithms, and machine learning. He developed the Neatsort adaptive sorting algorithm (NeatSort—A practical adaptive algorithm, M. La Rocca and D. Cantone, 2014, https://mng.bz/aEMx).

In this chapter

- welcome to this book

- what are data structures

- why do you need data structures

- examples of data structures making a difference

- step-by-step guidelines to apply data structures
  in a project

Data structures make the world go round: information is the gold of the Internet Age, and data structures are necessary for handling and making sense of information. Data structures allow us to shape data in meaningful ways and query it to find what is relevant to us.

Welcome to Grokking Data Structures

Welcome to *Grokking Data Structures*! I'm super excited to accompany you on this journey through data structures.

In this book, I want to dispel some misconceptions about data structures: they are extremely useful in your everyday work. Even if you are not a researcher, they do make a difference, and they are not hard to learn: you do not need to be a math expert to understand and use data structures!

During our journey, I will show you that data structures are not boring theoretical stuff. They have become part of our lives so much that I can claim you certainly use them regularly without even realizing it. Besides coding, you have used or seen in action some of the data structures we will describe in normal life situations.

Data structures are everywhere

You don't believe me? We could make it interesting with a little bet, but that would be so unfair of me!

Let's see. Do you ever go to a grocery or department store? When you go shopping, you fill your physical cart with items you want to buy: there it is, a *container*. But which container in particular? I don't want to spoil it for you, but you'll be able to tell after reading this book.

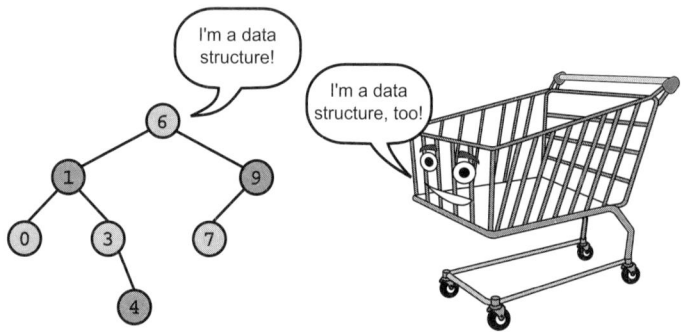

Once you find everything you need, you go to the cashier to pay. While you wait your turn, you are literally in another data structure, a *queue*!

Did I manage to convince you? If you are a software developer, convincing you will be even easier because if you write code, you must have used at least arrays. Not to mention that, of course, if you are reading a digital version of this book, your e-reader uses many data structures to hold pages of the book, its words, the bookmarks you might add, and so on.

Data structures are for everyone

This book teaches data structures to anyone, regardless of their background. You don't need advanced math; you don't need to have taken CS101 or any other course; you don't need to be a coding ninja, although some knowledge of Python might help. This book, like every book in the Grokking series, will provide you with an understanding of how things work, explaining what a data structure is, what the basic structures are, and how you can objectively decide which data structure is better for your task. It's a book for beginners, meaning that it assumes no previous knowledge, and it relies on your intuition and visual memory. However, even if you are familiar with the subject, you might find it useful to brush up on your skills and get an even deeper understanding of some of the topics.

What are data structures?

If you are reading this book, you are probably aware that we live in the so-called Age of Data, an era in which data has become an integral part of our lives. We are flooded with information, the production of which is accelerating at an unprecedented, exponential rate, fueled by technological advances. This stream of data is changing the way we live, work, and interact.

To make sense of this huge amount of information and avoid being overwhelmed, we need to organize it somehow. That's where data structures come in.

Data structures are a way of organizing and storing information in a computer or a program. They help to efficiently manage and manipulate data.

For example, if you want to find out whether a friend from school is on Facebook, you can. This is only possible because there is a data structure that organizes users in a way that makes it easy and fast to search among a billion users.

Algorithms and data structures

You often hear the term *data structures* used in conjunction with *algorithms*. In fact, you hear the term so often that you might ask whether they are the same thing. No, algorithms and data structures are not the same, although they are closely related.

An algorithm is a set of well-defined instructions, a step-by-step procedure designed to solve a specific problem or perform a particular task. In our Facebook example, we use an algorithm that searches through all the users' names and returns the most promising matches.

A data structure is a way of organizing and storing data in a computer or a programming language. It defines the relationship between the data elements, the operations that can be performed, and the rules or constraints for accessing and modifying the data. Facebook users are stored in a database that organizes its data in a way that makes it efficient to search for users by name.

> **NOTE** Algorithms are used to describe the operations performed on data structures. To use an analogy, data structures are like nouns, while algorithms are more like verbs.

Data structures and algorithms are interdependent, just like a meaningful sentence in English requires subjects, objects, and verbs to describe an action.

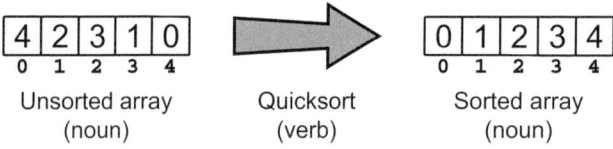

Algorithms transforming data like verbs acting on nouns

Data structures provide the organization and representation of information (the data), and algorithms serve as instructions for transforming that data. Each data structure implicitly defines algorithms for operations, such as adding, retrieving, and removing its elements.

Some data structures are specifically designed to allow the efficient execution of certain algorithms, such as hash tables for key-based search. (Don't worry if you don't know these terms at this point: they'll all be covered later in the book.)

Thus, describing a data structure requires accurately explaining the algorithms behind its methods. In other words, in this book, you will learn about many algorithms.

Why should I care about data structures?

Data structures are the building blocks of computer science. They are important because they help organize data, solve difficult problems, improve efficiency, optimize memory usage, and avoid security risks. They are essential tools for effectively managing and manipulating information in computer programs.

Recently, new trends in computer science that take advantage of data structures have emerged, such as graph neural networks, an even more powerful version of the machine-learning building blocks that power deep-learning models.

The database landscape is also evolving, and the concept of *flexible indexing* has recently been introduced. This is an indexing model based on data structures that can be nested in any combination and at any depth. It is an extremely powerful tool, and you can only harness this power if you master data structures.

However, I can give you an even more powerful reason: learning about data structures can make you a better software developer. Knowing about data structures and algorithms is like adding a tool to your tool belt.

Have you ever heard of Maslow's hammer, also known as the law of the instrument? It states that if your tool belt only has a hammer, you will be tempted to treat everything as a nail.

It's an observation that people tend to apply what they know to all sorts of different situations, even when it's not appropriate.

With data structures, if you only know how to use the data structure called a *hash table*, you'll be tempted to use it in every situation, even when you need to efficiently perform operations such as *next* and *previous* and would be better off using a *tree*.

Don't worry if the previous example sounds obscure and not obvious right now or if you don't know some of the terms used there: it's a good reason to keep reading because we will cover this topic later in the book.

This book gives you more tools to use when approaching a problem such as this one and trains you to recognize opportunities to use these tools to improve your code.

A hammer is unlikely to help if you need to tighten a bolt.

When do I need data structures?

In theory, you need data structures when you must organize your data in a way that makes it easy and efficient to store and retrieve it according to some special rules. That's a very formal definition, and despite being formally correct, it feels somehow far away from our daily routine, from the world as we make sense of it.

Let's see some examples of data structures in action to give you a better idea.

Searching like a pro

Tom has a large collection of items—imagine thousands of baseball cards or, on a larger scale, millions of products on his e-commerce site. These items have attributes, some of which (such as a name) uniquely identify the items.

How should Tom search that collection? For example, how would he search for Joe Di Maggio's card among all his cards?

He could, of course, go through them one by one until he finds the card he was looking for. If you like collecting cards as much as I do, you know that when you have thousands of them, searching for a specific card could take a long time. Imagine how long it would take to search for a product in an online catalog with millions of items!

Tom needs a better way to store and search for items, and to learn about the tradeoffs that are required to balance different needs. This book offers a few different options for search-efficient data structures and can help you find the right one for your needs. So, how about starting with sorted arrays and binary search?

So many users!

Let me describe another scenario. For Kat's web application, she needs to keep track of logged-in users and their IPs.

First, she implements IP tracking by herself. Locally, it works fine. But when she deploys her changes to production, the data structure she has used is too slow to support the amount of traffic on her web application, so it crashes the application server.

Then, considering how urgent fixing the problem has become, Kat out-sources the solution to a consulting firm, hoping they know better. Their solution is indeed fast. It even works well in production...until it doesn't. It turns out that a hacker has figured out that, with the right sequence of calls, they can overload the data structure the external company used and crash Kat's application again at will.

What happened here? The first time, performance was the problem because the wrong data structure was used, and it was too slow to operate at scale.

The second time, a better option was chosen. Unfortunately, the new solution was used carelessly, leaving a vulnerability to an adversary sequence (a sequence of inputs chosen ad hoc to cause problems to the data structure). This vulnerability, in turn, allowed a *denial of service* (DoS) attack. In such a scenario, a hacker can use a vulnerability to make an application so slow that its legitimate users won't be able to interact with it. Is there any hope? We will see that hash tables, if used properly, could solve most of Kat's problems. When talking about hash tables, we will learn more about the problem that made the DoS attack possible, how to fix it, and, more importantly, what to look for: even if you buy a finished product from a third party, you need to know what questions to ask, to make sure they did everything right.

Modeling relationships

Sandra is launching the next generation of social networks that will change the way we connect. Well, at least that's her dream. She is still implementing a minimum viable product and hoping to get some funding.

She is making good progress, but she has hit a bit of a roadblock when it comes to tracking the relationship between users. She wants to try something like a spreadsheet or a tabular structure, but she is not sure how to store it or implement queries about "friends of friends" relationships.

Sandra tries a naive solution by iterating through the entire list of users several times, but this somehow makes her application unresponsive, and she becomes very frustrated.

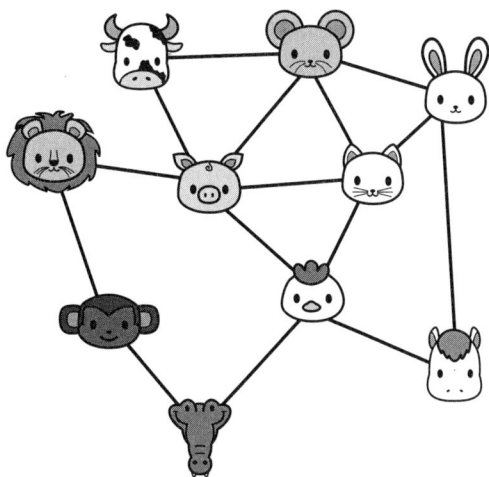

Sandra has only tried to do this in memory: What if she needs to add persistence to this data? And what if she later needs to find even more distant relationships such as "friend of a friend of a friend" or the six degrees of Kevin Bacon? Unfortunately, an SQL database doesn't seem to support everything she needs.

Later in this book, you'll learn that graphs would help Sandra tame highly relational data and that she could use the breadth-first search algorithms to explore indirect friend relationships. With graphs come graph databases, a different way of storing highly relational data that allows us to quickly run queries based on the relationships between different pieces of data.

Will I ever write code for these data structures?

Except for positions that involve some research, most software engineering positions won't require you to write your own algorithms or data structures on a daily or weekly basis. Most of the time, you'll just be using someone else's code. Yet, even then, studying data structures will help you make the right choices or be aware of the better solutions.

There are still certain situations in which you may need to roll up your sleeves and write your own implementation—for example, if you're using a brand-new programming language for which there aren't many libraries available or need to customize a data structure to solve a special case.

But regardless, even if you never have to write your own implementation, only firsthand knowledge of data structures will give you a better understanding of the tradeoffs you are making in your code and how to make your code more efficient.

How should I choose a data structure?

From the examples in the previous section, it's clear that choosing your data structures wisely is important. A less obvious point is that it's not about choosing the perfect data structure. You don't always have to choose the best possible one; most of the time, you can get away with a near-optimal alternative. But what's fundamental is avoiding the wrong choice, which would be a data structure that would crash your application or cause a security problem.

The most important thing I hope you take away from this book is a method for evaluating and choosing which data structure to use in any given context.

How do you do that? The ability to choose the right data structure is like a muscle that you need to train. Throughout the book, we'll build your knowledge and intuition by showing you the dangers you might face, how to systematically identify them by evaluating the complexity of algorithms, what aspects to balance, and what tradeoffs to consider.

How do we use data structures in a project?

At this point, you have an idea of what is in this book and why it is important. The next step is to understand how you can use what you learn here in your daily work.

Data structures and algorithms are not a technology, so it's hard to even imagine a manual on how to use them. They are used everywhere; most of the time, you use them without even realizing it.

The point is not how to add data structures to your code because, one way or another, you are already using them. Rather, it's about developing a process that will allow you to make conscious, informed choices about the data structures you use and expanding your knowledge of data structures so that when you face a problem, you remember the possible alternatives.

A mental model for applying data structures

As mentioned, it's not easy to distill an expert's experience and knowledge of data structures and algorithms into a step-by-step process. Perhaps it can be considered as part science and part art, with tacit knowledge built up through experience making the difference. It's a challenge, but I believe it's possible to extract some guidelines that can assist you and raise the level of your coding.

At a high level, the process of going from a problem to a solution using algorithms and data structures can be described in a few steps, illustrated in the following figure.

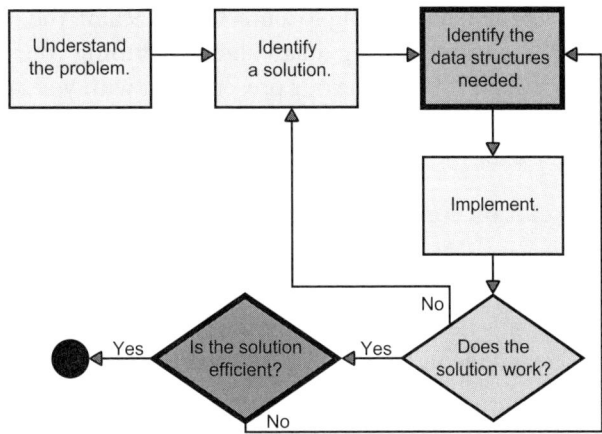

The steps are as follows:

1. Understand the problem you are solving.

2. Sketch out a possible solution.

3. Identify the data structures you need.

4. Implement a solution.

5. Check whether the solution works; if not, iterate.

6. Check whether the solution is good (efficient) enough; if not, iterate.

The key parts for us are steps 3 and 6:

- We think about the data structures we can use in our solution (step 3).

- We evaluate whether our (working) solution is too slow, uses too much memory, or breaks our requirements in any other way (step 6).

The implementation step is also relevant if we are implementing the data structures from scratch. In that case, we must also thoroughly test the code of the data structure for correctness and performance. But implementation is not our focus here: for simplicity, we will assume that there is a third-party library that we can use.

Identify what data structures are needed

So, assuming you've understood the requirements of your problem (a step that should not be neglected!) and sketched out a solution that you think you might work on, now it's time to think about what you need to build that solution. This is where you go from a high-level idea of what you need to solve a problem to a more concrete plan that includes what you will use to solve it.

For example, if your problem is getting to a meeting by 9 a.m. the next morning, your high-level solution might include setting up an alarm, planning your trip from home to the meeting, and making sure you have your presentation with you. Your next step is to identify the tools you can use: your phone to set the alarm, a bus or your car to get to the meeting, and your laptop for the presentation.

Check whether your solution is good enough

Identifying a possible way to solve your problem may not be enough. You also need to be able to solve it in a reasonable amount of time with the resources you have available. For an e-commerce website, it's not acceptable to take 10 minutes (or 1 minute!) to return your search results. For a video game, it's not acceptable to have requirements beyond home computers.

Then again, you don't want to overengineer, or overbuild, your application. You don't need a supercomputer to run your school's website, just like you don't need an overly complicated data structure for something that can be solved efficiently with an array. To avoid premature optimization, you'll usually want to start small and try more complicated data structures only if you already know, or find out in this step, that you have a bottleneck.

What about tests?

Looking at the flow we previously sketched, you might be concerned and remark that testing your code, cleaning it up, and making sure that, for example, variable and method names are not confusing are all important phases of software development. You'd be right—they certainly are. These phases are not included here because we are looking at the process at a high level and focusing on an abstract solution, leaving out the implementation details.

Data structures in action

Now that you are familiar with the steps you can take to include data structures in a project, let's look at an example to make the flow clearer and to illustrate the importance of selecting the most appropriate data structure.

Our scenario is an emergency room for pets. In this scenario, our little furry (and talking!) friends come to see the doctors, waiting for their turn in the lobby until they are admitted. We must triage patients, decide who gets admitted and when, and try to keep things running smoothly. We do not want to upset our patients, especially the alligators, who have a notoriously bad temper.

Understanding the problem and sketching out a solution

This may seem trivial, but underestimating a task would be a huge mistake. The most important thing in any project is to understand your client's requirements; the sooner you clarify them, the less painful the project will be. Here, the problem definition is vague enough to allow multiple interpretations: Do we need to worry about who's in the room? Can cats, dogs, alligators, and rabbits be in the same room? Is there a capacity limit (for the lobby or in terms of visits per day)? These (and many more) are all questions you should ask when faced with a similar task.

In this case, let's keep it simple: we just want to handle the registration and admission of the patients, and we assume that the lobby has infinite capacity and no other constraints. So, what we need is a device, a piece of software, that registers patients and then admits them in a certain order.

The next sections show how we can iterate the remaining steps until we find a good solution.

First try: Order agnostic

We understand our inputs and outputs. The next step is to understand how we are going to make this device.

Working on a solution means writing your own algorithm to transform an input and get to your goal, but it is a more high-level operation based on domain knowledge. Now it's time we start thinking about details.

We need a container, a data structure that can hold the patient registrations and return the next patient to be admitted each time we ask. But which container?

Keep in mind that all of the data structures mentioned in the following are covered in the book; you don't need to understand them right now. For our first attempt, we put the forms in a suggestion box at registration, and when a doctor gets free, we just blindly fish out one of these paper forms. The container we used is a *bag,* which is perfect if you don't care about the order in which you read the elements stored.

For this example, we assume the implementation phase produced code without bugs. Thus, we move directly to the questions: Does this solution work, and does it work well?

👍 Easy to implement

👎 No control over the order

Randomly choosing who gets in next has some problems: on average, everyone gets served within an acceptable time. However, patients tend to notice when someone who arrived after them cuts the line, especially when there are only a few patients. Fights start, and when an alligator eats a rabbit who cut into the line in front of her, it's clear that this is not a good solution.

Reverse order

We need to iterate on our solution. The high-level solution works, but we need to change the data structure we use.

This time, the forms are stored in order, in a pile with the oldest at the bottom and the newest at the top. Unfortunately, because of a misunderstanding, the triage operators take the next form from the top of the pile: they are implementing a *stack*, so the last registered patient is the first one admitted! At the end of the first day, when they have to deal with an angry lion who had been waiting the whole day to get a splinter removed from his paw, everyone realizes that this stack solution doesn't work at all.

A stack is good when we need to process the most recent entries first, but it's terrible to handle a waiting line.

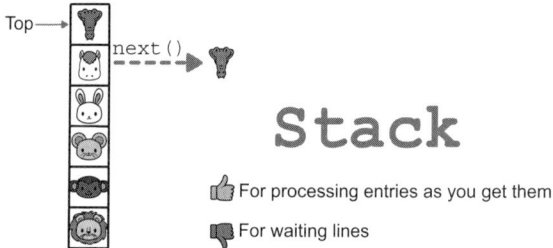

First come, first serve

This time, the correction is conceptually simpler: we take the next forms from the bottom of the pile, so the first patient to arrive will be the first to see a doctor. For this approach, we are using a *queue*, a data structure that allows us to iterate through the elements in the same order in which they were added.

And the solution works pretty well: no more arguments, no more endless waiting; patients are happier, and triage is less stressful. Finally, the implemented solution works.

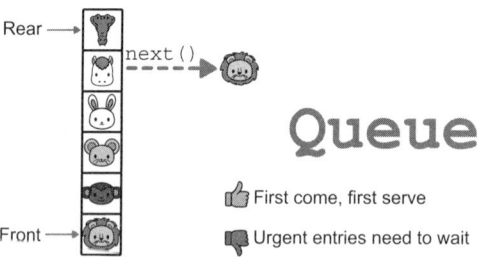

Now the final step. The question is, does it work well enough? After a few weeks of working with the new triage system, the doctors realized that in a few cases, some complications could have been avoided had the patients been seen immediately instead of waiting their turn.

Do you know what that means? We can do better. It's time to iterate.

Emergencies first

What we need is a data structure that allows us to take into account more than just the arrival time. Triage operators have the registration forms on which they write down a patient's initial anamnesis: they can estimate the urgency of a case and reorder the forms so that, even if the lion with the splinter arrived at the ER first, he would get in after the python who ate a computer mouse and the turtle who twisted her ankle while running.

Luckily, we have the right data structure for this: a priority queue. If we add all our cases to a priority queue, we can later ask it to return us the most urgent case, followed by the next most urgent one, and so on.

This solution works, and it works well. Are we done? That depends. First, it depends on the real requirements, which might require more guarantees. Then, we should consider the real implementation of the system to decide which kind of priority queue is fast enough or handles memory well enough for our needs.

But you get the point: you can measure the performance, compare it to your requirements, and then decide. For this example, because we understand how to choose the right data structure, we found a solution that works perfectly for our needs—understanding how to choose the right data structure.

Recap

- A data structure is a way to organize and store data in a computer or a programming language by defining the relationship between data, operations that can be performed, and rules or constraints for accessing and modifying data.

- Data structures are fundamental to organizing and storing data efficiently.

- An algorithm is a set of well-defined instructions, a step-by-step procedure designed to solve a specific problem or perform a particular task.

- Algorithms and data structures complement each other the way nouns and verbs complement each other in a sentence.

- Choosing the wrong data structure can have dire consequences, such as crashing your website or causing security hazards.

- There is a step-by-step process that can help you decide which data structures to use in a project.

- The process is iterative and requires checking the quality of your solution until you meet all your requirements.

Static arrays: Building your first data structure | 2

In this chapter

- a few basic ideas concerning data structures

- introducing a fundamental data structure—arrays

- the difference between statically and dynamically
  sized arrays

- introducing typical operations that can be done
  on arrays

- using arrays to solve a problem

In this chapter, we'll begin to talk about how data structures work and how to implement them. The chapter is special in that it will slowly introduce you to the process we are going to follow throughout the book as we talk about the technology we are introducing. However, it will also familiarize you with some basic concepts that you will need for the rest of the book.

What is an array?

We will begin our journey to the land of data structures with *arrays*, specifically static arrays. Arrays organize data by holding a collection of elements and making them accessible through an index.

But right now, the most important question I want you to be able to answer is, why arrays? Let me explain by using an example.

Memory and drawers

First, we need to take a step back and talk about how memory is organized. For the sake of simplicity, I like to think of memory as a modular shelf holding removable drawers.

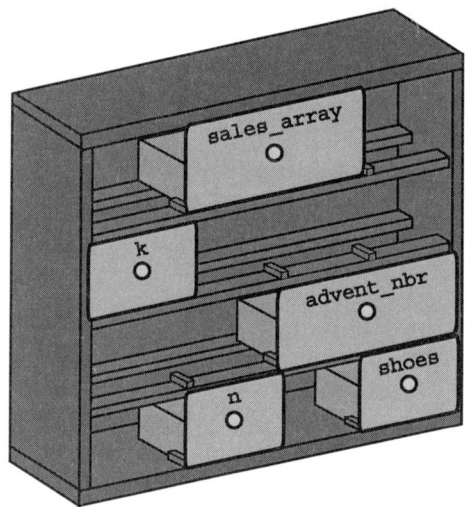

If the shelf structure is memory, then drawers are variables—a programming concept I assume you're already familiar with. Think of memory as potential: if you want to use some memory, you can create variables, the drawers that can hold your data from which you can retrieve it.

The size of the shelf determines the maximum number of drawers. You can create variables (drawers) of different sizes, as long as they fit into the space of the shelf. You can also fill those drawers with data, and larger drawers can hold larger data types. For example, you'll need a larger drawer for a floating-point value than for characters or (short) integers.

When do I need an array?

Meet Mario! He loves sweets, and he really loves chocolate. There is a drawer in his parents' kitchen where Mario keeps his chocolate truffles, his favorites. Right now, Mario has five truffles left. A drawer is like a variable, a container for data. In this case, an integer variable named `drawer` would contain the value 5.

To get from integer variables to arrays, let's look at another example. December is coming, and Mario's family prepares an Advent calendar for their children. The calendar is in the shape of a gingerbread house, with little drawers marked with numbers from 1 to 24.

If you are not familiar with an Advent calendar, it's similar to *Advent of Code*, except that instead of coding problems, you get a sweet treat every day between the 1st and the 24th of December (funny how the analogy usually works the other way around for everyone except software engineers!). Each drawer of an Advent calendar holds a cookie, some chocolates, or other candy, and the kids can open each drawer only on the day corresponding to the drawer number.

Going back to our shelf analogy, suppose you reuse part of the big storage shelf for the Advent calendar. The 24 drawers could be created anywhere on the shelf: they don't even have to be next to each other, and they don't have to be in any particular order. But if we were to create these numbered drawers, we would want to put them in ascending order and next to each other. Otherwise, it would be hard to find them.

Similarly, if we wanted to model an advent calendar in software, we could create 24 little variables and call them `advent_drawer_1`, `advent_drawer_2`, and so on. No one would stop us from doing so (although, hopefully, *someone* would stop us before we get this mess into production!).

It would already be painful to create 24 different variables by hand, but what's worse, every time we'd need to access one of the drawers in code, we'd have to use the correct variable name, so normally, in most programming languages, we'd have to know which variable we need at compile time (that is, when we write code).

Sometimes, however, we only get this information at *runtime*, when code is executed. For example, if we have a program that asks the user which drawer we need to check, we wouldn't know in advance which variable we need because we only get the information through I/O as our program runs. And if this is not your first code rodeo, you are probably familiar with loops: Can you imagine what a mess it would be to go through all the drawers without a `for` loop? (Don't worry if you can't because we'll see an example shortly.)

That's where arrays come in. An array is a data structure that holds multiple entries accessed by index. We'll define arrays properly in the next section, but for now, remember that, as a general rule of thumb, you use arrays when you need to store, iterate over, or manipulate a collection of values of (roughly) the same type without knowing much about how the individual values are correlated. (For cases when you have more information about the inner structure of your data and how the elements are related to each other, this book will introduce you to other data structures that will help you further.)

Definitions: Statically vs. dynamically sized

What is an array, then? Here is what our Advent calendar would look like as an array.

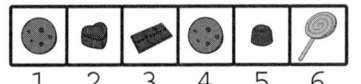

4	1	2	7
1	2	3	4

3	5	9
23	24	25

An integer array for the Advent calendar

Arrays aren't limited to storing integers or numbers in general: they can store fractions, strings, and other types of objects. As an example, how about an array of candies?

An integer array for candies

In its simplest definition, an array is an indexed collection of data. Indexed means that an array stores a sequence of items (usually called *elements*), and you only can access them by their position (also known as their index). For example, in the Advent calendar, we can access the drawer indexed with 1 to get the treat for December 1st, but we can't access the drawers by their content—for example, we can't easily find the drawer with seven truffles, nor in the candies array can we just say, "Get the strawberry lollipop."

Now that we are getting closer to formal definitions, we need to make a distinction because we can look at the definition of array from different angles.

If we focus on the functionality of arrays at a high, semi-abstract level, the array data structure has a few key characteristics:

- It stores a collection of data.

- Its elements can be accessed by index.

- Elements don't have to be accessed sequentially; that is, if I need the 10th element of an array, I can access it directly without having to read the 9 elements stored in the array before it.

These few points define an array at an abstract level. Technically, these points define an array as an *abstract data type*. Keep this term in mind as we will encounter it again in chapter 7.

From a different point of view, arrays are one of the core features of many programming languages. This is also where things get more concrete. Looking at arrays from this point of view, we have to deal with implementation details that vary depending on the programming language we choose.

Yet, many programming languages adhere to a few common characteristics when implementing arrays as a core language feature (we continue the previous list):

- Arrays are allocated in memory as a single, uninterrupted block of memory with sequential locations, which is both memory and time efficient.

- Arrays are restricted to storing data of the same type. This restriction also stems from the need for optimization because it allows the same memory to be allocated for each element in the array and the compiler/interpreter to quickly know the memory address of each element. We'll talk about this in detail in the next section.

- The size of arrays, that is, the number of elements contained in an array, must be decided when the array is created, and that size can't be changed.

The last three points represent a *lower-level* definition that describes *static* (aka *statically sized*) arrays, a core feature of many programming languages such as C, C++, Java, and so on.

In this chapter, we focus on static arrays. *Dynamic* (aka *dynamically sized*) arrays, whose size can change at runtime, are another variant of this data structure. We'll learn more about dynamic arrays in chapter 5. Note that it's also possible to relax the fourth point of the list and allow heterogeneous content for arrays, which means that you can mix different data types for the array's elements: Python, the programming language we use in this book, natively provides *lists*, a dynamically sized kind of array that allows any data type for its elements.

Values and indexes

In the previous section, we learned that arrays are an indexed data structure. This means that an array associates an index to each of the elements it contains, and only through an index can we access the corresponding element.

When we talked about static arrays, I pointed out that in many languages, arrays force all their elements to be of the same data type. This requirement is useful for several reasons.

First, as the next figure illustrates, it allows you to allocate the exact amount of memory needed for the array. Second, it makes it possible to quickly compute the memory address for each element because all elements will have the same size and thus be equally spaced, which makes computing the memory location of an element straightforward.

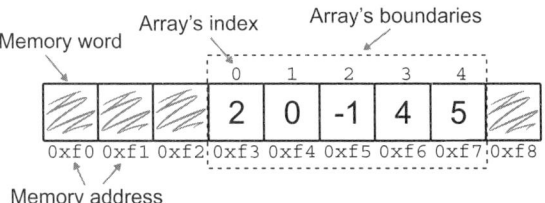

Arrays implementation and memory addresses

You may noticed that in the examples of the Advent calendar array shown in the previous section, the indexes of the array elements start at 1. In other words, each index corresponds nicely to one of the first 24 days of December. Some of you may have an eyebrow raised because you're used to indexes starting at 0, so let's talk about it.

While many programming languages start indexes at 0, some have array indexes starting at 1. A few of the most well-known examples are Julia, MATLAB, R, and Fortran.

Python is one of those languages that use zero-based indexing, and so we follow the convention throughout the book of having the indexes of arrays start at 0.

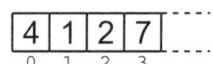

Zero-based indexing, as you can imagine (and may already have experienced), forces developers to be careful when thinking about indexes, especially if they need to implement algorithms that access specific positions or when they need to be careful about staying within the bounds of the valid indexes. For example, the last element of a zero-based indexed array of size n will be at index n-1, and trying to access the element at index n will result in an error.

A zero-based-indexing version of the Advent calendar array

Initialization

As discussed earlier, the rest of this chapter focuses on static arrays. One key point I briefly mentioned is that when you create a static array, you need to decide its size in advance. For example, if you need to store five elements in an array, you'll need to allocate the memory for all those elements when you create the array. That is, by declaring an array, we create the structure that will hold five values of a certain type, which must also be decided at that moment.

We are preparing the space to hold those elements, but what happens before we actually assign values to them?

To get started, there are two ways to create an array: we can just declare it, or (in most programming languages) we can *initialize* the array elements at the same time we declare it.

Initializing an array means assigning (valid) values to all of its elements. In this case, the compiler, while translating your code into a program that can run on your machine, simultaneously allocates memory for the array and fills it with the values we decide at compile time, before moving on to the next instruction.

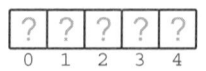

An "empty" array: What values will we find? We just don't know!

What happens when you just declare the array without initializing it? Are its elements kept "empty"?

There is no concept of empty, which means that when you declare a variable, the compiler must assign a value to it. In the case of arrays, all elements must be assigned a value.

The actual value depends on the programming language and the type of the array; for example, in Java, an array of integers will have all its elements set to 0 if it is created without initialization. Some programming languages have a special value to represent emptiness;

for example, Python has the value `None`, and Java uses `null`. Note that these are special values that are explicitly assigned to the array elements.

The gist is that you must be careful when creating an array if you plan to access its elements without first assigning them. When in doubt, check the language specifications to understand what will actually happen.

Arrays in Python

OK, that's enough theory. Let's get a taste of arrays in action. Young Mario not only loves candy but also computer programming. He is learning Python and wants to keep track of his Advent calendar, so every morning, as soon as he opens his drawer for the day, he wants to update his digital version of the calendar. He also plans to update it every time he eats a piece of chocolate, so he can keep an eye on his little brother Ian, who is strongly suspected of stealing Mario's treats on Halloween.

Let's help Mario build a simple application using arrays!

Python lists vs. the array.array class

I already mentioned that Python offers the `list` class as its native array-like solution. *Python* lists are closer to dynamic arrays, and they also don't have the limitation of holding data of the same type: you can create a list with numbers, strings, or other lists, all together.

Python *lists* are more powerful than static arrays: for example, they support dynamic resizing, while `array.array`, which comes with Python's standard library, doesn't. But you know how it is: with great power comes great responsibility—and a price to pay. In general, the price for supporting dynamic resizing is degraded performance and a slower data structure (we'll talk more about this in chapter 4). To be clear, in many cases, you'll be fine using *lists*, and you won't notice the difference in your application. But if you are writing critical sections of your code, potential bottlenecks where performance is critical, then you may want to make sure to use the most performant option.

> **TIP** Just remember that optimization also has a cost (in terms of development time, maintenance, and clarity), so avoid optimizing too early or without real benefits. Before you decide to optimize some code, make sure you run it and identify the critical sections where optimization would make the most difference.

It's important that you understand how static arrays work before we approach their dynamic counterpart in a later chapter. Unfortunately, Python doesn't offer a native static array alternative. The closest we get is Python's array module, which enforces type consistency but is still a dynamic array. A true static array can be found in the NumPy library, which is a math library fine-tuned to be efficient at vector computation. With `numpy.array`, you can create fixed-size arrays of doubles, still somewhat different from Java arrays.

This is not the place to explore the pros and cons of all the possible solutions, although it's important that you know they exist. Instead, to help you experiment with static arrays, we created a custom class based on `array.array`, which simulates how a static array works. (You can find this custom class in the book's repo: https://mng.bz/VxpG.) At this point, you shouldn't worry about the details of how we implement a static array. The important point is that once you import the class, you can create a new array of size n using the following code:

```
from arrays.core import Array
a = Array(n)
```

Then you can access all elements of a, from index 0 to n–1, and assign them like a regular array. On the flipside, you can't expand or shrink this array.

By default, an array of *integers* is created. If you want to create an array (of five elements) of *floats*, you can use

```
b = Array(5, 'f')
```

Then, for example, you can run

```
print(b)
print(b[2])
b[3] = 3.1415
```

Note that all elements of the newly created array are initialized to 0 (or 0.0 for floats).

Indexing

As mentioned previously, Python uses zero-based indexing for arrays, which means that for an array with *n* elements, the first element of the array is always at index 0, and the last element is at index n–1.

Sometimes zero-based indexing is a bit inconvenient, like in our Advent calendar example. We'll find day 1 at index 0, when it would have been more intuitive to find it at index 1.

Sometimes, it's more than inconvenient: you have to be careful about indices to avoid going past the end of an array. For an array of size n, n–1 is the last valid index. Even with Python lists, while –1 is a valid index (specifically, the index of the last element in the array), accessing a[n] will crash your application. Now you could be asking: What about a[-n]? And a[n+1]? Only one of them will work: Can you guess which one?

To avoid having to deal with this kind of Jedi mind trick, we have disabled negative indexes for our class of static arrays.

Operations on arrays

Now that you know how to create an array, the next question is what to do with it.

Initially, our array is an *empty* container—not in the sense that its elements are actually empty, but rather that the values assigned to the array's cells are meaningless. Our helper class arbitrarily initializes every array element to 0, like it's done in many programming languages.

However, the details of each programming language are not important now. The only assumption you need to make is that, unless or until you initialize the array, its data is *meaningless*.

You can fill the array however you like. You don't have to follow any order when assigning new values to its elements, but here's the caveat: you might want to keep track of which elements are *meaningful* to your application. I'll go further: you definitely want to; I can't think of an example where you wouldn't.

In most cases, the order in which we store the elements won't matter. If that's the case, we can simply add the new elements at the first unused index in the array and keep the array left-justified: this means that if we add k≤n elements to our array, they will be at the indexes from 0 to k-1.

?	7	?	?	3	-1	?
0	1	2	3	4	5	6

An array with some
elements assigned and
some "empty" elements

7	3	-1	?	?
0	1	2	3	4

A left-justified
array

With left-justified arrays, it becomes quite convenient to keep track of which elements are meaningful, and we only need to store the size of the filled chunk of the array.

> **NOTE** This is one possible way to do it—in fact, one of many. If you choose to work with a left-justified array, it's your responsibility to keep track of how many elements are currently stored in the array.

Now let's see how to perform some basic operations on our (unsorted) array.

A class for unsorted arrays

We could write a set of global functions that take a core.Array object as an argument and manipulate it. However, I'm not going to take this approach. I know we can have a cleaner implementation by writing an UnsortedArray class that wraps around and isolates (*encapsulates*) our array.

Why? There are many good reasons to prefer object-oriented programming over the imperative paradigm. If this debate is a new topic for you, I suggest you take some time to research and read about it.

One thing you may have already considered is that we need to keep track of the size of the filled part of the array. With a left-justified array, that's enough to separate the part of the array that holds data from the empty part.

If we implement a class for the unsorted array, we can store its size in an attribute and update it as part of the operations on the array. Without wrapping our unsorted array in a class, we would have to store the size of the array in a global variable and pass that value to each of the functions that manipulate the unsorted array.

These methods, in turn, would have to trust the caller and still perform some sort of validation on the input. Anyone using these methods could, by accident or design, pass an incorrect value for the size of an array. Even worse, whoever owns the array has to keep the size variable in sync: for example, they have to remember to update the array after inserting and deleting values.

Encapsulation: A pillar of modern programming

The fact that anyone can change the variable with the size of the array is frighteningly prone to errors. Instead, we need to strive for something called *encapsulation*. Each instance of an array needs to have this value bundled with it and, ideally, only modifiable internally by the instance itself. (Python does not help us much here as it has no real private access to class attributes.)

So, we're going to implement unsorted arrays as a class. You can find the full code on GitHub (https://mng.bz/x2dX):

```
class UnsortedArray:
    def __init__(self, max_size, typecode = 'l'):
        self._array = Array(max_size, typecode)
        self._max_size = max_size
        self._size = 0
```

In the constructor, we keep the same signature as for our core static array helper class. In fact, we even use one of those static arrays internally to host the data.

Note that while we could inherit from `core.Array`, we instead create an instance of `core.Array` and assign it to an attribute of the object: we use composition with an instance of `core.Array`.

> **TIP** A general rule of thumb is to favor composition over inheritance: it gives you more flexibility in design.

If you are not familiar with composition, inheritance, and their tradeoffs, a good read would be Dane Hillard's *Practices of the Python Pro* (Manning, 2019).

Adding a new entry

For context, we create our array `arr = UnsortedArray(n)`, where n is the number of elements we allocate for the array (its maximum capacity). Let's say we have already added k elements to the array. We can't make any assumptions about the order of the elements, and we even don't care about their order.

Under these assumptions, we can add the next entry of the array at index k, right after the last entry, that is, if there is room in the array! The first thing we have to do is check that k is a valid index. If it is, we can proceed with the assignment, remembering to increment k, the current size.

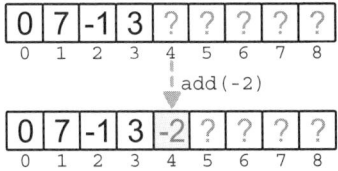

If the array is full, we raise an exception to alert the caller to the problem.

Adding the fifth entry to an array with size n=9

Here is how the code would look like as a method of our class:

```
def insert(self, new_entry):
    if self._size >= len(self._array):
        raise ValueError('The array is already full')
    else:
        self._array[self._size] = new_entry
        self._size += 1
```

Removing an entry

Adding new elements to an unsorted array is pretty straightforward, right? Things get a little more interesting when we want to remove an existing entry.

In the most common scenario, you'll want to remove an entry somewhere in the middle of the array. Unfortunately, simply "clearing" the entry at the given index would leave a gap in the middle of the chunk of the array where we store our valid entries, breaking our assumption that the entries are left justified.

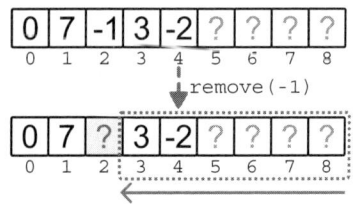

Removing an entry leaves a gap; therefore, we need to shift all elements to the right of the gap.

To fix this situation, in the abstract, we would have to shift all the entries to the right of the gap one position to the left. This would solve the problem, but it would also be a lot of work.

This is unfortunate: it would be much easier if we just had to remove the last entry of the array instead! We could just update the size of the array to ignore that last entry.

There is a special case, a data structure called a *stack*, which only allows you to remove its last entry. We'll study stacks in chapter 8, but in the meantime, it turns out we are in luck after all: there is a way to manipulate unsorted arrays and get into the same scenario, where we only remove the last entry.

Since the array is unsorted, and we assumed that the order of the entries doesn't matter, we can just swap the last entry and the one we want to remove, and then we can always remove the last entry!

We have to take care of a few edge cases, especially checking whether the array is empty, but then things are much easier than we thought:

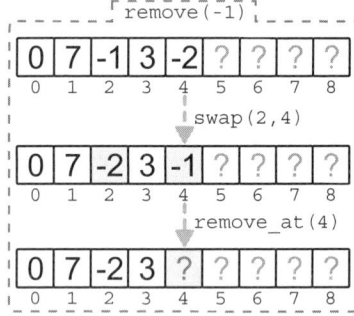

Swapping the entry to be removed with the rightmost one in the array, and then deleting it

```
def delete(self, index):
    if self._size == 0:
        raise ValueError('Delete from an empty array')
    elif index < 0 or index >= self._size:
        raise ValueError(f'Index {index} out of range.')
    else:
        self._array[index] = self._array[self._size-1]
        self._size -= 1
```

The last element will be outside the populated chunk (a word of caution: array loitering).

"Smart swapping" by overwriting the deleted element (we don't need to store the value that we are going to delete.)

Searching for a value

Another important operation we want to be able to perform is searching: given a certain value, is it stored in the array, and at what index? If we look more closely, we need to ask a few more questions. For example

- What happens if there are multiple occurrences of the same value? Do we return the first occurrence, any occurrence, or all of them?

- If the target value isn't in the array, what do we return? One way would be to return -1, which works in many languages. However, in Python, -1 is a valid index for lists, because you can use negative numbers to index elements from right to left. Therefore, returning -1 could backfire and cause an error to go unnoticed if the caller doesn't check the method output.

Let's make the following assumptions: we will return the index of the first occurrence of the target entry found, or None (an invalid index) if not found.

So how do we do a search? Unfortunately, because the entries are stored without any ordering, we have no better way than to iterate through all items until we find a match. It's not very efficient, but we don't have any information that would allow us to do better:

```python
def find(self, target):
    for index in range(0, self._size):
        if self._array[index] == target:
            return index
    return None
```

If it got to this point, it couldn't find the target.

The search method can be used in conjunction with the delete method to remove elements by value. First, we find the index of the value we want to remove, and then we can call the delete method defined in the previous section.

Traversal

Sometimes, we want to apply the same operation to all elements of a data structure, and the same goes for arrays. It could be printing them or squaring them. What we want is to traverse our array, going through all its elements (exactly once, in some order that depends on the data structure), and applying some method that we'll take as an argument.

For more advanced data structures such as trees and graphs, this gets more complicated, as we'll see. But for arrays, it only requires a for loop:

```python
def traverse(self, callback):
    for index in range(self._size):
        callback(self._array[index])
```

We'll assume that the operation we want to perform has some sort of side effect and that we don't need to collect its output (otherwise, we'd be talking about a map operation).

Once defined in its simplest form, we can try calling it with the print method to get the gist of how it works:

```python
array.traverse(print)
```

Arrays in action

Now that we have seen how arrays work, let's see how we can make use of them.

Statistics

Mario and Tony play this game that they invented where Tony picks the lower three numbers on a die, and Mario picks the top three. So, if the result of a dice roll is 1, 2, or 3, Tony wins, and if it's 4, 5, or 6, Mario wins.

That's a 1! Tony, you win again

They take turns rolling the dice, betting their baseball cards on each roll. Whoever rolls the dice at any given time decides how many cards to bet, and the other one can double the bet.

After playing the game for a while, Mario has lost half of his card deck. He thinks that Tony is winning a bit too much and doesn't understand why. When Mario tells his father about this game, Mario's father suggests that Tony may be (unknowingly) using an unfair die: a die with certain numbers coming up more often than others.

With a fair die, he continues, over a large number of rolls, each of the six numbers should come up about one-sixth of the time. The more rolls you try, the closer the actual frequencies will be to each other.

Therefore, one way to prove that a die is unfair is to record the statistics of the results of many rolls and then check how the results are distributed. After breaking the ice with programming and arrays, Mario feels on a roll (pun intended), and he wants to use arrays to prove that Tony is cheating. So, his father helps him write a mobile application that Mario will use to record the results of the dice rolls.

Whenever Mario registers a dice roll on his phone, the application registers the result in array `counters` with six elements. All elements of `counters` are initialized to 0 when the app is first run. When the die comes up with, say, a 4, the app increments `counters[3]`. Remember that the possible values go from 1 to 6, but the array indexes go from 0 to 5 (in Python and many other languages), so if we want to update the number of times k has been drawn, we need to increment `counters[k-1]`.

For this particular application, we don't need to fill the array incrementally or keep track of meaningful entries: we know exactly how many entries to allocate from the start, and they can all be considered meaningful once initialized to zero. In other words, we populate the array at initialization. But, in the next example, we'll see how to use what we've learned about incrementally filling arrays.

Once Tony and Mario have played enough, and Mario has recorded hundreds, even thousands of dice rolls, here comes the interesting part: How does he check that the values are

0	0	0	0	0	0
0	1	2	3	4	5

	0	0	0	1	0	0
	0	1	0	1	0	0
	0	1	0	1	1	0
	0	1	0	2	1	0
	0	1	1	2	1	0
	0	1	2	3	4	5

An array with six counters. Each time a die is thrown, the corresponding counter is incremented.

those of a fair die? There are a few ways, but most of them would probably be way beyond the math of a primary school kid. So Mario's father suggests to start by finding the maximum value in the array for the number that shows up more often. Let's assume that there is a single maximum value or that, in case of a tie, we can indifferently return the one with the lowest index.

Then what Mario needs to code is a variation of array traversal. We go through all the elements, one by one, and check: Is this the one with the highest frequency?

Notice that instead of assuming that the maximum value in the array is nonnegative (which would be true in our case), we can write a safer, slightly more general method by initializing the variable max_value to the first element in the array and then start iterating from the second element.

This variant makes the code more robust (we don't have to rely on the caller passing an array with nonnegative values) and more widely applicable.

For each element, we compare it to the currently stored value for max_value, and if the current element is greater, we update both the value and its index. In the end, we can just return the value found and the index where it is. But in our use case, we need to remember to add 1 to the index we get to have the most frequent value that came up when rolling Tony's dice:

```python
def max_in_array(array):
    if len(array) == 0:
        raise Exception('Max of an empty array')
    max_index = 0
    for index in range(1, len(array)):
        if array[index] > array[max_index]:
            max_index = index
    return max_index, array[max_index]
```

The second task Mario's father gives him is to write a similar function that returns which face of the die comes up least often and how often that happened.

"Once we have these four values," Mario's father says, "we can check if Tony's die is fair."

```
max_in_array(counters)
> 1, 234
min_in_array(counters)
> 5, 107
```

They find that the most common result showing up is 2 (remember we get the index, which is 1 minus the actual value on the dice), and the least common is 6, with a large difference in their frequency.

"That's weird," says Mario. "What does that mean?"

"It means I'm going to call Tony's parents. You should get your cards back."

EXERCISES

2.1 Write the code for a function returning the minimum value in an array and its index.
Hint: Can you adapt the function `max_in_array`?

2.2 Can you write a method returning both the max and min values at once? What's the advantage of computing both within the same method?

Collections

Another use case for arrays is to keep track of things as they appear. For example, Mario loves collecting baseball cards (or any kind of cards).

His parents gave him a special binder in which he can put his most valuable cards. The binder has a limited capacity, so Mario has to choose wisely which cards to put in it.

If we want to model the binder on a computer, an array is a good analogy. An unsorted array, like the one we saw in the previous section, is an even better analogy.

You can make the array as big as the size of the deck. The array would start out empty, meaning we would keep track of the cards we added to it—initially none.

As we buy or trade cards, we can add new entries to the array: we don't care about the order. We can just have them in any order. Once the deck/array is full, we can remove some of the cards/entries to make room for the new memorabilia we want to keep in the deck. If we have an idea about which card we want to remove (maybe a Billy Ripken 1989 Fleer?), we can run a search on the whole array to find the index to free up.

Finally, to complete the analogy, if we want to write down some data for each card, such as the player's name and age, then we should be thinking about running `traverse` with a function printing that information.

Multidimensional arrays

Arrays are not limited to holding only numbers. Their entries can be characters, strings, objects, and other arrays. In particular, an array of arrays is a *multidimensional array*. Matrices are used in many fields such as graph theory, linear algebra, machine learning, and physics simulations. To learn more about multidimensional arrays, check out the book's repo: https://mng.bz/Adlx.

Recap

- Arrays are a way of storing a collection of elements and efficiently accessing them by position.

- The term *array* usually serves as a synonym for a statically sized array (or static array for short), a collection of elements accessed by an index, where the number of elements is fixed for the entire lifetime of the collection.

- Dynamically sized arrays are also possible. They behave like static arrays, except that the number of elements they contain can change.

- Many programming languages, such as C or Java, offer static arrays as a built-in feature.

- Arrays can be initialized at compile time. If a language allows you to skip initialization, then the initial value of the array's elements depends on the language.

- Arrays can be nested: you can create an array of arrays. As for static arrays, we call them multidimensional arrays or matrices.

- If we don't mind the order of its elements, adding and removing elements to and from an array can be done easily.

- We can search all (generic) arrays by traversing them until we find what we are looking for.

- It's possible to use arrays for many applications. For example, counting items and computing statistics are perfect use cases for arrays.

In this chapter

- why keep an array sorted

- adjusting the insert and delete methods for sorted
  arrays

- the difference between linear search and binary
  search

In chapter 2, we introduced static arrays, and you learned how to use them as containers to hold elements without worrying about the element's order. In this chapter, we take the next step: keeping the array elements sorted. There are good reasons for ordering arrays, such as domain requirements or to make some operations on the array faster. Let's discuss an example that shows the tradeoffs and where we can get an advantage by keeping the element of an array in order.

What's the point of sorted arrays?

In the previous chapter, we looked at arrays as containers where the order of their entries doesn't matter. But what if it does? Well, when the order does matter, it changes everything, including how we perform the basic operations we have implemented.

Before we look at how, let's try to understand when a sorted array can be useful.

The challenge of the search ninja

Our little friend Mario got excited about both coding and baseball cards. He started saving his lunch money to buy cards to play with his friends. He bought so many cards that it became difficult to carry and find them. His father bought him a binder to make them easier to carry around, but with hundreds of cards, even with the binder, it was still hard to find the ones he needed.

After seeing him struggle, Mario's mother, a software engineer, suggested that he sort the cards by team and name.

Mario was skeptical: sorting all those cards seemed like a lot of work. He'd rather play now than spend the time. So, it was time for the big talk—the one about fast searching in sorted lists.

Mario's mom explained that if he sorts the cards first, it will be much easier to find what he is looking for. Mario was still not convinced, so she challenged him: they will split all of Mario's cards and take half each, and then each of them will randomly choose five cards for the other to find in their half. They can only search for one card at a time, so the next card they need to search for is given only after they find the previous one. Mario can start searching while his mom sorts her deck. Whoever finishes first wins.

Now the challenge begins, and Mario's mom takes 5 minutes to calmly sort her half, while Mario finds his first card and giggles and taunts her for her efforts—Mario considers himself a search ninja: he is the fastest among his schoolmates.

But once Mario's mom finishes sorting her cards, little does he know that, before Mario finds his third card, his mother has already completed her task. Mario is astonished: "How did you manage to be so fast?"

Good question! But you will have to wait until the next chapter to find out why her method was faster! In this chapter, we will instead focus on how to implement what Mario's mom used to win the challenge.

Implementing sorted arrays

In the rest of this chapter, we take a closer look at how the basic operations on a sorted array work and how to implement them in Python. As for unsorted arrays, I'm going to create a class, `SortedArray` this time, that internally handles all the details of a sorted array. You can find the full code on GitHub (https://mng.bz/x24Y), but we also discuss the most important parts here.

For sorted arrays, encapsulation becomes even more important because we need to guarantee another invariant: that the elements in the array are always sorted. As we discuss in the next section, the insert method looks very different for sorted arrays, and if this method were to operate on an array that is not sorted, it would behave erratically and almost certainly produce the wrong output.

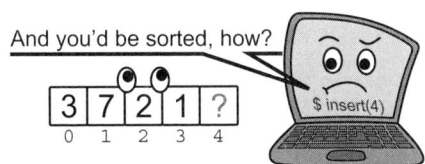

This is also why we ideally don't want to let clients directly assign the array's entries and mess up their order. So, we only allow modifying the array through the `insert` and `delete` methods.

Let's start with the class declaration and constructor:

```
class SortedArray():
    def __init__(self, max_size, typecode = 'l'):
        self._array = core.Array(max_size, typecode)
        self._max_size = max_size
        self._size = 0
```

In the constructor, we keep the same signature as our core static array helper class and, similarly to what we did for the `UnsortedArray` class, we internally compose with an instance of `core.Array`.

Note that the behavior and meaning of some methods will be different between `SortedArray` and `core.Array`. First, compared to the `core.Array` class we provided, the meaning of "size of the array" is different: for the core type, it means the capacity of the array, but it has a different meaning here. We still need to set and remember the capacity of the array, but, like with the unsorted arrays, we want to keep track of how we fill that capacity as we add entries to the array.

Therefore, the behavior we expect when we call `len(array)` is different in this case. For the core array, we always return the array capacity, but here we keep track of how many entries the array currently holds (keeping in mind that the maximum number of entries it can hold is given by the capacity of the underlying core array—a constant value returned by the `max_size` method).

Now we have a *class* for our next data structure, the sorted array. However, a data structure is not really useful until we can perform operations on it. There are some basic operations that we usually want to perform on most data structures: *insert*, *delete*, *search*, and *traverse*.

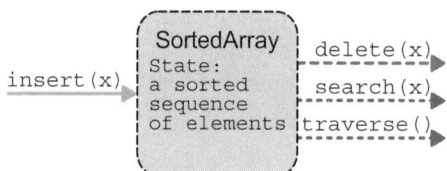

Some data structures have special versions of some of these (for example, some only allow you to remove certain elements, as we will see when we discuss the *stack*), and some others may not support all operations. However, by and large, we'll often implement these core operations.

Insert

We start with insertion. When we need to add a new element to a sorted array, we must be more careful than with the unsorted version. In this case, the order does matter, and we can't just append the new element to the end of our array. Instead, we need to find the right place to put our new entry, where it won't break the order, and then fix the array. (I'll soon explain how.) Because of the way arrays work, this is not as easy as we might hope.

Let's see a concrete case: a sorted array with five elements, to which we want to add a new value, 3. (For the sake of simplicity, we avoid duplicates in this example, but the approach would be the same if we had duplicates.)

Once we find the right position for our new entry 3, we create a split of the old array, basically by dividing it into two parts: a left subarray `L` containing the elements smaller than 3 (namely, 1 and 2) and a right subarray `R` containing the entries larger than 3 (namely, 4, 5, and 6).

Theoretically, we would have to break the old array at the insertion point and then patch [1,2]–[3]–[4,5,6] together, connecting these three parts. Unfortunately, we can't do this easily with arrays (it's easier with linked lists, as we discuss later in the book).

Since arrays must hold a contiguous region of memory, and their entries must be in order, from the lowest-index

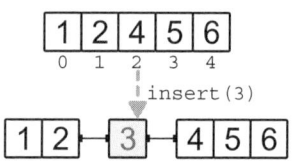

memory cell to higher indexes, we need to move all elements in the right partition R one entry to the right of the array.

There are a few ways to implement insertion, but we will go with this plan:

1. Start with the last (rightmost) element in the array—let's call it X (6 in our example)—and compare it to the new value K to insert (3).

2. If the new value K is greater than or equal to X, then K must be inserted exactly to the right of that position. Otherwise (as in our example, where 3 < 6), we know that X will have to be moved to the right, so we might as well move it now. We choose our new X element (5) as the element to the left of X and go to the previous step. We repeat until we find an entry X that is less than or equal to K or until we reach the beginning of the array.

3. Once we have found the right place, we can just assign K to that position without any other change because we already moved all the elements that needed to be moved to the left of this position.

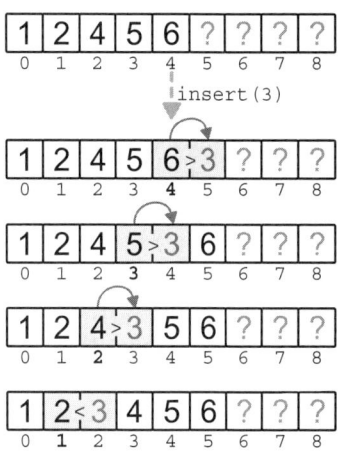

An example of insertion in a sorted array

These steps are the core of a sorting algorithm called *insertion sort*. It sorts an existing array *incrementally* by building a sorted subsequence used as a starting point and adding the elements of the array from left to right, one by one. Although there are faster sorting algorithms than insertion sort, it's still a good choice whenever you need to build your sorted sequence incrementally, like in our case. If you are interested in learning more about sorting algorithms, I suggest reading *Grokking Algorithms, Second Edition* (Manning, 2023), especially chapters 2 to 4.

Now that we know what we have to implement, we just need to write some *Python* code to do it:

```python
def insert(self, value):
    if self._size >= self._max_size:
        raise ValueError(f'The array is already full, maximum size: {self._max_size}')
    for i in range(self._size, 0, -1):
        if self._array[i-1] <= value:
            self._array[i] = value
            self._size += 1
            return
        else:
            self._array[i] = self._array[i-1]
```

Found the spot in the middle of the array

```
self._array[0] = value
self._size += 1
```

If it gets here, the right spot is
at the beginning of the array.

As you can see, the only other thing we needed to add was a check at the beginning of the method to make sure we didn't overflow the array's capacity.

Delete

The same considerations we made for inserting apply symmetrically to deleting existing elements. Suppose we need to delete the fourth element (the one at index 3) of an array with seven entries. We can't leave a "hole" in the array, and we can't use the same trick as for unsorted arrays, filling the deleted position with the last entry of the array.

Instead, we need to shift all elements between the fifth and the seventh positions. We need to move these elements one position to the left so that the element previously at index 4 is moved to the cell at index 3, and so on.

> **TIP**   The general rule is the following: shift all elements from the index after the deleted element to the end of the array.

Typically, with a sorted array, we are more interested in deleting a specific value than the element at a specific position. That is, it's more common for the client to know the value they want to delete rather than its position.

How do we reconcile this need with what we have discussed so far and provide a user-friendly interface? All we need to do is find the position of the value we want to delete, and to do that, we can reuse a search method, which we'll discuss in the next section. When implementing the `delete` (by value) method, we'll assume that we have already defined a `search` method: for the purposes of this section, we don't need to know the details of how it works, just that it returns the index of the value we're looking for, or `None`, if it's not available.

Once we have the index we are looking for, we simply have to shift all elements to the right of the index one position to the left:

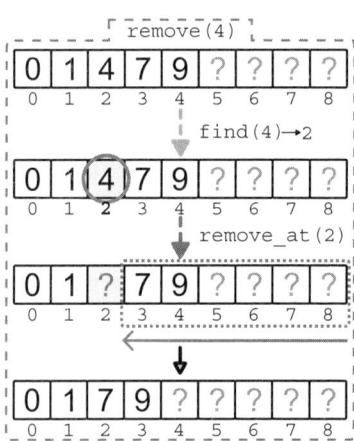

To remove an element from a sorted array, first we find its index, and then we shift all the elements to its right, overwriting the deleted element.

```
def delete(self, target):
    index = self.search(target)
    if index is None:
        raise ValueError(f'Unable to delete element {target}: the
entry is not in the array')
```

```
    for i in range(index, self._size - 1):
        self._array[i] = self._array[i + 1]
    self._size -= 1
```

EXERCISE

3.1 What if we want to implement the delete-by-index method? Describe the abstract steps this algorithm should perform, and then implement it in Python, as part of the `SortedArray` class.

Linear search

We implemented the delete-by-value method using search, so the next step feels kind of obvious: implementing the `search` method. This is also the point of this whole section on sorted arrays: we want to keep an array sorted so that we can search it faster.

One immediately apparent advantage of searching in a sorted array is that if we go through all the elements from left to right, we can stop an unsuccessful search (one that discovers that our target is not in the array) as soon as we find an entry larger than the target itself. Since the elements are sorted, the ones on the right can only be even larger, so there is no point in searching further:

```
def linear_search(self, target):
    for i in range(self._size):
        if self._array[i] == target:
            return i
        elif self._array[i] > target:
            return None
    return None
```

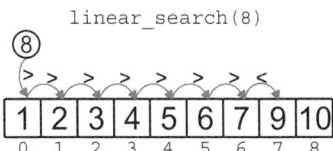

linear_search(8)

The advantage we get is already something, but it's not a game changer. Sure, if we search for one of the smallest elements, we'll be much faster, but if we look for one of the largest, we'll still have to go through the whole array, more or less.

That begs the question: Is there a faster way to find the target value without traversing the entire array? Pause for a moment and think about what we could do differently.

Now, would you believe me if I told you that we can do much better?

An unsuccessful linear search in a sorted array. We need to scan every element from the beginning of the array until we find an element (9) that is larger than our target 8. Note that it took eight comparisons to find out that the searched value was not in the array.

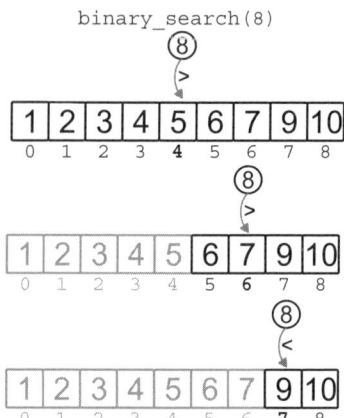

An unsuccessful binary search. After one comparison, we have ruled out more than half of the array. After two, more than 75% of it is excluded. In this example, by the third comparison, when we have only two elements where our target could be, we discover that the target is not in the array.

Binary search

You should believe me, because it turns out that we can. Although we will discuss the reasons more formally in the next chapter, by the end of this section, you will have a clear idea that binary search is a different game than linear search.

Meanwhile, I'll tell you how. We start by looking at the middle element of the array, and if we find our target, just like that, we're done (and extremely lucky).

Otherwise, since the array is sorted, we can still squeeze some information out of the comparison. If our target is larger than the middle element M, then it can't be to the left of it, right? Because the array is sorted, all the elements before the middle one are smaller than or equal to M. Similarly, if it's smaller, it can't be to the right of our current position. One way or another, we can focus our search on either half of the array and repeat the process as if we were dealing with a smaller array.

This method is called *binary search*. The implementation may not seem too complicated: we define two *guards*, the left and the right index, which delimit the subsection of the array where we know the target should be. Then, we bring these two guards closer at each step until we either find our target or find out that it's not in the array:

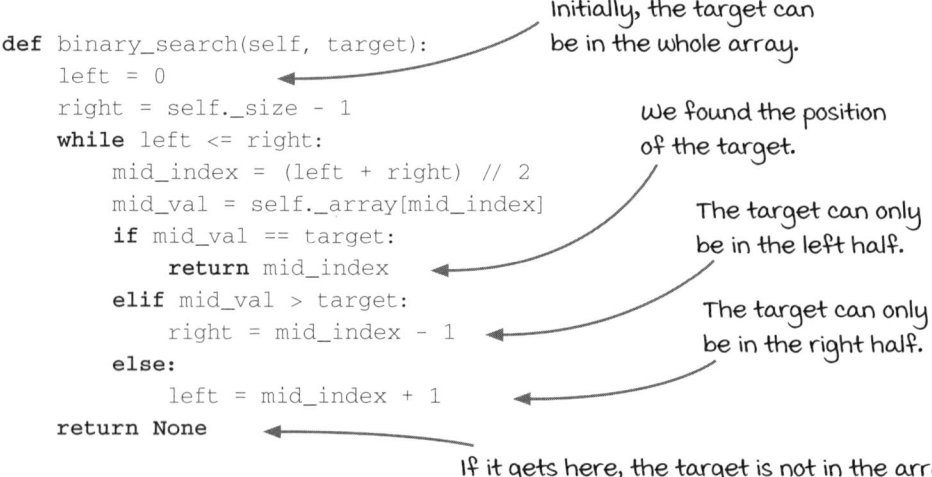

```
def binary_search(self, target):
    left = 0
    right = self._size - 1
    while left <= right:
        mid_index = (left + right) // 2
        mid_val = self._array[mid_index]
        if mid_val == target:
            return mid_index
        elif mid_val > target:
            right = mid_index - 1
        else:
            left = mid_index + 1
    return None
```

Initially, the target can be in the whole array.

We found the position of the target.

The target can only be in the left half.

The target can only be in the right half.

If it gets here, the target is not in the array.

But trust me, this is one of those algorithms where the devil is in the details, and it's hard to get it right the first time you write it. So, you better test it thoroughly, even if it's the hundredth time you write it!

Why it's called a binary search and why it's more efficient than the `linear_search` method, you'll find out in the next chapter. But for now, a word of caution: if your array contains duplicates, and you need to find the first (or last) occurrence of a target value, then this method will not work as is. You could (and will) adapt it to find the first occurrence, but that makes the logic of the method a little more complicated and the code a little less efficient. It is still faster than linear search, but obviously, if you return the first occurrence that you find, you'll be even faster. So, you only worry about duplicates if you have a good reason to return the first occurrence, or if not, all occurrences are the same.

And that concludes our discussion of static arrays. I know that I mentioned a fourth operation: traversal. As a reminder, traversal is the process of accessing each element in an array exactly once. Now you have all the elements to perform this operation yourself. Just remember that in the context of sorted arrays, traversal is typically performed in ascending order, from the smallest element to the largest.

EXERCISES

3.2 Implement the traverse method for sorted arrays. Then use it to print all the elements in the array in an ascending sequence.

3.3 Implement a version of binary search that, in case of duplicates, returns the first occurrence of a value. Be careful! We need to make sure that the new method is still as fast as the original version. Hint: Before doing this exercise, be sure to understand the difference in running time between binary and linear search. Reading chapter 4 first can help with this part.

Recap

- A *sorted array* is an array whose elements are kept in order as they change.

- To maintain the elements of an array in order, we need a different approach when inserting and deleting elements. These methods must preserve the order and therefore require more effort than their counterparts for unsorted arrays.

- On an already sorted array, we can run *binary search*, a search algorithm that can find a match by looking at fewer elements than *linear search* (which simply scans all elements until it finds a match).

- With sorted arrays, you have faster search, but you also have an extra cost to keep them sorted. Therefore, they should be preferred when there is a high read-to-write ratio (many more calls to the `binary_search` method than to `insert` and `delete`).

Big-O notation:
A framework for measuring algorithm efficiency | 4

In this chapter

- objectively comparing different algorithms

- using big-O notation to understand data structures

- the difference between worst-case, average, and
  amortized analysis

- a comparative analysis of binary and linear search

In chapter 3, we discussed how binary search seems faster than linear search, but we didn't have the tools to explain why. In this chapter, we introduce an analysis technique that will change the way you work—and that's an understatement. After reading this chapter, you'll be able to distinguish between the high-level analysis of the performance of algorithms and data structures and the more concrete analysis of your code's running time. This will help you choose the right data structure and avoid bottlenecks *before* you dive into implementing code. With a little upfront effort, this will save you a lot of time and pain.

How do we choose the best option?

In chapter 3, you were introduced to two methods for searching a sorted array: *linear* and *binary search*. I told you that binary search is faster than linear, and you could see an example where binary search required only a few comparisons, while linear search had to scan almost the whole array instead.

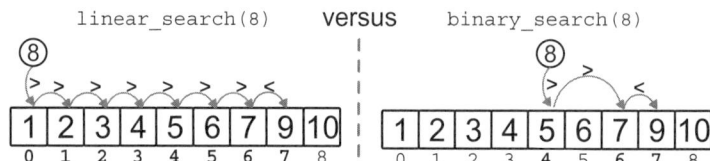

You might think this was just a coincidence or I chose the example carefully to show you this result. Yes, of course, I totally did, but it turns out that this is also true in general, and only in edge cases, linear search is faster than binary.

However, to determine which algorithm is faster, we need a consistent method to measure their performance. We may want to know not only how fast it is but also, maybe, how much it consumes in terms of resources (memory, disk, specialized processor's time, etc.).

So, how can we measure algorithm performance? There are two main ways:

- Measuring the implementation of an algorithm, running the code on various inputs, and measuring the time and the memory it takes. This is called *profiling*.

- Reasoning about an algorithm in more abstract terms, using a simplified model for the machine it would run on and abstracting many details. In this case, we focus on coming up with a mathematical law describing the running time and the memory in terms of the input size. This is called *asymptotic analysis*.

Profiling

The good thing about profiling is that there are tools already available that do most of the work for you, measuring the performance of your code and even breaking down the time by method and by line.

In Python, `cProfile` and `profile` (https://docs.python.org/3/library/profile.html) are available to everyone. You only have to import the one you want to use and set up some code that calls the methods you want to profile.

Profiling looks great, but does it solve all our needs? Not really.

We profile a specific implementation of an algorithm, so the results are heavily influenced by the programming language we choose (some languages may handle the operations we need better than others) and also by the actual code we write. Thus, the implementation details can affect the overall result, and bad implementation choices can make the implementation of a good algorithm slow. Moreover, the machine on which the profiling is run and its software, such as the operating system, drivers, and compilers, can also affect the final result.

In other words, when we profile linear and binary search, we compare the two implementations, and we get data about the implementation. We can't assume that these results will hold for all implementations, and, for what is worth, we also can't generalize the results and use them to compare (only) the two algorithms.

The other notable shortcoming of profiling is that we are testing these implementations on finite inputs. We can, of course, run the profiler tool on inputs of different sizes, but we can only use inputs as large as the machine we are using will allow.

For some practical situations, testing on these inputs may be enough. But you can only generalize the result so much: some algorithms outperform their competition only when the size of the input is larger than a certain threshold. And you can't generalize the results you get on a smaller machine for larger machines or from a single machine to a distributed system.

Asymptotic analysis

The main alternative to profiling is asymptotic analysis. The goal of asymptotic analysis is to find mathematical formulas that describe how an algorithm behaves as a function of its input. With these formulas, it's easier for us to generalize our results to any size of the input and to check how the performance of two algorithms compares as the size of the input grows toward infinity (hence the name).

The results we obtain are independent of any implementation and, in principle, valid for all programming languages.

You can imagine that there is also a downside. Of course, we have to work harder to get those formulas, and it requires working out the math, sometimes a lot of math. Occasionally, it's so hard that there are algorithms for which we haven't found the formula yet or we don't know if we found the best formula to describe their running time.

However, this challenge in finding the right formula does not occur with the algorithms used by the data structures described in this book and with many others. You won't even have to figure out these formulas yourself, and in fact, this book will not discuss the math involved. You'll just be working with the results that have been proven by generations of computer scientists.

My goal is to show you how to use these results and what to look for when deciding which algorithm or data structure to use.

Which one should I use?

Both profiling and asymptotic analysis are useful at different stages of the development process. Asymptotic analysis is mostly used during the design phase because it helps you choose the right data structures and algorithms—at least on paper.

Profiling is useful after you have written an implementation to check for bottlenecks in your code. It detects problems in your implementation, but it can also help you understand if you are using the wrong data structure in case you skipped the asymptotic analysis or drew the wrong conclusions.

Big-O notation

In this book, we are going to focus on asymptotic analysis, so we will briefly describe the notation commonly used to express the formulas that describe the algorithms' behavior. But before we do so, remember what we said about asymptotic analysis? It uses a generic (and simplified) representation of a computer on which we imagine running our algorithms. It's important that we begin by describing this model because it deeply influences how we perform our analysis.

The RAM model

In the rest of the book, when we analyze an algorithm, we need a touchstone that allows us to compare different algorithms, and we want to abstract away as many hardware details (such as CPU speed or multithreading) as possible.

Our fixed points are a single-core processor and *random-access memory* (RAM). This means that we don't have to worry about multitasking or parallelism and that we don't have to read memory sequentially like in tapes, but we can access any memory location in a single operation that takes the same time, regardless of the actual position.

From there, we define a *random-access machine* (also abbreviated as RAM), a computation model for a single-processor computer and random-access memory.

> **NOTE**   When we talk about the RAM model, RAM stands for random-access machine, not random-access memory.

This is a simplified model where memory is not hierarchical like in real computers (where you can have disk, RAM, cache, registries, and so on). There is only one type of memory, but it is infinitely available.

The random access machine

In this simplified model, the single-core processor offers only a few instructions—mainly those for arithmetic, data movement, and flow control. Each of these instructions can be executed in a constant amount of time (exactly the same amount of time for each).

Of course, some of these assumptions are unrealistic, but in this context, they are also fine. For example, the available memory can't be infinite, and not all operations have the same speed, but these assumptions are fine for our analysis, and they even make sense to a certain point.

Growth rate

Now that we have defined a computational model for studying algorithms, we are ready to introduce the actual metrics we use. Yes, that means this is the math part! But don't worry! We are going to take a visual approach and greatly simplify the notation used—we are going to define and use it very informally.

As mentioned earlier, we want to describe the behavior of algorithms using some formulas that relate the size of the input to the resources used.

There are times when we need to go through this mathematical analysis. We are interested in how the resources needed change as the input gets larger. In other words, we are interested in the rate of growth of these relations.

For a given resource, for instance, the running time of our algorithm, we are going to define a function $f(n)$, where n is typically used to define the size of the input. To express the rate of growth of function f, we use the big-O notation.

> **NOTE** The name big-O comes from the symbol used for the notation, a capital O.

We write $f(n) = O(n)$ to state that the function f grows as fast as a line in the *Cartesian plane*. Which line? Well, we don't say as we don't need to know. It can be any line passing through the *origin*, except the vertical axis.

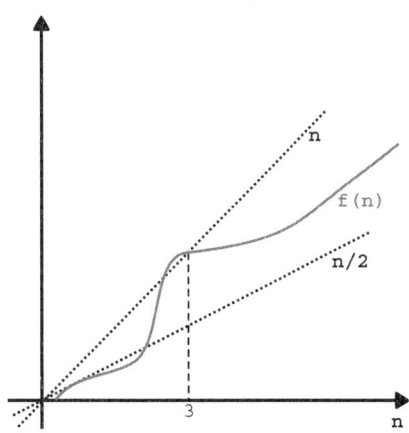

In practice, if a resource, such as the memory used by our algorithm, grows at a rate given by a function $f(n) = O(n)$, this means that as the input to our algorithm gets larger, the memory it uses is bounded between two straight lines on the graph.

More formally, we could say, for example, that for $n > 3$, it holds $n/2 < f(n) < n$. Or, equivalently, we could say that for $n > 30$, it holds $n/4 < f(n) < 5n$. It doesn't matter whether we choose the first pair of lines, $y = n/2$ and $y = n$, or the second pair, $y = n/4$ and $y = 5n$: asymptotic analysis just asks us to find one such pair of lines that, for sufficiently large values of n, act as bounds for f.

In fact, the notation $O(n)$ doesn't define a single function but a class of functions—all the functions that grow as fast as straight lines—and writing $f(n) = O(n)$ means that f belongs to this class.

However, the important thing that $f(n) = O(n)$ tells us is that there is at least one line that will outgrow $f(n)$ when n becomes large enough.

So, when we say that our algorithm runs in $O(n)$ time (aka linear time), it means that if we drew a graph showing how long it took for the algorithm to run on inputs of different lengths, the graph would look like a straight line. There would be tiny bumps here and there due to random things that can happen in computers as programs run, but if you zoom out of those details, it looks like a straight line.

Common growth functions

You might ask, though, which line is it going to be? If we look at the lines in the next figure, there is a lot of difference between them: one grows much slower than the other! (Note that we will focus on the first quadrant for the rest of the graphs, restricting to positive values for both axes.)

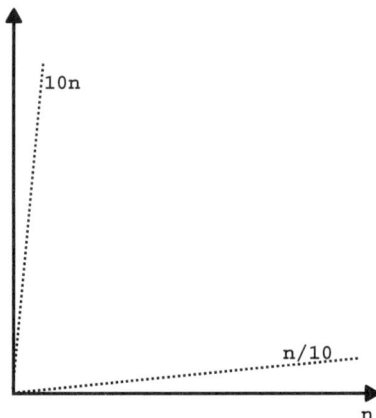

With this notation, we can't tell upfront which line our growth is going to be close to. That's too bad, but we are okay with it. Some functions grow a lot faster than straight lines, and we have ruled them out! Other functions grow more slowly (significantly more slowly!) than our running time, and that's unfortunate, but at least we know.

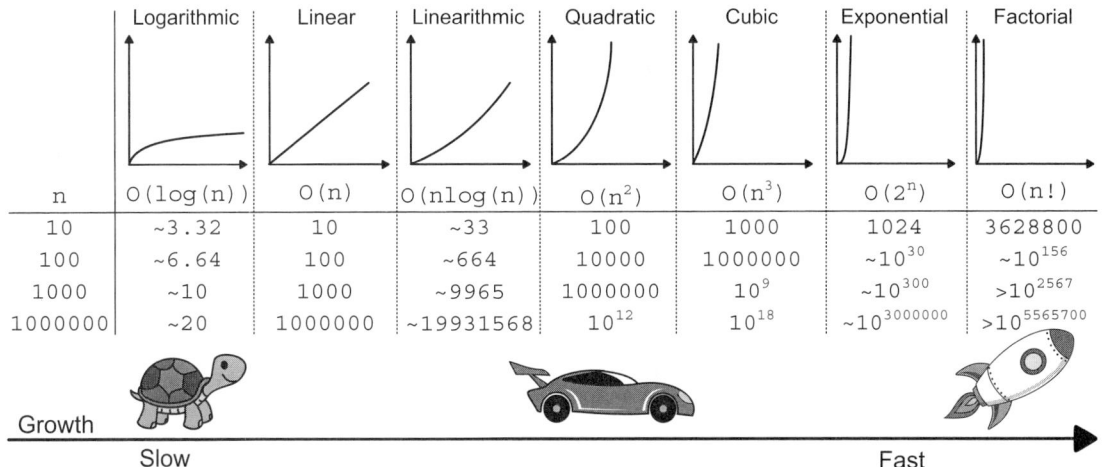

n	O(log(n))	O(n)	O(nlog(n))	O(n²)	O(n³)	O(2ⁿ)	O(n!)
	Logarithmic	Linear	Linearithmic	Quadratic	Cubic	Exponential	Factorial

n	O(log(n))	O(n)	O(nlog(n))	O(n²)	O(n³)	O(2ⁿ)	O(n!)
10	~3.32	10	~33	100	1000	1024	3628800
100	~6.64	100	~664	10000	1000000	~10^{30}	~10^{156}
1000	~10	1000	~9965	1000000	10^9	~10^{300}	>10^{2567}
1000000	~20	1000000	~19931568	10^{12}	10^{18}	~$10^{3000000}$	>$10^{5565700}$

Growth
Slow   Fast

Some of the growth rates you might encounter when studying algorithms. From left to right, the functions grow increasingly faster.

If you look at some examples of cornerstone functions that we might often encounter in algorithms, you can see that logarithmic functions grow very slowly, and linear functions grow at a constant rate. With linearithmic functions (in the order of O(n * log(n))), we see a bit of acceleration, meaning that the growth is faster with larger inputs (for example, the growth is less when we go from 100 to 200 elements than when we go from 200 to 300). Linearithmic functions, however, do not grow too fast. Polynomial functions such as n^3 or $3n^2 - 4n + 5$, conversely, accelerate rapidly with input size, and exponential functions such as 2^n or 5^{n+2} really skyrocket.

The set of functions I've shown you doesn't include all the possible function classes: it's impossible to list them all. But there is one that it's worth adding: the constant function, a function whose value doesn't change with the size of the input. The class of constant functions is denoted by O(1).

In our RAM model, we can say that all the basic instructions take O(1) time.

Growth rate in the real world

In the previous section, we have only talked about how these functions grow, but are they good or bad? Is a logarithmic function better than an exponential one? Of course, functions are not good or bad inherently—that depends on what quantity a function describes. If your formula describes your income based on units sold, I bet you'd prefer that it featured a factorial term!

In asymptotic analysis, we usually measure the resources needed to run an algorithm, so we are usually happy to find that our algorithm is associated with a slowly growing function. It's time we look at a concrete example to give you a better idea.

Imagine that we are trying to understand whether we can afford to include some algorithms in our code, based on their running time. In particular, we want to look at the following five algorithms that operate on arrays:

- Search in a sorted array.

- Search in an unsorted array.

- *Heapsort*, a sorting algorithm that we will discuss in chapter 10. Sorting takes the array [3,1,2] and returns [1,2,3].

- Generating all pairs of elements in an array. For example, for the array [1,2,3], its pairs are [1,2], [1,3], and [2,3].

- Generating all the possible subarrays of an array. For example, for the array [1,2,3], its subarrays are [], [1], [2], [3], [1,2], [1,3], [2,3], [1,2,3].

How do we figure out which is fast and which is slow? Should we run all these algorithms on many inputs and take note of how long it took? That might not be a good idea because it would take us a long time—a really long time, as we'll see.

The good news is that if we know a formula that describes the asymptotic behavior of an algorithm, we can understand its order of magnitude, an estimate of the time it will take for inputs of various sizes (not the exact time it will take to run, but an idea of whether it will take milliseconds, seconds, or even years!).

I have summarized in another figure an estimate of how the five algorithms would perform, assuming that each one of the basic instructions on our RAM model takes 10 nanoseconds (ns) to run. For each algorithm, the figure shows the formula for its asymptotic running time. You'll have to trust me on these, but we'll soon see an example of how to derive these formulas.

	Algorithm				
	Binary search	Linear search	Heapsort	All the pairs	All the subsets

Input size	Running time				
n	$O(\log(n))$	$O(n)$	$O(n\log(n))$	$O(n^2)$	$O(2^n)$
10	33 ns	100 ns	330 ns	1 us	10 us
20	43 ns	200 ns	864 ns	4 us	10 ms
30	49 ns	300 ns	1.4 us	9 ns	10 s
60	60 ns	600 ns	3.5 us	36 us	317 years
100	66 ns	1 us	6.6 us	100 us	10^{18} years
1000	100 ns	10 us	100 us	10 ms	10^{300} years
1000000	200 ns	10 ms	19 ms	2.7 hours	
10^9	298 ns	10 s	5.5 min	3171 years	

How long does it take to run an algorithm? That depends on the order of growth of its running time. All results are approximated.

As you can see, logarithmic functions are pretty nice. We could run a binary search on a billion elements, and it would still take the time it takes some atoms to decay, which is too fast for us to notice, anyway. Sorry to break it to you, but most algorithms won't be that fast. The range of acceptable growth rates includes linear functions, which take the blink of an eye (or maybe a few blinks—in this analysis, it's the order of magnitude that matters), even for large inputs.

Linearithmic functions, like good sorting algorithms, are still manageable: we are talking about minutes to sort a billion elements—just the time to take a break and make a cup of tea or coffee. Quadratic functions, however, are already hard to run on large inputs: we are talking about thousands of years on the same one-billion-element array, so if such a job were finished today, it would have started about the time the Pyramids were built. Now I hope you understand why it is important that you choose a sorting algorithm that is linearithmic, like *mergesort* or *heapsort*, over one that is quadratic, like *selection sort*.

> **TIP** If you'd like to learn more about sorting algorithms, Aditya Bhargava explains them nicely in his highly popular *Grokking Algorithms, Second Edition* (Manning, 2023)!

Finally, we talk about the exponential functions: small inputs are usually manageable, but you can see that with 60 elements, it would take us centuries (and so many subsets!), and with 100 elements, we are already in the order of magnitude of the age of the universe.

Big-O arithmetic

When I gave you the definition of the big-O notation, I told you that to be able to state that `f(n) = O(n)`, we do not care which straight line can grow beyond `f`, as long as there is one. It doesn't matter which line we choose, whether it is `y = n`, `y = 5n`, or some other. The important thing is that for sufficiently large values of `n`, the line is always above our `f(n)`.

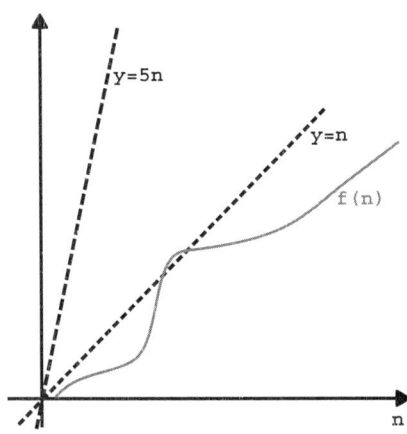

This property allows us to look at the big-O definition from a different angle: we can say that $O(n)$ is the class of all straight lines. This means that, for asymptotic analysis, two lines are considered asymptotically equivalent, so two functions $f(n) = n$ and $g(n) = 3n$ are considered equivalent—their growth is of the same order of magnitude.

But obviously, $3n$ grows much faster than n, by a factor of 3. So, how can they be equivalent?

Beyond the math, the key point is that if you compare them to any function in $h(n) = O(log(n))$, both will outgrow h, at some point. And if you compare f, g, or any $c*n = O(n)$ with $z(n) = O(n*log(n))$, they will all be outgrown by z, no matter how big the value of the constant c is.

These considerations have direct consequences for how we write expressions in the big-O notation and also how we compute expressions with terms expressed in the big-O notation.

First, as we have seen, constant factors can be ignored, so $c * O(n) = O(c * n) = O(n)$ for all real (positive) constants c. The second important conclusion we can draw is that we only need to remember the largest factor in a polynomial. $O(c * n + b)$ simplifies to $O(n)$: in fact, $O(c * n + b) = c * O(n) + b * O(1) = O(n)$. Geometrically, this means that we don't need a line to pass through the origin to find a line with a steeper growth trajectory.

Perhaps the best way to show what this means and why it holds is with an example. Let's consider the function $f(n) = 3n + 5$.

Plotting function f in the Cartesian plane, we can see that we can find (at least) two lines, $g(n) = 5n$ and $h(n) = 2n$, which bound f for $n \geq 3$, that is, for $n \geq 3$ we have $2n < 3n + 5 < 5n$. But this satisfies the requirements of big-O notation, and so we can conclude that $3n + 5 = O(n)$.

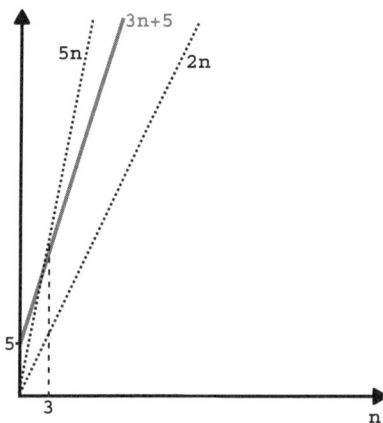

Now, the best part is that this simplification rule is not limited to lines! It's true for polynomials of any order and, in general, for expressions that sum any class of functions:

$$O(6 * n * log(n) + 110 * n + 9999) = O(n * log(n)) + O(n) + O(1) = O(n * log(n)).$$

Finally, you must be more careful when there are nonconstant terms that are multiplied or combined with other nonlinear functions.

With `O(n)*O(log(n))`, we can't simplify anything except the notation, bringing all the formulas together as `O(n * log(n))`.

Worst-case vs. average vs. amortized analysis

Now that you have covered the notation, there are a few more considerations about asymptotic analysis that we need to make.

When doing asymptotic analysis, we usually, unless otherwise stated, consider the worst possible situation. Think about linear search in a sorted array. There are searches where the result is found after only a few comparisons, if it's near the beginning of the array, and other searches where we have to scan almost the whole array, if the target is near the end of the array. Which case should we consider? Well, we want to be thorough and consider the worst possible case, and we call this *worst-case analysis*.

There are other situations where we can still have different behaviors depending on how lucky we are, but the probability of good behavior is much higher than for linear search. In these cases, along with worst-case performance, we can also discuss the *average-case analysis* of the algorithm's performance, which takes into account the likelihood of many different inputs to compute an expected value for the performance of the algorithm.

Finally, for some data structures, there is a guarantee that by performing the same operation on the data structure many times, even with different inputs, the average performance will be better than we can guarantee for a single run. For example, in chapter 12, we will learn that if we repeat `search` and `insert` on a hash table many times (say a million) under certain conditions, we can guarantee that the sum of all the running times will be better than the worst-case running time of a single operation multiplied by a million.

When this happens, the guarantee is never on a single operation, which can be unusually slow if you are unlucky. If we run a large number of operations, however, we can amortize the cost of the single unlucky operation by spreading it over the total time taken by all the operations. In fact, this is what we call *amortized analysis*. While average-case analysis tells us what to expect on average but gives us no guarantees for a single run, amortized analysis establishes a worst-case bound for the combined performance of a large number of operations.

For example, you might have a data structure `D` for which insertion normally takes `O(1)`, but once in a hundred runs, it takes `O(n)`, where `n` is the number of elements the data structure stores. We know that

- Worst-case analysis tells us that insertion for `D` is as slow as `O(n)` in some cases. That's technically correct but also quite misleading, isn't it? It's only going to be a slow linear operation once in a hundred operations!

- Average-case analysis tells us that if D has n elements, the average running time is $O(n/100)$ for a single insertion, which still means a linear bound for large values of n. And it still doesn't tell us the whole story, because only one in a hundred operations takes linear time.

Now suppose we insert $m = 1000$ elements into an initially empty D. Here's what each type of analysis can tell us:

- Worst-case analysis: $T(m) = O(m^2)$.

- Average-case analysis: $T(m) = O((m/100)^2) = O(m^2)$.

- Simplifying, we assume that exactly 990 of these operations will take $O(1)$, and only 10 of them take $O(m)$. So, the time spent on all m operations is $T(m) = (m - 10) * O(1) + 10 * O(m) = O(m)$. We can do a similar reasoning for $m = k * 100$, where k is constant.

Amortized analysis matches our intuition when we need to measure the performance of an algorithm over a large batch of operations, each of which is usually fast and only sometimes slow. In these cases, we can use amortized analysis to get a tighter bound on all the operations combined. We will look at a very similar example in chapter 5.

> **TIP** To avoid unpleasant surprises, it's very important that, when you evaluate an algorithm, you pay attention to what kind of analysis the results refer to. Amortized analysis is great, but sometimes—for example, in real-time systems—you need guarantees on the worst possible case.

Measured resources

There can be many resources you may want to measure, depending on the context, but in this book, we focus on two. You have already seen that we are interested in running time to understand how long it will take for an algorithm to compute its result. To say that algorithm *A* takes linear time, we write $T_A(n) = O(n)$.

The other critical resource is memory. There are cases where you may want to differentiate between RAM and disk consumption or cache usage. But, in general, we just use the term *space* to refer to all the memory used by an algorithm or a data structure, without worrying about where it's hosted.

For data structures, we want to keep track of how much *extra space* an algorithm (applied to the data structure) uses. Extra space means any memory in addition to what is already occupied by the data structure.

For example, suppose you need to invert an array A. We can do this using a second array B of the same size and assign the last element of A to the first of B, and so on. This way, we use $O(n)$ extra space for an array of size n, and we can write $S(n) = O(n)$.

Alternatively, we can invert the array in place, using a single variable to swap the first and last elements of A, then the second and penultimate, and so on. Since we are using only a single variable whose size doesn't depend on n, we only need a constant amount of extra space, so we can write that as $S(n) = O(1)$.

An example of asymptotic analysis

Now that we have defined the nomenclature we will use throughout the rest of the book, we need to close the circle for this chapter and use big-O notation to evaluate the performance of the two search algorithms we have defined on ordered arrays.

How do we do this? We can reason about the steps the algorithm performs abstractly. Or we can look carefully at our code and note the expected asymptotic running time for each instruction. Then, we derive an expression from which we can compute the final formula—most of the time, this is enough.

By the way, our main goal in our analysis will be to find an upper bound on the running time and extra space of the algorithm (that is, to find a formula that limits the maximum running time of the algorithm).

Proving that the formulas we derive are also lower bounds (that is, that it's not possible to find a function that grows more slowly) is beyond the scope of this book.

Linear search

If we reason about the algorithm, our intuition immediately tells us that, in the worst case, we have to scan the whole array. But let's look at the code as an exercise:

```python
def linear_search(self, target):
    for i in range(self._size):            # repeat F(n) times
        if self._array[i] == target:       # cost: O(1)
            return i                       # cost: O(1)
        elif self._array[i] > target:      # cost: O(1)
            return None                    # cost: O(1)
    return None                            # cost: O(1)
```

The first instruction is a `for` loop: `for` loops are multipliers, meaning that the cost of the instructions inside the loop must be multiplied by the number of iterations. This `for` loop is repeated, let's say, $F(n)$ times (we still need to find the value of F), and the four instructions in the loop each take a constant amount of time. The last instruction, after the end of the loop, is executed only once and also takes constant time.

So the formula for the running time of linear search is $T(n) = F(n) * [O(1) + O(1) + O(1) + O(1)] + O(1) = F(n) * O(1) + O(1) = O(F(n)) + O(1) = \mathbf{O(F(n))}$.

Now we need to find an expression for F (that is, we need to understand how many times the `for` loop is repeated). The `for` loop is set to repeat n times, but there are two return statements inside of the loop that cause the flow to break out of the loop. For example, if we find what we were looking for in the first element, we will exit the loop after just one iteration.

Conversely, with an unsuccessful search (when a search doesn't find a match), the loop completes all n iterations.

How do we reconcile these opposite scenarios? We can do one of two things:

- Consider the *worst-case scenario*: then, if we are unlucky, we need O(n) iterations.

- Consider the *average* number of elements scanned before finding a match.

Would we get a better result by going with the average? Not necessarily: on average (without any prior knowledge of the array element distribution and the calls), we can say that it would take us n/2 tries to find a match. But we can simplify constants in big-O notation, and O(n/2) = O(n).

Therefore, we can say that for linear search, T(n) = O(n): unsurprisingly, *linear* search takes *linear time*!

Two important points:

- By analyzing code, we are evaluating this implementation of an algorithm. Our analysis will be as good as the implementation itself.

- Watch out for hidden costs. Take the for loop, for example: at each iteration, there is some extra cost to increment the loop variable and check the exit condition. In this case, it's all constant-time operations, but it doesn't have to be. And every time you call a method inside a loop, you have to remember to factor in its cost.

Finally, how about extra space? It's easy to show that this method only takes a constant amount of memory.

Binary search

So much for linear search. Now let's look at binary search, starting directly from its code:

```python
def binary_search(self, target):
    left = 0                                # O(1)
    right = self._size - 1                  # O(1)
    while left <= right:                    # O(1), G(n) iterations
        mid_index = (left + right) // 2         # O(1)
        mid_val = self._array[mid_index]        # O(1)
        if mid_val == target:                   # O(1)
            return mid_index                    # O(1)
        elif mid_val > target:                  # O(1)
            right = mid_index - 1               # O(1)
        else:
            left = mid_index + 1                # O(1)
    return None                             # O(1)
```

Each line of code executes in constant time, except for the while loop—once again, we must watch out for hidden costs, but luckily, there is none here.

The expression can be roughly simplified as `T(n) = O(1) + O(1) + G(n) * [O(1) + O(1) + O(1) + O(1) + O(1)+ O(1)] + O(1) = O(1) + G(n) * O(1) = O(G(n)) + O(1) = O(G(n))`.

So, what we need now is to find an expression for `G(n)`, a function that describes the number of iterations of the `while` loop.

The loop goes on until the left pointer goes beyond the right pointer. We begin by considering that `left` initially points to the first element of the array and `right` points to the last element: all the elements of the array are contained between the two pointers. It's hard to anticipate how `left` and `right` will be updated because it depends on the actual values of the elements and of the target being searched, so the way they evolve is erratic. But we can make some considerations about their distance.

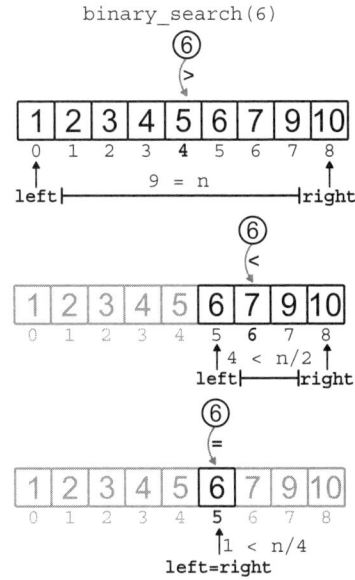

At first, as we know, their distance (the number of array elements in the range from `left` to `right` included) is n. After one comparison, if we don't have a match, we discard more than half of the elements in the array. In other words, one of the two pointers will advance at least half of the distance. And their distance keeps halving until we either find a match or the distance becomes 0.

How many times can we halve this distance? As many times as we can divide n by 2 until it becomes 0 (assuming integer division). This number is exactly $\log_2(n)$, so we can only have `O(log(n))` iterations of the main loop of the method. Replacing `G(n)` with `O(log(n))` in the expression for `T(n)`, we can finally say that for binary search, `T(n) = O(log(n))`, which, as you should know by now, is great, much better than linear search, especially when we have to do a lot of searches! But remember, the catch is you can only perform binary search on a sorted array, while for linear search, there is no difference, in terms of asymptotic analysis, between sorted and unsorted array. In terms of memory, like *linear search*, we only use `O(1)` additional space.

So, now you know how, in chapter 3, Mario's mother won the search competition, and why it was a good idea to sort the cards beforehand!

This concludes our introduction to big-O notation and asymptotic analysis: we will use it a lot in the rest of the book.

EXERCISE

4.1 Using big-O notation and asymptotic analysis, derive the running time and extra memory used for `insert`, `delete`, and `traverse` on sorted arrays. How do they compare to the same methods on unsorted arrays?

Recap

- To evaluate the performance of an algorithm, we can use asymptotic analysis, which means finding out a formula, expressed in *big-O notation*, that describes the behavior of the algorithm on the *RAM model*.

- The *RAM model* is a simplified computational model of a generic computer that provides only a limited set of basic instructions, all of which take constant time.

- *Big-O notation* is used to classify functions based on their asymptotic growth. We use these classes of functions to express how fast the running time or memory used by an algorithm grows as the input becomes larger.

- Some of the most common classes of functions, the ones you will see more often in this book, are

  - *O(1)–constant*—Whenever a resource grows independently of *n* (for example, a basic instruction).

  - *O(log(n))–logarithmic*—Slow growth, like binary search.

  - *O(n)–linear*—A function that grows at the same rate as the input, like the number of comparisons you need in a linear search.

  - *O(n*log(n))–linearithmic*—We'll see this order of growth for priority queues.

  - *O(n²)–quadratic*—Functions in this class grow too fast for resources to be manageable beyond about a million elements. An example is the number of pairs in an array.

  - *O(2ⁿ)–exponential*—Functions with exponential growth have huge values for *n* > 30 already. So if you want to compute all the subsets of an array, you should know that you can only do this on small arrays.

In this chapter

- what are the limitations of static arrays

- overcoming problems with static arrays by using
  dynamic arrays

- tradeoffs and when to use dynamic arrays

- what does it mean to build a dynamic array

- the best strategies to grow and shrink dynamic arrays

In these first few chapters, we have discovered how versatile arrays are and discussed some of their applications. But have you noticed in all the examples we have seen, the maximum number of elements we can store, and thus the size of the array, is determined in advance and can't be changed later? This can work in many situations but, of course, not always—it would be naïve to think so.

There are many examples of real-world applications where we need to be flexible and resize a data structure to meet an increasing demand. When the ability to adjust their size is added to arrays, we get *dynamic arrays*. In this chapter, we look at examples where flexibility gives us an advantage and then discuss how to implement dynamic arrays.

The limitations of static arrays

Arrays are cool, right? Our little friend Mario sure thinks so: they are quite handy for storing items, and you can access these items quickly if you remember their position in the array (that is, their index).

Mario is so excited about learning how to use arrays that he can't stop talking about it! He shares his passion for STEM and computers with his friend Kim from school, who is just as geeky.

Kim has already read something about arrays in her CS class and tries to curb Mario's enthusiasm by raising some objections and highlighting their limitations. Their discussion goes on for a while without a clear winner. So, at home, after dinner, Mario looks for his mother's help. She explains to him that he has only seen static arrays so far and that they do have some shortcomings.

Fixed size

The most obvious problem with statically sized arrays is that they can't be resized! I believe we can all agree on that, but what does it really mean? What are the consequences? It's a twofold problem.

A primary limitation of static arrays is their fixed size. Once full, a new, larger array must be created, and elements must be transferred from the old array to the new one.

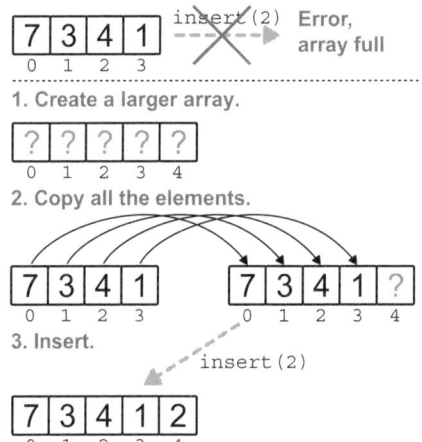

This problem has less to do with arrays as abstract data structures than with arrays as low-level features of programming languages (as a reminder, we discussed this distinction in chapter 2) because arrays are implemented as a contiguous block of memory. As you can imagine, creating a new array to replace another one is expensive, both in terms of data to be moved and memory to be allocated and released. The second problem is a direct consequence of the first one: since changing the size of an array is expensive, we need to allocate enough space upfront to avoid the need for such resizing.

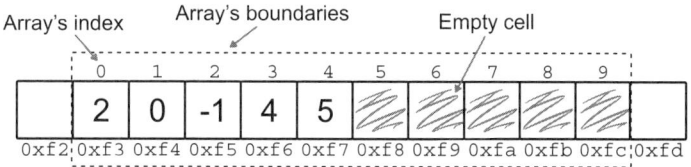

In chapter 3, when we defined our `SortedArray` class, we added an argument to its constructor specifying the maximum capacity of the array so that we could pre-allocate all the memory needed for the maximum number of elements the array could hold.

But this is also a waste. For example, if I know that I will need to support 10,000 elements on peaks, but most of the time, the array will only hold about 100, the remaining 99% of the space allocated to the array is sitting there unused. In such a situation, we are forced to think about the tradeoffs between allocating a larger array and wasting memory versus allocating the space we need "just in time" when we need it, but having to periodically move the elements we have to a larger (or smaller, when we are deleting many elements) array.

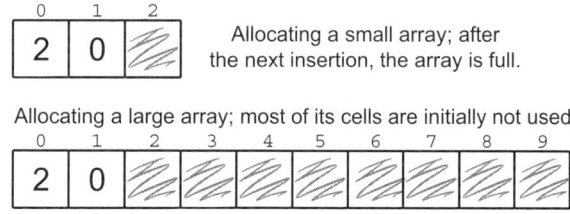

Tradeoffs

How nice would it be if there was a more powerful version of arrays that could grow and shrink as we need, without much overhead? Well, unfortunately, there isn't. In the next chapter, we discuss *linked lists*, a data structure that is more flexible than arrays and can be easily resized. But this flexibility comes at a price. In a linked list, if we want to read the fourth element, we can't do it directly—we must read the first three before.

You might object that if there isn't any version of arrays that is more powerful and flexible, why is this chapter titled "Dynamic arrays"?

I understand you may feel confused right now—you have a good reason. Here's the thing: dynamic arrays are not another data structure or a different programming feature that magically lets us have our cake and eat it too (that is, resizing arrays for free and keeping all their benefits).

From a developer's point of view, a dynamic array behaves much like a static one, except that if you try to add a new element to a full dynamic array, you won't get an error. In fact, you won't have to worry about the size of a dynamic array at all: the data structure manages its size for you.

Full disclosure: dynamic arrays are implemented with static arrays, and we still have to pay the price of allocating a new array and throwing away the old one every time we need to resize it. The key to dynamic arrays—what makes them a good compromise—is the strategy they use to grow and shrink the underlying static arrays.

The caveat is that dynamic arrays make some of the operations a little slower. That's natural—we have to pay the cost of resizing the array from time to time. So, if we know in advance that an array will hold a certain number of objects or that the number of elements will slightly fluctuate around a certain value, then we should definitely prefer a static array. If, however, the number of elements grows or varies greatly over time (even shrinking significantly at some points), then a dynamic array would be preferable to avoid wasting memory and provide flexibility.

In the next section, we discuss why these strategies are important and which strategies work better. Then, after consolidating the understanding of how they work, we can move on to their implementation.

How can we grow an array's size?

We know there is no shortcut to growing an array, and we know we must endure the pain of creating a new array every time the old one fills up and we need more space. But the following questions emerge:

- When should we resize the array?

- How much larger should the new array be?

- What should we do when we delete elements? Should we shrink the array as well?

It's time to meet our little friend Kim again, who will help us figure out the answers.

The trophy case

Kim is passionate about STEM, but what she really loves is robotics. She won several competitions, from the school to regional level, and every time she wins something, she puts the robot that won the prize in a trophy case in her family's living room. She is so good at robotics and wins so many competitions that the case has run out of space.

Her parents want to clean out the cabinet and get rid of some of the oldest robots, at least the ones she made in primary school. But that's out of the question for Kim. She does not want to throw anything away, demanding a bigger cabinet for the new prizes.

After a lot of tears and pouting, Kim's parents have to give in, and they agree to provide new cases to house Kim's new trophies. But there is one caveat: the old cabinets can't be extended and will have to be disposed of, so Kim will have to pay for the new cabinets (and the disposal of the old ones) herself with money from her piggy bank. If she runs out of money and can't afford a new cabinet, she'll have to get rid of some of the older robots.

So, Kim has no choice but to find the best strategy to save as much money as possible in the long run. (You might wonder why not use modular furniture. While that's a valid point, for this analogy, let's consider that modular solutions aren't available.)

Strategy 1: Grow by one element

To establish a baseline, Kim evaluates the simplest possible growth strategy. After the case is full, as soon as she has a new robot to showcase that wouldn't fit, she throws the old case away and has a new case built, one that can hold exactly the new number of robots and nothing more.

It's already filled up!

Old size: 2   Added: 1

If her first case could hold four robots, when she wins a fifth prize, she will have a new case built to hold five robots, then one for six robots, and so on. The cost of the cases is (let's assume) linear considering the number of robots they can hold (say, $200 per robot).

So, she would have to pay $200 * 5 + $200 * 6 + $200 * 7, and so on. At the third case replacement, she would have paid $200 * (5 + 6 + 7) = $3600, and she could probably say goodbye to her weekly allowance until high school.

Kim is not very enthusiastic about this prospect, so she keeps working to come up with better options.

Strategy 2: Grow by X elements

Growing the case by one unit at a time doesn't seem like a good option. Intuitively, we can see that the new case is already filled up when created, and when a new robot has to be added, it will trigger the process again.

Maybe we can have a buffer instead, and when Kim builds a new trophy case, she makes it four units larger? That will cut Kim some slack and give her time to save more money from her allowance while winning trophies before needing to pay for a new case.

But is four units the right amount? In the spring, there are a lot of robotic fairs, and Kim usually participates in as many as she can. What if she wins a medal in 5 of them, or 10, or all of them? She might not even get the new case built in time to use it if she wins more than four medals in a week before the wooden shop delivers it.

Maybe she should make them 5 units larger, or 8, or 10? What's the sweet spot?

Strategy 3: Double the size

Finally, Kim considers a third strategy. Instead of increasing the size of the case by a constant amount, she doubles the size of the case each time she has to build a new one. This ensures that each new case will accommodate her trophies for a duration equal to the combined lifespan of all previous cases.

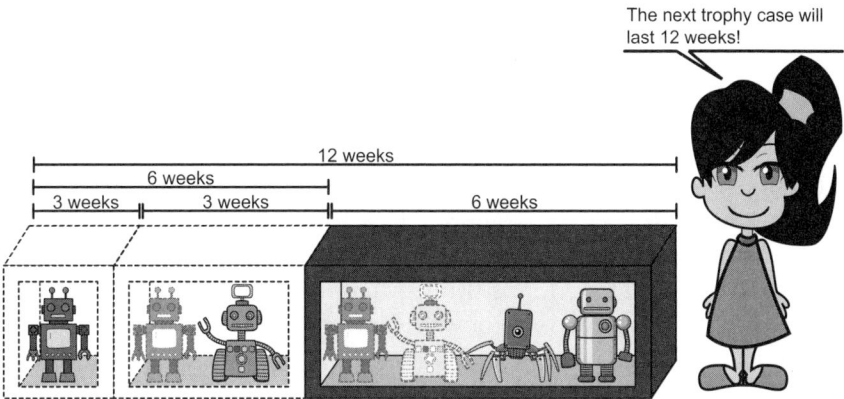

By doubling the case size, the expected life of each new case is the same as the sum of the expected lives of all the previous cases because we can add as many robots to the new one as there were in the case we are replacing.

Now that her four-unit case is full and she has won a new trophy, she will have an eight-unit case built. The next one will be a 16-unit case, and the one after that will be able to hold 32 robots.

Sure, if she builds bigger cases, she will have to advance more money, but then she won't have to worry for a while. And if she wins more trophies faster, the new cases will keep pace.

But will she end up spending more or less money? What's the best strategy?

Comparing the strategies

There is only one way to know: do the math.

Kim has an ambitious goal—to win 60 medals by the time she enters high school. So, all she has to do is calculate how much it would cost to build increasingly larger trophy cases until she gets one that can hold at least 60 of her robots and see how they compare. And no, her parents aren't going to buy a 60-unit case now. That would kind of defeat their purpose of getting their living room back without giving it over to robots.

Table 5.1 provides a cost comparison for the three strategies.

Table 5.1   Comparison of costs for strategies to gradually increase the size of a trophy case

Strategy	Total cost (expression)	Final cost
Increase size by 1	$200 * (5 + 6 + 7 + 8 + ... + 60)	$364,000
Increase size by 4	$200 * (8 + 12 + 16 + 20 + ... + 56 + 60)	$95,200
Double the size	$200 * (8 + 16 + 32 + 64)	$24,000

So, with the first solution, Kim would have to give up her college fund. The second option would be somewhat better, but she would still have to get a scholarship just to pay it back. The third option, while still expensive, is a lot cheaper than the other two.

You might have noticed that the last strategy has fewer terms to add—that might be a clue! In fact, she would only have to buy a new trophy case four times, which is a big improvement!

Still, $24,000 is a lot of money to waste on trophy cases, so in the end, Kim might listen to her parents, settle for a trophy case for 10 robots, and display only her best creations.

Nevertheless, the same reasoning can be applied to arrays, and it's of great value.

Applying the strategies to arrays

So, from the examples we have seen and the math we have worked out, it seems that the best strategy is to double the size of the array every time we need more space.

Before you are sold, you might still ask: What if, instead of growing by 4 units, we grew the case by 16?

Doing the math, $200 * (20 + 36 + 52 + 68) yields $35,200, closer to the doubling strategy but 50% costlier. A constant-increase strategy might have an optimal point, but it's tailored to specific situations (like our 60-robot example). If we precisely knew our space needs, we could simply use a static array!

As mentioned earlier, the same reasoning can be applied to dynamic arrays. Suppose we need to implement a dynamic array by starting it with a single element and then allocating a new larger array each time the old one fills up. Let's also imagine that we will eventually add 100 elements to the array.

Each time we create a new array, we have to allocate the memory, but we also have to copy the elements of the old array into the new one. For example, for the +1 strategy, the first time we resize the array, the old array has one element that we need to copy to the new array (of size two). Then we copy those two elements into a new array of size three, and so on.

It works similarly for the other strategies. The expressions for the cost (in terms of elements copied from the old array to the new array) and the final costs are summarized in table 5.2.

Table 5.2 A comparison of the number of assignments for strategies to insert 100 elements into a dynamic array

Strategy	Number of assignments (expression)	Total assignments
Increase size by 1	$1 + 2 + 3 + 4 + 5 + 6 + \ldots + 98 + 99$	4851
Increase size by 4	$1 + 5 + 9 + 13 + \ldots + 93 + 97$	1225
Double the size	$1 + 2 + 3 + 6 + 12 + 32 + 64$	127

The difference in the results is astounding! We won't go into the math, but let me give you an idea of why we have this result. The expression for the first strategy is the sum of the first 99 integers, and it generalizes to any integer n: there is a long-known formula that says the result of summing the first n integers is $n * (n + 1) / 2$. In other words, the number of elements to be copied would be quadratic.

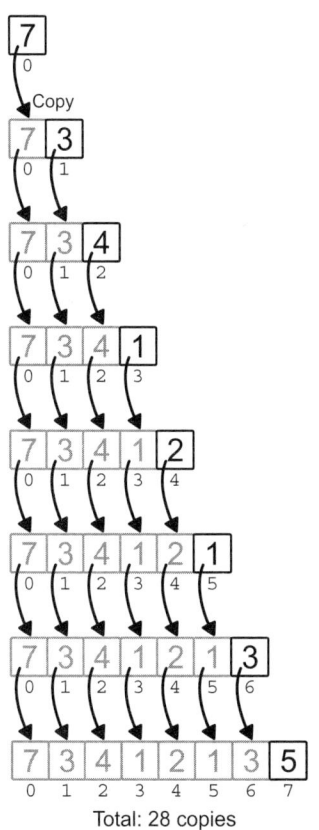

Total: 28 copies

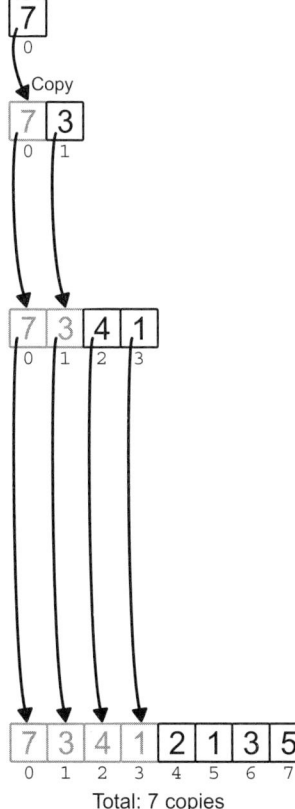

Total: 7 copies

Resizing an array with the +1 strategy versus resizing an array with the x2 strategy. There is a clear difference in terms of the number of times we need to copy the old elements over.

With the last strategy, instead, we double the number of elements at each step, which means that we wait twice as long before resizing the array again. This is also a known mathematical progression, and we could prove that to get an array of size n, starting with an array of size 1 and using this strategy, we will only need to copy $O(n)$ elements in the worst case.

In chapter 4, we saw that a quadratic function grows much faster than a linear function, so we do not doubt that we want a strategy that guarantees us linear overhead.

Should we also shrink arrays?

There is another aspect that we have ignored so far. We have agreed that it can be a good idea to double the size of a dynamic array as it fills up, but we haven't talked about what to do when we delete elements.

In our trophy case example, we didn't face this situation at all because Kim never wanted to remove any trophies or robots from the case. So, let's look at a different example to understand better what we need. The new example will be something more intangible, closer to computer science—let's imagine we need to implement a dynamic array to keep track of orders that are currently being worked on at your e-commerce company. When a new order comes in, it's added to the array; when the order is fulfilled and closed, it's removed. The entries remain in the array in the same sequence they were received (but any order can be deleted at any time).

Vinyl player to Abbey Road	HD camera to 21 Jump Street	180" plasma screen	∅
Created: 09/26/1969	Created: 07/06/1990	Created: 01/10/2022	
0	1	2	3

So, we start with a small array and double its size each time we fill the array—more precisely, each time we need to add a new element to a full array. The array keeps growing as new orders are received, but at some point, we also start deleting closed orders. So, how should the array adjust when orders are removed? Do we need to do something when we delete elements? Do we want to?

It depends heavily on the pace and timing of new orders coming in and old orders being closed, but, in general, we know that we should be ready to adjust when many elements are deleted. Why is that? Let's consider the following situation: you get a spike in orders for Black Friday, so the array needs to be expanded many times to accommodate them all. For example, you get a peak of 10,000 open orders at the same time during the holidays, while normally, you only have 100 open orders at any given time. If you don't resize the array after the Black Friday orders are closed, you'll waste 99% of the memory on a huge, mostly empty, container. And if your company grows by a factor of 100 or more, we are talking about millions of empty elements (and thus gigabytes of memory).

So, it seems that we need to also shrink a dynamic array somehow. But what exactly should we do?

Halve on delete

One possible strategy, probably the first that comes to mind, would be to shrink the array by halving it as soon as half of its elements are unused. This strategy has the advantage of reducing unused space, which would never be more than half of the total space. However, there is another edge case that we could look at to understand why this strategy might not be a good idea.

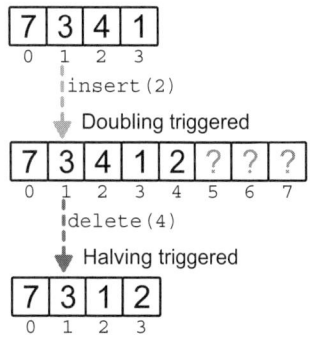

Consider a full dynamic array A with eight elements. Adding a ninth element X requires us to double the array's size. So, we make a new 16-slot array B, transfer the elements, and add X. However, if we soon remove an element, half of B becomes empty. Our current approach would shrink the array by half, creating an eight-slot array C. Now, C is full again, and any addition would need another resize. This back-and-forth resizing, especially with very large arrays, can severely degrade performance. We need a more efficient approach.

Smarter shrinking

Let's try another approach: when deleting an element causes the array to be half empty, we don't panic. Instead of resizing the array immediately, we will wait. How long should we wait? Well, there could be many good options, but I'm going to stick with a safe one: we wait until only a quarter of the array is used. This means that, for an array of capacity eight, we only halve it when there are six unused elements.

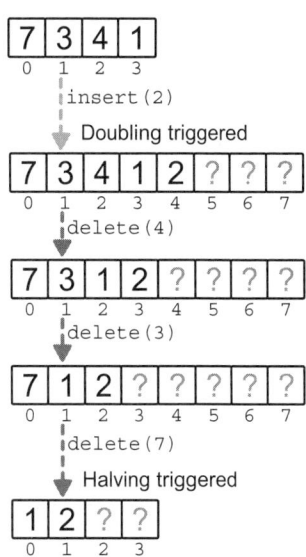

This way, after the resizing, the new array will be half empty, and we will still be able to insert new elements for a while before it fills up. Is this the perfect solution?

> **NOTE** There is no perfect solution because the perfect choice could only be made if we knew the sequence of insertions and deletions in advance. But this is a reasonably good solution that works well in most cases.

Implementing a dynamic array

Now that we have revealed the trick behind dynamic arrays, we can even implement them. To recap what we have discussed in this chapter: dynamic arrays can be implemented by using static arrays underneath and seamlessly (to the client) resizing these arrays as needed. For how to resize the helper static arrays containing data, we will use the following strategy:

1. We start with an array of size one (unless the client specifies an initial capacity).

2. If we need to insert a new element and the static array is already filled to its maximum capacity, we resize the array by doubling its size.

3. After we remove an element from the array, we resize the array by halving its size if only a quarter of the maximum capacity is filled.

All set! We just need to write some code to do the magic for us.

The DynamicArray class

In the rest of this chapter, we will implement an *unsorted* dynamic array. This means that the order of the elements is not guaranteed. We'll make the following assumption: the elements will be stored in the same order as they are inserted. When an element is deleted from the array, the elements after it are shifted to fill the hole left by the removed element (we will discuss this decision in detail in the section about the delete method).

Let's dive into the implementation. As always, you'll find the full code, along with documentation and tests, in the book's repo on GitHub: https://mng.bz/67J6. We'll begin with

```
class DynamicArray():
    def __init__(self, initial_capacity = 1, typecode = 'l'):
        self._array = core.Array(initial_capacity, typecode)
        self._capacity = initial_capacity
        self._size = 0
        self._typecode = typecode
```

As with the SortedArray class, we reuse the core.Array base class with composition, creating the static array as an internal attribute, that the DynamicArray class will handle behind the curtain.

As you can see, it's a simple constructor, very similar to the one for SortedArray. But notice that this time, we need to store the type of the array's elements, that is, the typecode argument. This is because we will need to create new static arrays each time we resize, and to do so, we need to pass the typecode argument to the constructor of core.Array.

Insert

Insertion doesn't change much from what we were doing with static arrays in chapter 2. The only difference is that, before performing the insertions, we need to check if there is any room left. If the static array is full, we need to resize it by creating a new array with twice the capacity and moving all the elements from the old array to the new one.

Let's start by defining a helper method to perform the resizing:

After saving a reference to the old array in a local variable, we can create a new array twice as large.

```python
def _double_size(self):
    old_array = self._array
    self._array = core.Array(self._capacity * 2, self._typecode)
    self._capacity *= 2
    for i in range(self._size):
        self._array[i] = old_array[i]
```

We need to copy all the elements from the old array to the new one.

It's nothing fancy. We only need to implement what we have discussed in this chapter and earlier in this section.

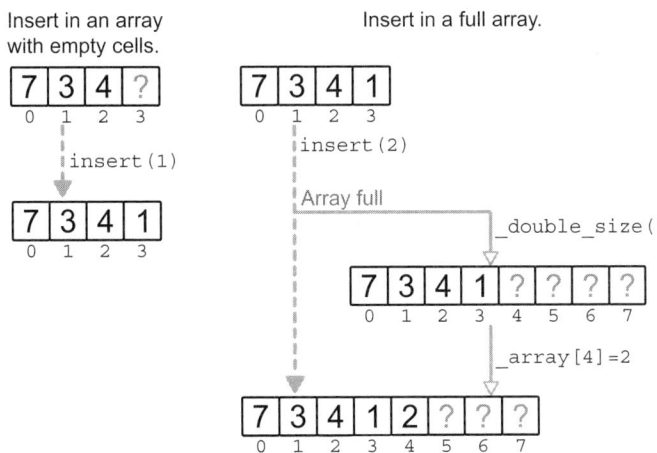

Now that we have the helper method for resizing the underlying static array, we can implement the insert method more easily and with a cleaner result:

```python
def insert(self, value):
    if self._size >= self._capacity:
        self._double_size()
    self._array[self._size] = value
    self._size += 1
```

When it gets here, we are sure that self._size < len(self._array).

What is the running time of the insert method, and how much extra memory does it use? Looking at the code, the instructions in insert take O(1) steps and require O(1) extra memory, except for the call to _double_size().

Remember, whenever we have a call to another method, the called method's running time contributes to the overall execution time, so we need to analyze the inner calls as well. And indeed, there is a catch here: when called on an array of size n, _double_size() creates a new array (using O(n) extra memory) and moves O(n) elements.

A word of caution about space analysis: don't let the fact that some memory is freed after it's been used confuse you. We need to include all allocated memory, even if it's freed later.

So insert, in turn, also takes O(n) time and uses O(n) extra space when the method to resize the array is called. This means that as the number of elements, n, grows, the resources needed by the method also grow linearly.

The fact that the worst-case running time and space requirements for insert are linear is bad news. We don't have a worst-case constant-time insert anymore, like we had with static arrays.

Upon deeper analysis, however, we can also find a silver lining. I said that these are the requirements for when the resize helper method is called: What about when we don't need to resize? In the best case, only the constant-time instructions are executed, and no extra space is used.

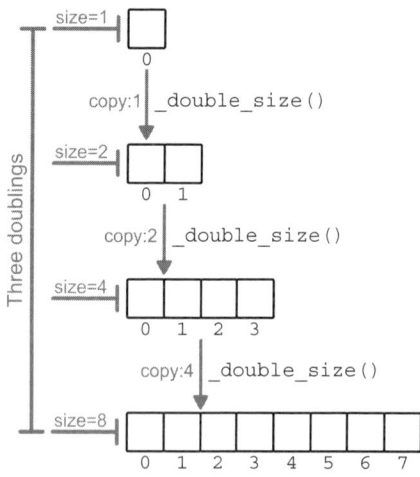

So, if we are lucky and we don't have to resize the array, insert is pretty fast. That's why it's important—if we have any idea of how many elements we might need to insert—to use the initial_capacity argument in the constructor and pre-allocate a larger static array (this is not just theory; you can find the same idea in Java standard library).

But there is more! We need to dig even deeper and ask how many times the _double_size method is actually called?

I won't go into the formal analysis, but here is the intuition. If we start with an array of size 1, we can only double it log(n) times before its size becomes n. And on each of those calls, we move only a fraction of those n elements.

For example, to get to eight elements, we call _double_size three times, and we move a total of 1 + 2 + 4 = 7 elements (1 the first time, 2 the second, and so on). This is generally true, and we can prove that we only need to copy O(n) elements and use O(n) extra space to insert n elements into a dynamic array.

Therefore, we can say that the *amortized time* for n insertions into a dynamic array is O(n). As mentioned in chapter 4, with an amortized analysis, we can't give any guarantee for the individual insertion, which can be slow if we are unlucky and need to resize the underlying array. But if we perform a batch of operations, we can guarantee that the total cost is of the same order of growth as for static arrays.

Find

There is nothing special about the `find` method for dynamic arrays. We can use the same methods we wrote for unsorted and sorted arrays, respectively, on both static and `dynamic` arrays.

In our case, for an unsorted array, we just have to bite the bullet and scan the whole array until we find a match (or don't). Thus, with an unsorted array, we already know that we can't do better than $O(n)$ for the running time (no extra space used).

The method is exactly the same as the linear search that we have already discussed in chapter 2:

```
def find(self, target):
    for index in range(self._size):
        if self._array[index] == target:
            return index
    return None
```

Delete

For the `delete` method, either we can either implement a delete-by-index method or we can reuse `find` to implement a delete-by-value variant. Here, I'll show you the latter, which only has three more instructions to find the index and check if the value exists.

Note that if there are duplicates, we delete the first occurrence of the value.

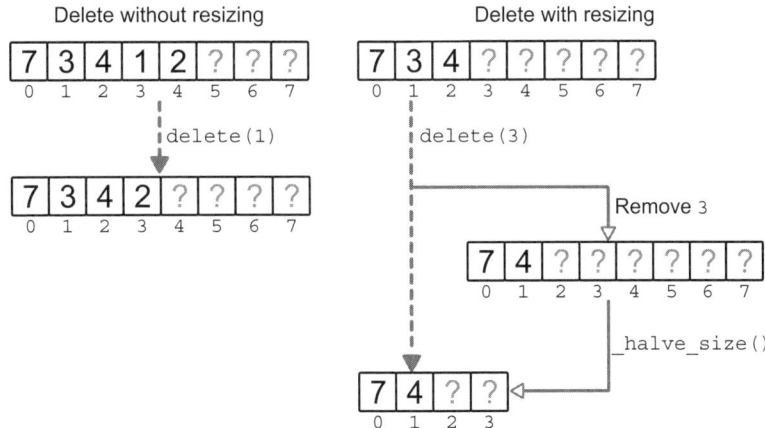

As with `insert`, we need to check whether we need to resize, but this time, the check is the last action we perform, and resizing means shrinking. So, first, we must find the element to delete and then remove it from the array, shifting all elements after it. Only at this point can we check whether the array is full for more than a quarter of its maximum capacity—otherwise we decide to shrink it:

```
def delete(self, target):
    index = self.find(target)
    if index is None:
        raise(ValueError(f'Unable to delete element {target}: the entry
is not in the array'))
    for i in range(index, self._size - 1):
        self._array[i] = self._array[i + 1]
    self._size -= 1
    if self._capacity > 1 and self._size <= self._capacity/4:
        self._halve_size()
```

Check if the array should be
shrunk after removal.

Similar to `insert`, the `delete` method uses a larger amount of resources in the calls where the resize is triggered. But unlike for `insert`, even if we don't resize the array, this version of the method has an $O(n)$ worst case for the running time. Here, we use linear search to find the index of the value to delete and then shift all elements after the deleted one (an operation that requires a linear number of assignments, in the worst case).

If we decided not to preserve the insertion order, we could implement a delete-by-index method (taking the position of the element to be deleted as an argument) that had a similar amortized performance as the `insert` method. Which version of the method is better? That depends on the context, that is, on the requirements of your application.

Note that the difference is not just a matter of implementation. We are choosing between different algorithms, each with its unique behavior and tradeoffs.

This concludes the implementation section—the same `traverse` method we implemented earlier can be used here as well.

EXERCISES

5.1 Implement the delete-by-index method and make sure that the amortized running time and extra space for n deletions are both $O(n)$. Hint: Suppose we don't need to preserve the insertion order of the elements.

5.2 If you implement the version of delete that removes elements by index, what are some possible drawbacks to swapping the deleted element with the last element instead of shifting the elements after the deleted one?

5.3 Implement the `DynamicSortedArray` class, modeling a dynamic array whose elements are kept in ascending order. What's the best possible running time for `insert` and `delete`?

Recap

- Arrays are great containers when we need to access elements based on their position. They provide constant-time access to any element, and we can read or write any element without sequentially accessing the elements before it.

- However, arrays are inherently static. That is, because of the way they are implemented in memory, their size cannot be changed once they are created.

- Having a fixed-size container means that we can't be flexible if we find that we need to store more elements. Furthermore, allocating a large array from the start to support the largest possible number of elements is often a waste of memory.

- Dynamic arrays are a way to get the best of arrays and add some flexibility. They are not a different type of data structure. They use fixed-size arrays but add a strategy to grow and shrink them as needed, reallocating the underlying static array each time it needs to be resized.

- The best strategy for dynamic arrays is to double the size of the underlying static array when we try to insert a new element into a full array and halve the size of the array when, after removing an element, three-quarters of the elements are empty.

- This flexibility comes at a cost: insert and delete can't be constant time as they are for static unsorted arrays. But for the insert method (and, under some assumptions, for the delete method as well), we can guarantee that n operations take an $O(n)$ amortized running time and additional memory.

In this chapter

- what linked lists can do better than arrays

- singly linked lists are the simplest version of linked
  lists

- doubly linked lists make it easier to read the list
  in both directions

- circular linked lists are good at handling periodic
  or cyclic data

In chapter 5, we discussed how static arrays have a weak spot when it comes to flexibility. *Dynamic arrays* may give us an illusion of flexibility, but, unfortunately, they are not a different (and flexible) data structure. They are just a strategy to resize static arrays as efficiently as possible. As discussed, the ability to resize arrays comes at a cost—slower insertion and deletion.

This chapter discusses yet another way of having a data structure that can be resized whenever needed, namely, *linked lists*. We will look at both singly linked lists (the simplest version) and doubly linked lists, which trade memory for better performance on some operations. As with dynamic arrays, we will find that there is again a price to pay for this flexibility, only this time, it's a different price.

Linked lists vs. arrays

It makes sense to start our discussion by making a comparison between linked lists and arrays. After all, we already have a data structure that can hold data and on which we can perform insert, delete, and search operations. Furthermore, we can traverse an array, that is, we can read its elements sequentially and perform some operation on each of the elements.

But how do linked lists differ from arrays in terms of functionality and efficiency?

Under the hood of a linked list

Let's start by explaining how linked lists work.

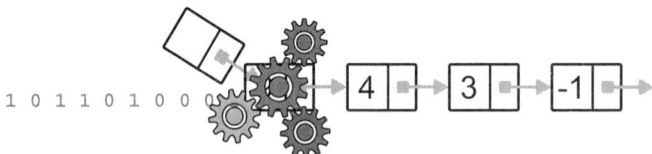

If you remember our discussion in chapter 2, an array is usually implemented as a unique, contiguous block of memory, divided into cells of equal size, each of which contains one of the array elements.

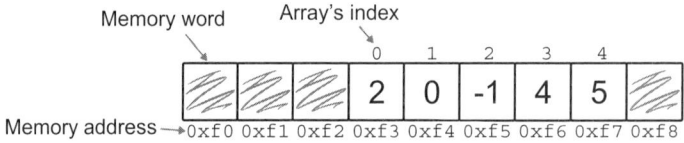

Unlike arrays, a linked list is a complex modular structure, made of building blocks called *nodes*: each node contains an element, a single value, of the linked list. But that's not all! Because the nodes are not in 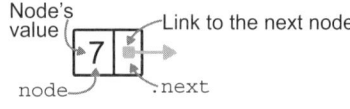 contiguous areas of memory, each must also contain a link to the next node, an extra piece of data that stores the location in the memory of the next node in the list.

This is the main difference between arrays and linked lists: in arrays, the location of each element is uniquely determined by the position of the first element and the elements' size. Therefore, if we know the memory address of the first element of the array (stored in the variable for the array), we can compute the address of each element by knowing its index (that is, its position in the sequence of elements).

Arrays and linked lists: A comparison

Let's compare how the same values are stored in an array and a linked list.

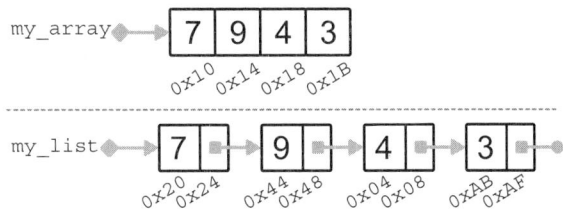

A linked list is a sequence of linked nodes, where each node is itself a small data structure that stores a single value and a link to the next node.

With linked lists, there are two main differences with respect to arrays:

- Nodes are not stored contiguously but anywhere in the available memory address space.

- Owing to the noncontiguous storage, the location of each node must be saved. This address is stored within the node itself, which means that each node of a linked list will take up more memory than the corresponding array element. As you can see, for each node, we have drawn an extra cell, allocated just after the value, which contains the link to the next node.

These differences have consequences, both positive and negative. On the positive side, as the nodes in a linked list don't have to be allocated contiguously, we have more flexibility: we are not forced to allocate the whole list in advance, and we can add as many nodes as we want at any time, as long as there is enough memory to allocate a new node. The negative consequence, however, is that since the addresses of the nodes are not predetermined, there is no formula to compute where a node will be given its index in the sequence of list elements. This means that, compared to arrays, we lose the ability to access any element by its index and are instead forced to read the linked list from its beginning, one node at a time, getting the address of the next node, and so on, until we get to the element we want to access.

Let's see a concrete example: What's the difference between reading the third element from an array versus from a linked list?

With an array, we can just access the element at index 2. It's a single, constant-time operation (that is, it takes the same time, regardless of whether we access the third, the fourth, or the hundredth element).

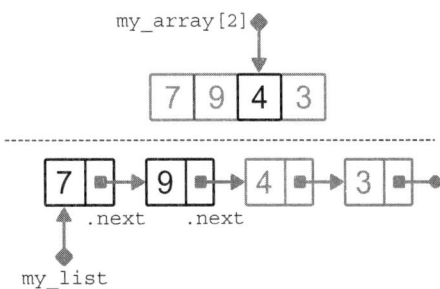

In a linked list, we start by accessing the first element and follow its pointer to the second and then to the third element. This operation requires accessing a linear number of nodes, and that's the main drawback of a linked list. But, of course, there are situations where this is too expensive and other situations where we won't care (for example, if we know that we won't be traversing the list much, while instead, we will always be accessing elements near the beginning).

Singly linked lists

What we have described in the previous section is called a *singly linked list*—yes, that means there are two kinds of linked lists. A singly linked list is a linked list with a single link per node, pointing to the next element in the list.

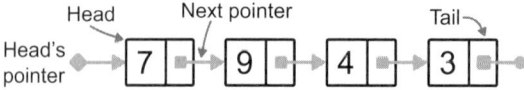

The first element of a linked list is called its *head*, and the last element of the list is called its *tail*. In a singly linked list, the characteristic of a head node is that no other node points to it, so we need to store a link to the beginning (aka head) of the list somewhere in a variable.

In a linked list, each node only knows about its successor: it is indirectly linked to all nodes after it, but it is isolated from its own predecessors.

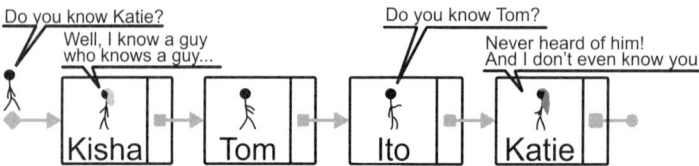

The characteristic of a tail node is that its next pointer doesn't point to another node (in programming languages such as Java or C, it's set to `null`). In this section, we are going to discuss an application of singly linked lists and then explore the characteristics and implementations of the same methods we defined on arrays: `insert`, `delete`, `search`, and `traverse`.

Orders management

In chapter 5, we discussed a situation where static arrays would struggle and where we would need the flexibility of dynamic arrays. This example is in the section "Should we also shrink arrays?" and it features an e-commerce company and the process that keeps track of the customers' orders. When a new order is received, it's added to the end of the list, and orders are kept in the same sequence as received. When an order is fulfilled, it gets removed from the list.

If we were to store the orders in a linked list instead of an array, what would change?

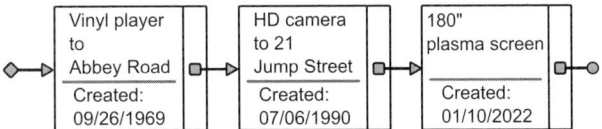

First and foremost, unlike arrays, linked lists wouldn't have any empty space allocated. We would only allocate nodes as needed.

When we get a new order, we create a new node (*just in time allocation*), and there is no need to allocate space in advance. When we remove a node, we won't leave any "hole," that is, no empty space will be created (we will see this in detail in the next sections). Of course, each node would need some space to store its value (the order, with items, address, and creation date) and also some extra space for the next link.

It seems that linked lists are perfect for our order management task. But are they too good to be true?

Implementing singly linked lists

Linked lists are different from any data structure we have seen so far. Arrays are just a contiguous area of memory divided into cells of equal size, so there is little overhead in implementing them (at least their simpler versions).

The implementation of linked lists is, however, less straightforward. I like to think of linked lists as two-tier data structures.

There is an external data structure that implements the linked list itself and provides an API for clients to interact with the list and perform our usual operations on it.

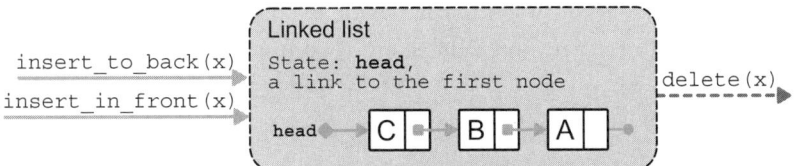

This is like a shell, a wrapper around the linked list. But internally, inside this wrapper, we need to use a different data structure—the nodes that we have described earlier in the chapter. They can be thought of as data structures that store a single value (to be picky, two values: a user-facing value, the data stored by the client, and an internal value, the link to the next node).

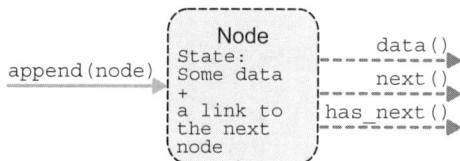

A linked list then consists of nodes sequentially ordered by their links. In addition, it includes some helper attributes, such as a reference to the first node in the list, and some associated methods. Therefore, to implement a linked list, we must first implement a class for the nodes.

As always, the full code for this chapter is also stored in the book's repo on GitHub: https://mng.bz/rVRD. This is the Python code for the Node class:

```python
class Node:
    def __init__(self, data, next_node = None):
        self._data = data
        self._next = next_node

    def data(self):
        return self._data

    def next(self):
        return self._next

    def has_next(self):
        return self._next is not None

    def append(self, next_node):
        self._next = next_node
```

This class is minimal, with only the attributes for the data and the link to the next node, two public methods to return their values, and two methods to set the link to the next node and check whether there is a link to the next node. That's all we need for the internal implementation of a singly linked list.

> **TIP** The `Node` class can also be kept hidden from clients by implementing it as a nested class within the list class. This is because users shouldn't directly manipulate the list's nodes.

The wrapper class for the list, the one class with which all clients will interact, is also minimal in its initialization section:

```python
class SinglyLinkedList:
    def __init__(self):
        self._head = None
```

Yes, that's it! All we need to do is initialize the internal attribute pointing to the head of the list (that is, the first node in the list) to `None`: when `head` is set to `None`, it means that the list is empty.

If you look closely, you will notice two important differences from the constructors for the array classes we have implemented in the previous chapter:

- We don't need to specify a size for the list; we don't need to allocate any space in advance, and the list can grow dynamically.

- There is no argument for restricting the type of data stored in nodes. That's because, in a loosely typed language such as Python, it doesn't make sense to restrict the type of the values of a container like a list (for arrays, it might make sense to achieve higher efficiency, as we explained in chapter 2).

    Of course, in strongly typed languages such as Java or C++, it makes sense to force the list to contain elements of the same type, and it would still be possible to restrict the type of data stored using Python type hints if there is a strong, context-related reason to do so.

Don't be fooled, though. The complexity in the `SinglyLinkedList` class is all in its methods.

Insert

The first operation that we usually want to implement on a data structure is insertion. But how do we do it for an unsorted, singly linked list?

Insert at the end of the list

If you remember from chapter 2, for unsorted arrays, we added new elements toward the end of the array, after the last element previously stored in the array. We can do the same for unsorted lists as well. We don't care about the order of the elements, and we can just append new elements to the end of the list.

To add a new element to the end of the list, we need to traverse the entire list, find its tail, and then add a new `Node` to it (which will be the new tail).

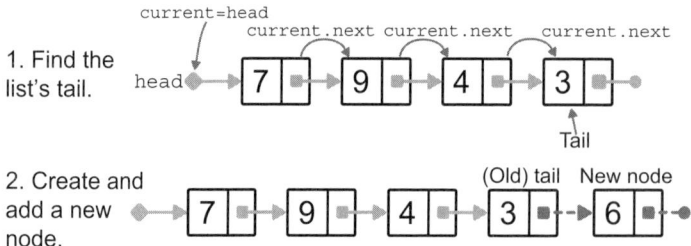

1. Find the list's tail.

2. Create and add a new node.

This works and keeps the elements in the same order as they were inserted. But can you see a problem here? We must traverse the whole list each time we insert a new element: this means that this method takes linear time, `O(n)` for a list of n elements. Another way to look at this is that inserting n elements into an empty list would take quadratic time:

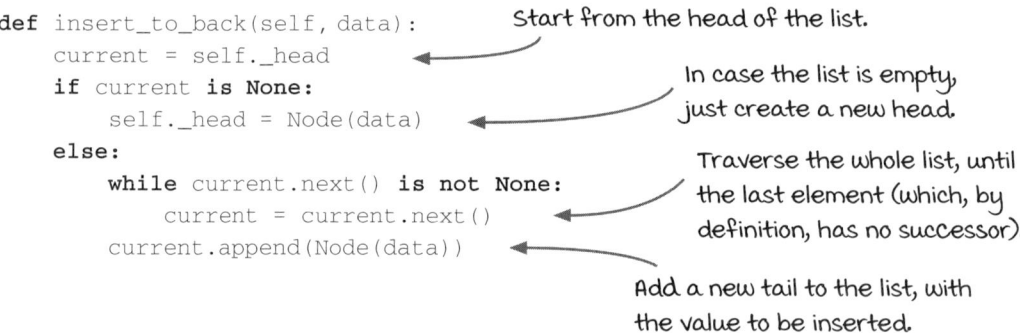

```
def insert_to_back(self, data):
    current = self._head
    if current is None:
        self._head = Node(data)
    else:
        while current.next() is not None:
            current = current.next()
        current.append(Node(data))
```

Start from the head of the list.

In case the list is empty, just create a new head.

Traverse the whole list, until the last element (which, by definition, has no successor).

Add a new tail to the list, with the value to be inserted.

With arrays, we can access their last element (or any element) in constant time but, unfortunately, this is no longer true for lists.

> **NOTE** With linked lists, we could theoretically store a link to the list's tail, and that would make insertion at the end easier; however, with singly linked lists, updating the link to the tail when we delete an element could be expensive.

So, we are stuck with linear-time insertion, and that's far from ideal: Can we do better? Of course we can!

Insert, smarter (in front)

Although it makes sense to insert elements at the end of the list, we are working with unsorted lists, and we don't care about the order of the elements. Instead, how about inserting a new element at the beginning of the list?

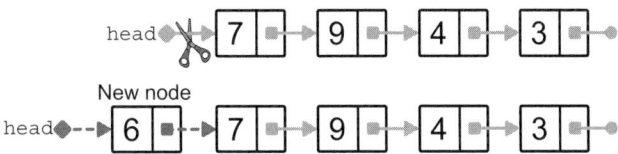

Not only is this possible, but it apparently works beautifully:

```
def insert_in_front(self, data):
    old_head = self._head
    self._head = Node(data, old_head)
```

There is a reason why inserting elements at the beginning of the list is fast, while inserting at the end is not. It's because of the asymmetry in nodes, where we only store the link to the node's successor but not its predecessor. Therefore, we can only traverse the list in a single direction, and, as we'll soon see, any change, insertion, or deletion is expensive unless made at the beginning of the list.

By growing the list from its head, we create a new list made up of the newly created node, followed by the old list. And this is as efficient as it gets: it takes only constant time, O(1).

Search

Now that we can populate our linked list with orders, we can start searching it to find any order we have added. The search method is a straightforward linear search: we can't do any better than traverse the entire list until we find what we were looking for or reach the end of the list trying.

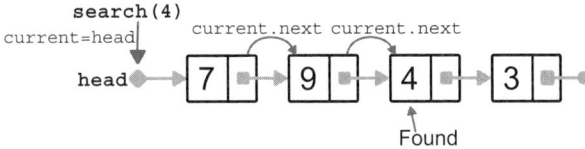

This implementation of the search method, which of course takes linear time and constant extra space, returns the node where the matching data is stored:

```
def _search(self, target):
    current = self._head
    while current is not None:
        if current.data() == target:
            return current
        current = current.next()
    return None
```

You may have noticed that the name of the method has an underscore in front of it—I implemented it as a private method. That's because this implementation should only be used internally. Why is that? There is more than one reason, actually: as a feature, it wouldn't be that useful, and design-wise, we shouldn't return `Node` objects.

First, feature-wise: there is no reason to return the node found to a client. With arrays, we return the index of the found value, but with linked lists, a user would not get any additional information from the node because they already have the data stored by the node (in this implementation, we compare the whole `data` field with the `target` value passed as an argument).

There are cases where we store composite data on the nodes, and we may want to perform the search on some fields. For example, in our order management application, we store the order itself, a composite field made of (presumably) order ID, product list, creation date, some sort of status for the order, and details about the buyer and the shipment. We could search by order ID, or by shipping address, and return the whole order.

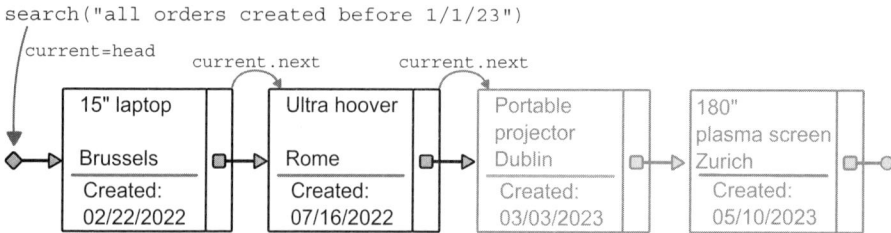

Even if we do so, we definitely don't want to return a reference to the list node: we shouldn't share the `Node` class with clients. The internal implementation of the linked list should be opaque to the users, who should rely only on the external interface provided by the linked list. By ensuring users rely only on the external interface, users can seamlessly switch without breaking any code if you later write an improved linked list implementation. By making the `_search` method private, we could also make the `Node` class private to `SinglyLinkedList`.

> **TIP**   Following the principle of least authority, we shouldn't give any client a reference to a list's `Node`: if a third party has a reference to an internal node, which is mutable, they can make changes and break the list.

This doesn't mean that search is useless. In the order management example, we can return a copy of the order's data, without providing any reference to the list nodes. By changing the returned value, we can implement a `contains` method, which tells the caller only whether the data is stored in the list. And we can always use the `_search` method internally, calling it from other methods of the same class.

Delete

When it comes to the `delete` method, we don't have the dilemma we had with arrays. We want to delete elements by value because, as we discussed, list elements are accessed sequentially: for example, we can't directly access the third element in the list without accessing the first two elements.

On the bright side, however, deleting an element in a list is much easier. All we have to do is bypass the element we want to remove, that is, make sure to update its predecessor's link, so that it points to the successor of the element we want to delete.

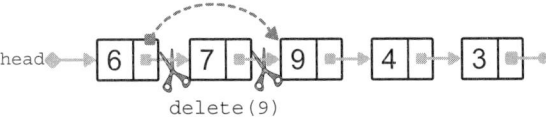

delete(9)

Easy, right? Not so fast!

First, there are two edge cases to consider:

1. If you delete the last node, then you have to make the previous node the new tail (in our implementation, its link is set to `None`).

2. If you delete the first node, the head of the list, then there is no predecessor! In this case, we just have to update the list's `head` pointer.

Once we have clarified the edge cases, you might think that we should reuse the search method to find the node to remove, and then perform the change. The sad news is, this won't work.

In the section about the insert method, I mentioned how nodes in singly linked lists are asymmetric. Because we only store the next pointer in each node, we can go from one node to its successor in the list, but we can't go to its predecessor.

Basically, when we have a link to a node N in the list, it's as if we can only see the section of the list from N onward, while all the nodes before it are invisible to us.

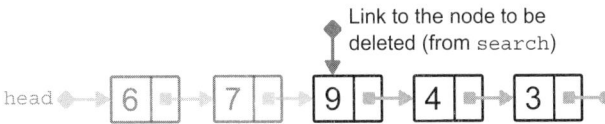

Link to the node to be deleted (from `search`)

So, we can't use _search to find the node that stores the value we need to delete because we wouldn't be able to update the `next` link on the node's predecessor.

However, we can still use what we have in the implementation for the search method: we just need to traverse the list and keep a link to the node before the one we are visiting.

Once we find our target, we can use that link to access the predecessor of the node we want to delete:

```
def delete(self, target):
    current = self._head
    previous = None
    while current is not None:
        if current.data() == target:
            if previous is None:
                self._head = current.next()
            else:
                previous.append(current.next())
            return
        previous = current
        current = current.next()
    raise ValueError(f'No element with value {target} was found in the
list.')
```

Edge case: delete the head of the list.

Average case: a node in the middle of the list (or the tail as well)

If it gets here, target is not in the list.

What's the running time of the `delete` method? We have to search the list first, so it's `O(n)`. As we have discussed, having a pointer to the node to delete wouldn't help us, unfortunately, because we would still have to traverse the list up to its predecessor, to update it. We will see later in this chapter how we could address this problem.

Finally, note that this method only requires a constant amount of additional memory.

Delete from the front of the list

Deleting the head of the list can be considered a special case. There are contexts where we do not need to delete elements at any position, but only at the beginning of the list—we will find the perfect example when we discuss the stack in chapter 8. As we discussed when talking about insertion, operations that only change the head of the list are cheap, and indeed, deleting the first node in the list would be a constant-time operation.

This concludes our section on singly linked lists. Now you have everything you need to implement a usable version of the list! The code on our GitHub repository (https://mng.bz/Vx00) also includes a few more helper methods that can be useful in many situations.

EXERCISES

6.1 Implement a `delete_from_front` method that removes and returns the head of the list. Hint: This is an edge case in the general-purpose delete method.

6.2 Implement the traverse method for singly linked lists. The method should take a function that can be applied to the data stored in the list and return a Python list with the result of applying such a function.

Sorted linked lists

We have implemented a singly linked list where the order of its elements doesn't matter. What changes if the order does matter? For instance, what if we want to store elements in our order management system not in the order in which they are received, but (for example) sorted by user, or by ID (in case IDs are not auto-incremented, but randomly assigned)?

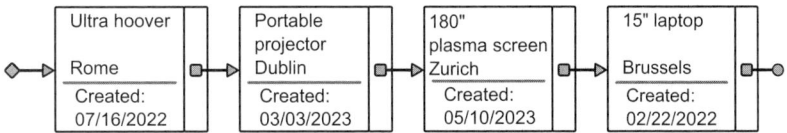

A list of orders sorted by name of the product (descending).

In this section, we will briefly see what we need to change to keep the elements of a singly linked list sorted.

Insert in the middle

If we need to keep our list of orders sorted, then we can't just insert new nodes at the beginning (or at the end) of the list. We are forced to traverse the list to find the right place to insert the new value—more specifically, we need to find the node after which the new value should be added and then update the links in the list (and in the newly created node) to include the node that stores the new value.

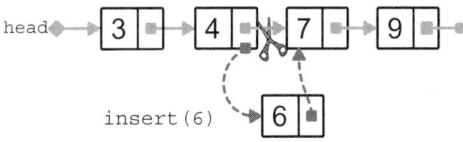

If we assume for the sake of simplicity that the node's data is directly comparable (that is, we can use the < operator on these data), the implementation of this new insertion method is very similar to the traversal we have in `delete`:

```
def insert_in_sorted_list(self, new_data):
    current = self._head
    previous = None
    while current is not None:
        if current.data() >= new_data:
            if previous is None:
                self._head = Node(new_data, current)
```

Edge case: insert at the beginning of the list.

```
    else:
        previous.append(Node(new_data, current))
    return
    previous = current
    current = current.next()
if previous is None:
    self._head = Node(new_data)
else:
    previous.append(Node(new_data, None))
```

General case: add the new node between **previous** and **current**.

Edge case: empty list

Edge case: insert at the end of the list.

As you can imagine, this version of the insertion method only works if the list is sorted and its running time is `O(n)` —we lose constant-time insertion.

EXERCISE

6.3 Can you think of a way to write the `insert_in_sorted_list` method by reusing the `insert_in_front` and `delete` methods and without making any other explicit changes to the nodes? What would be the running time of this method?

Can we improve search?

In chapter 3, we discussed sorted arrays, and we learned that we have to give up constant-time insertion to keep the elements sorted. We also learned that, in exchange, we get to use *binary search*, a more efficient search method, which only needs to look at `O(log(n))` elements in the worst case, much better than *linear search*, whose running time is `O(n)`.

So, maybe we get the same improvement for linked lists? Take a minute to think about it before you read the answer.

The main advantage of binary search is that we can pick an element from the middle of the array, and then (if we don't find a match) we can ignore half of the remaining elements. With linked lists, to get to the middle element of the list, we would have to traverse all the elements before it. And then, to find the middle element of the half of the list we kept, we would have to traverse half of those elements (even if we kept the left half of the list, we would still need to traverse those elements again). This would make the running time worse than linear search.

The key to binary search is the constant-time access to any element in the array by its index. Since lists lack this feature, generally, they can't be more efficient than linear search.

That means that `insert` was the only method we had to change to keep the list's elements sorted and also that we don't get any advantage unless, for example, we want to have fast access to the smallest element, which would always be at the head of the list. Anyway, in some contexts, you might be required to keep your list sorted, so this variant might come in handy.

Doubly linked lists

We have learned that singly linked lists (SLL) do offer greater flexibility than arrays, but they have important drawbacks. First and foremost, we are forced to read the list's elements sequentially, while with arrays, we can directly access any index in constant time. This is an intrinsic limitation of linked lists, and there is nothing we can do: it's the price we have to pay to have a data structure that can be allocated "just in time" when we need it.

We can't get general-purpose constant-time access with linked lists, but doubly linked lists address another quirk specific to singly linked nodes: their asymmetric nature. SLL nodes only maintain a link to their successor, which makes some operations on a list more complicated and slower.

In this section, we discuss how we can overcome this limitation and at what cost.

Twice as many links, twice as much fun?

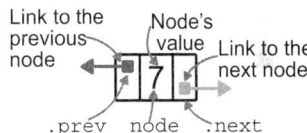

You might have already figured this out: a doubly linked list (DLL) is a linked list whose nodes store two links, throwing in the link to the node's predecessor.

This trivial change has important consequences:

- We can traverse a DLL in both directions, from its head to its tail, and from its tail to its head.

- If we have a link to a single node of the list, we can reach any other node in the list, both before and after it. We experienced how important this is when we discussed the delete method for SLLs.

- On the negative side, each node of a DLL takes up more space than the corresponding SLL variant. On large lists, the difference can affect your applications.

- Another negative consequence is that for each change we make to the list, we need to update two links—maintenance becomes more complicated and more expensive.

As for the implementation, the `Node` class, in addition to the new attribute, now has a few more methods to set, access, and check this link to the previous node. Notice that we no longer pass an optional argument to `Node`'s constructor to set the next pointer. It's better to force clients to create a disconnected node and use the append method explicitly.

Also, for doubly linked lists, the logic of appending a new node is more complicated because, for consistency, we must also set the predecessor link of the node we are appending. Similarly, when we prepend a node, we must set its successor:

```
class Node:
    def __init__(self, data):
        self._data = data
        self._next = None
        self._prev = None

    def data(self):
        return self._data

    def next(self):
        return self._next

    def has_next(self):
        return self._next is not None

    def append(self, next_node):
        self._next = next_node
        if next_node is not None:
            next_node._prev = self

    def prev(self):
        return self._prev

    def has_prev(self):
        return self._prev is not None

    def prepend(self, prev_node):
        self._prev = prev_node
        if prev_node is not None:
            prev_node._next = self
```

In the wrapper class for the list, we also have some changes:

```
class DoublyLinkedList:
    def __init__(self):
        self._head = None
        self._tail = None
```

Specifically, we also set a link to the tail of the list. This allows us to quickly delete from the end of the list but at the cost of keeping this link updated when we make any changes, as we will see in the next sections.

From these implementations alone, it's clear that doubly linked lists are more complicated to implement and maintain than their singly linked counterparts. Are DLLs worth the tradeoff? Well, that depends on your application. Before we delve into the implementation of the methods for DLLs, let's look at one such application where they do make a difference.

The importance of retracing your steps

Meet Tim! He is working on his first video game, a side-scroller where the hero has to move from one room to another inside a building, from left to right.

Tim has carefully designed the rooms, implemented each room individually, and now he needs to model the sequence of progress between the rooms.

"How do I do that?" he wonders.

The framework Tim is using offers an out-of-the-box singly linked list, which would save him a lot of development time. But if he uses a singly linked list, the game hero can go to the room on the right but won't be able to go back.

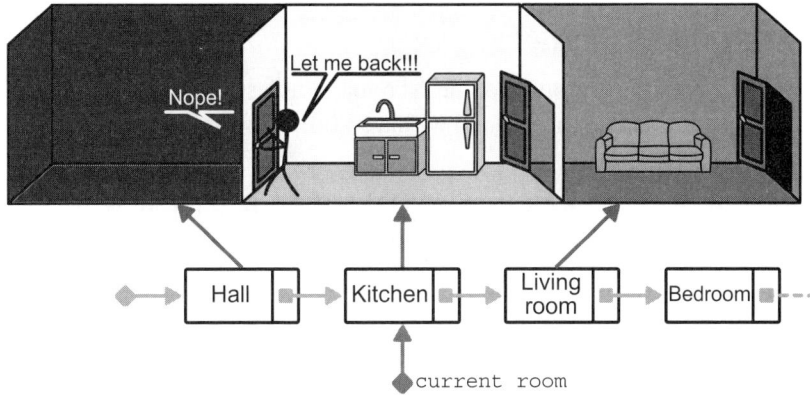

The problem is that for the gameplay Tim is designing, the players need to be able to trace back their steps because there are rooms where some interactions can only be unlocked later in the game. Then a singly linked list can't work, and Tim needs to implement a doubly linked list.

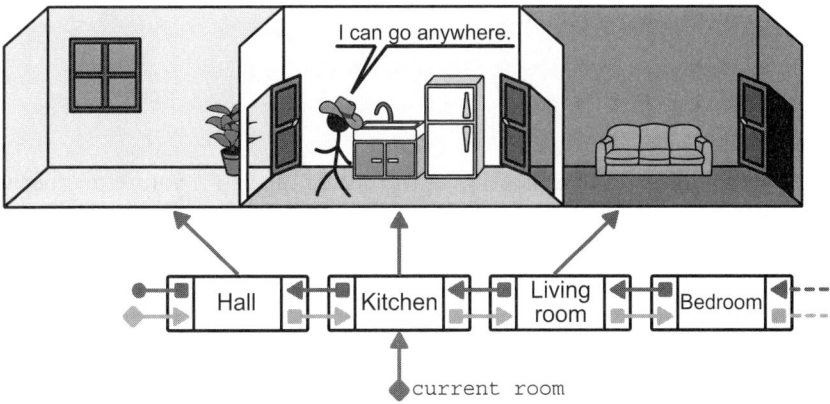

Whenever we need to move back and forth through a list, in both directions, that's a use case for a doubly linked list. It can be layers in a multi-layer document or actions that can be undone and redone. There are many use cases in computer science where the space used by the extra link of DLLs is not only worth it but necessary.

Insert

We have discussed how the extra link stored in doubly linked lists can create new opportunities and, ultimately, value. Let's now see the price we must pay, starting with the insert methods.

As before, we have the opportunity to insert elements at the beginning, at the end, or at an arbitrary point of the list.

Insert at the beginning of the list

Inserting a new node at the beginning of the list remains as fast as it was for singly linked lists: we still have to get the head of the list (and we have a link to it) and prepend the new node.

There is a little more maintenance to this operation for DLLs, because we need to update the previous pointer of the old head, and possibly we might have to update the link to the list's tail, in one edge case—when we insert in an empty list:

```
def insert_in_front(self, data):
    if self._head is None:
        self._tail = self._head = Node(data)
    else:
        old_head = self._head
        self._head = Node(data)
        self._head.append(old_head)
```

Insert at the end of the list

Things get interesting with the insertion at the end of the list. If you remember what we discussed earlier in this chapter: inserting at the end of the list is particularly inefficient for SLLs. It takes linear time.

For DLLs, however, two things are game changers:

- We can store a pointer to the tail of the list, which can then be accessed in constant time.

- From any node, we can access (and update) its predecessor in constant time.

This means that we can follow the link to the tail of the list, and add a new node as its successor, all in constant time.

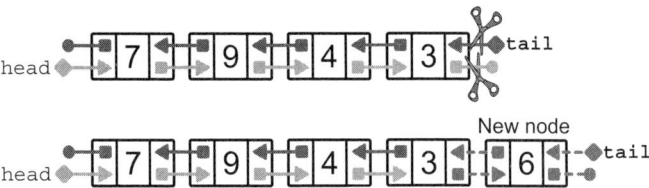

With a doubly linked list, we can efficiently insert the elements at either end of the list indifferently. Even more, since we can traverse the list in both directions, we can access the elements in both the direct and inverse order of insertion:

```
def insert_to_back(self, data):
    if self._tail is None:
        self._tail = self._head = Node(data)
    else:
        old_tail = self._tail
        self._tail = Node(data)
        self._tail.prepend(old_tail)
```

Insert in the middle

Finally, what if we want to insert an element in an arbitrary position in the middle of the list (that is, neither at the end nor at the beginning)?

There are two possible situations. If we have the link to either of the nodes between which we need to add the new element, then the operation of adding the new node consists only of updating the `next` and `prev` pointers on those nodes, and it only takes constant time: compared to arrays, we don't need to shift the elements to the right, and that's a huge saving!

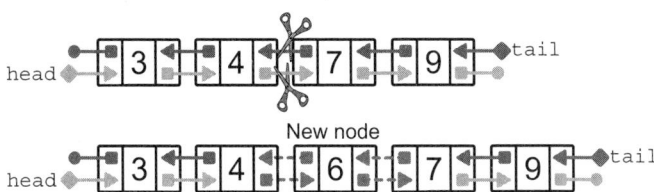

If we need to find the insertion point, especially when we want to keep the list sorted, this requires traversing the list. And list traversal takes linear time. The good news is that, even in this case, we wouldn't need to store a reference to the previous node while traversing the list, which makes the operation easier than with SLLs.

Search and traversal

When it comes to searching a doubly linked list, the extra links to the predecessors can't really help us. Our best option is still linear search, which means traversing the list from its beginning to its end, until we find the element we are looking for, or until we reach the end of the list. Sure, we can now traverse the list in both directions, but (unless *domain knowledge* suggests otherwise), there is generally no advantage in doing so. Therefore, we can reuse the `_search` method written for SLLs exactly as it is—we don't need to repeat the code here.

Obviously, the same consideration applies to the `traverse` method. But as an exercise, you can add a method to traverse the list in reverse order, from tail to head.

Delete

Conceptually, `delete` on DLLs works exactly the same way as `delete` on SLLs: we traverse the list until we find the element we want to delete, E, and then update the links of the nodes before and after E, bypassing it. And then, we are done.

There is one big difference, however: nodes store a link to their predecessor, so we can reuse the search method to find the node with the element to delete. Another difference is that we must pay attention to edge cases and update the `_tail` link for the linked list when needed.

The implementation of the method, therefore, looks a lot different for doubly linked and singly linked lists:

```
def delete(self, target):
    node = self._search(target)
    if node is None:
        raise ValueError(f'{target} not found in the list.')
    if node.prev() is None:
        self._head = node.next()
        if self._head is None:
            self._tail = None
        else:
            self._head.prepend(None)
    elif node.next() is None:
        self._tail = node.prev()
        self._tail.append(None)
    else:
        node.prev().append(node.next())
        del node
```

Delete the node at the beginning of the list.

In this case, the list's head was the only element in the list.

Delete the node at the end of the list.

General case

The running time for the delete method remains O(n), like for SLLs, because we still need to traverse the list to search the node storing the element to be deleted.

Concatenating two lists

Imagine you have two or more lists, for example, lists of tasks, one list per day, where the tasks must be completed in the order they appear in the list, and today's task must be completed before tomorrow's tasks.

Suppose at some point we need to compress two days' worth of errands into a single day—some travel is suddenly scheduled for tomorrow, and you need to complete your tasks by today. Concatenating two lists by appending one to the other is super easy—we just need to append the head of the second list to the tail of the first list.

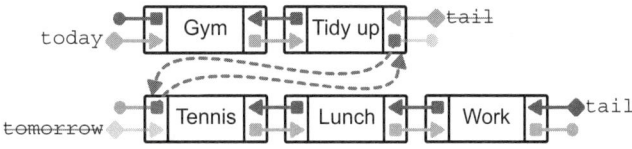

In code: `today._tail.append(tomorrow._head)`. That's it! Lists, and especially doubly linked lists, offer constant-time concatenation.

Now, imagine if we had to merge two arrays! We would have to allocate a new array whose size would be the sum of the sizes of the two original arrays and then move all the elements of both arrays into the newly created array.

Now imagine you have large lists of unsorted items that need to be merged often. This is the perfect example of an application where a linked list can perform much better than an array.

And that's all for the doubly linked list. As always, you can find the full code for this class on the book's repo on GitHub: https://mng.bz/x2Re.

EXERCISES

6.4 Implement a method to insert a new element after a certain node in the list. This node must be passed as an argument. What's the running time for this method? Is there any edge case?

6.5 Implement the `SortedDoublyLinkedList` class, modeling a DLL whose elements are kept sorted. Hint: Follow the example of what we did with the `SortedSingleLinkedList` class. What methods do we need to override in this case?

Circular linked lists

So far in this chapter, we have been discussing linear lists that have a clear distinction between their beginning and end. In other words, we assume that once we have traversed a list and reached its end, we are done. Sometimes in life, it doesn't work that way.

Sometimes you need to start over instead of just stopping. In this section, we will look at some examples where this happens, and we will briefly discuss how we can modify our linked list data structures to adapt.

Examples of circular linked lists

There are cyclical activities whose steps are repeated many times in the same sequence. For example, the agricultural cycle repeats the same steps each season, and the seasons themselves repeat in a perpetual cycle.

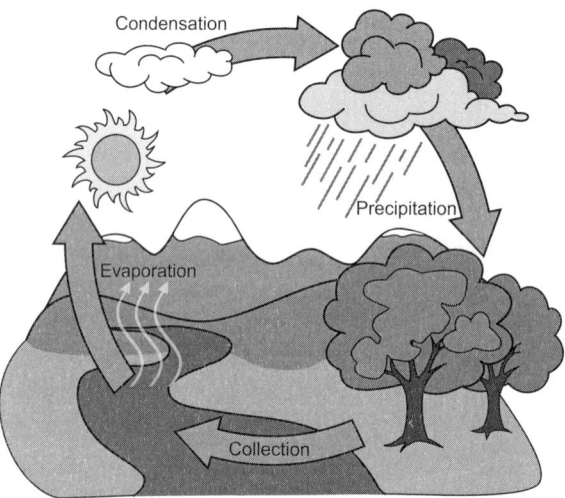

There are cyclical processes that go through stages, over and over again, like the process of building and launching a startup or a product, or the water cycle. Some resources are used cyclically, ranging from agricultural examples such as crops to computer-science-related instances such as cache nodes or servers. Another computer-related resource that is used cyclically and that you are probably familiar with are pictures in slide shows and carousels.

In all these contexts, instead of using a regular linked list, we might want to turn to one of its variants, a circular linked list.

Circular linked lists can be implemented as either singly linked or doubly linked lists indifferently. The choice between singly and doubly linked is independent and is based on the traversal requirements, as discussed earlier in the chapter.

For example, a singly linked list is sufficient to model a slideshow, a presentation where images are shown cyclically in the same order, without the possibility of manually going back. Similarly, if we need to represent the agricultural cycle, or route incoming calls to a list of servers, we can use a singly linked list, because we will only be traversing the list in one direction.

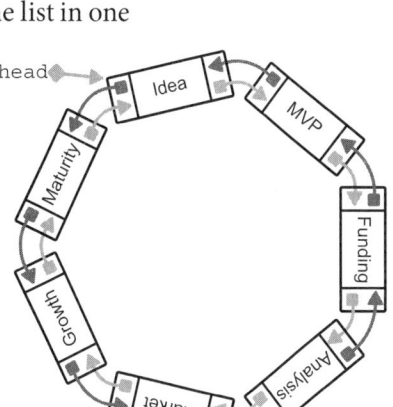

If, instead, we need to be able to move in both directions in the list, we have to use a doubly linked list. In contrast to the slideshow above, imagine a carousel that allows users to go back and forth between pictures. An example of this would be modeling the process of creating, building, and growing a startup, where we might need to go back to a previous step at any time. For example, we could go back from the market phase to the analysis phase to adjust a product, without having to start from scratch.

Implementation tips

We won't go into detail on how to implement circular linked lists, mainly because it requires only minimal changes with respect to the classes we already implemented in this chapter.

There are, however, a few things to keep in mind when designing a circular linked list:

- While in regular lists the last node had no successor (and the head, in doubly linked lists, has no predecessor), in circular lists, we set the successor of the tail of the list to its head. This means that we must be careful when traversing the list, or we will end up in an infinite loop.

- For a circular doubly linked list, we don't need to store a link to the tail of the list: it's just `head.prev`.

- For circular linked lists, it is common to have some sort of iterative way to traverse the list: one element at a time, as we would do with a Python iterator. This means that we need to add another attribute to the list to store the node currently being traversed, plus a method that returns its data and, at the same time, advances to the next node.

- If we provide step-by-step traversal, we will have to be very careful when deleting or inserting elements to the list—we will have to make sure to update the pointer to the current element when needed.

EXERCISE

6.6 Implement a circular linked list, with step-by-step traversal. You can implement either a singly or doubly linked version. Can we reuse anything from the classes we have defined earlier in the chapter? Is composition an option? Is inheritance an option, and what are pros and cons here?

Recap

- *Linked lists* are an alternative to arrays because they can be expanded and shrunk more easily, without reallocating or moving elements other than those being added or removed.

- A linked list is a two-tier data structure that is internally implemented as a sequence of instances of a data structure called *node*. Each node contains some data, namely an element of the list, and at least one link to the next node in the list.

- Linked lists with only one link, the one to the successor of each node, are called *singly linked lists* (SLL). They are the simplest version of linked lists. Singly linked lists can only be traversed in one direction, from their beginning, called its *head*, to their end, called its *tail*.

- Singly linked lists are fast for operations on the list head: inserting a node before the head of the list and deleting or accessing the head are all constant-time operations. Other operations take linear time.

- In a *doubly linked list* (DLL), each node also stores a pointer to its predecessor. Therefore, doubly linked lists can also be traversed from their tail to their head, making it easier to read the list from both directions.

- DLLs require more memory than SLLs to store the same elements.

- Operations such as `insert`, `delete`, and `search` are, for the most part, as fast in SLLs as in DLLs. Doubly linked lists are faster when we need to insert or delete an element from the end of the list.

- The best reason to choose a DLL over an SLL is the need to move through the list in both directions.

- *Circular linked lists* are lists (either DLLs or SLLs) where the successor of the tail of the list is the head of the list (and vice versa, for DLLs). All nodes have a successor, and in DLLs, all nodes have a predecessor.

- Circular linked lists are used whenever we need to traverse a list repeatedly (for example, to cyclically use resources or perform tasks).

Abstract data types: Designing the simplest container—the bag

7

In this chapter

- the difference between an abstract data type and a data structure
- arrays and linked lists: are they data structures or data types
- the key properties of a container
- meet the bag, the simplest possible container

By now, you should be familiar with arrays and linked lists, which were the focus of our first six chapters. These are core data structures, ubiquitous in computer science and software engineering. But more than that, they are also *foundational* data structures, which means that we can—and will—build more complex data structures on top of them.

In chapter 2, we discussed how arrays can be approached as concrete language features or as abstract data types. In this chapter, we will discover that this duality isn't limited to arrays. We will then talk about an important class of abstract data types—containers—which will be our focus in the next five chapters.

This chapter is a bridge between the first half of the book, where we have discussed core data structures and principles, and the second half, where we focus on data structures that build on top of what we have learned so far.

Here, we bridge the gap by introducing the first of many examples taken from the containers class—bags.

Abstract data types vs. data structures

What's the difference between a data structure and an abstract data type? We have scratched the surface of this question when we discussed arrays.

An abstract data type (ADT) focuses on what operations you can perform on the data, without specifying how those operations are implemented. A data structure, conversely, specifies more concretely how data is represented, as well as algorithms for performing operations on that data.

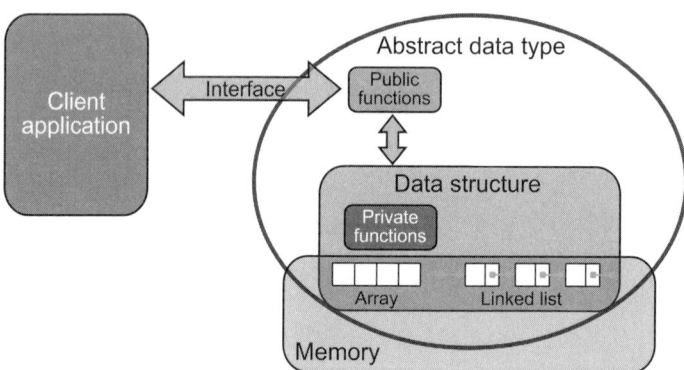

For example, we can look at arrays as the concrete language feature provided by some programming languages, that is, contiguous blocks of memory that can be divided into cells of equal size, each of which can hold an element of a given (and fixed) type. Or, we can consider a higher abstraction of arrays, focusing on the operations they can offer—constant-time read/write of the elements based on indexes—and ignoring how they are implemented.

In this section, I will first give a more formal definition that highlights the differences between these two views, and then we will look at a few examples to illustrate what we have learned.

Definitions

Designing and building software is a complex process that usually starts with an abstract idea and refines and enriches it until we get to a code implementation. For data structures, we can think of a three-level hierarchy to describe this design process.

An *abstract data type* (ADT) is a theoretical concept that describes at a high level how data can be organized and the operations that can be performed on the data. It provides little or no detail about the internal representation of the data, how the data is stored, or how physical memory is used. ADTs provide a way to reason at a high level about ways to structure data and the operations that this structuring allows.

We described what a *data structure* (DS) is in chapter 1, but let me give you an alternative definition here: a data structure is a refinement of the specifications provided by an ADT where the computational complexity of its operations—how data is organized in memory (or disk!) and the internal details of the DS—are normally discussed.

There is a third level in this hierarchy: the *implementation*. At the DS level, we don't worry about the language-specific problems and quirks involved in coding a data structure. For a linked list, we define how a node is designed and what it contains, but we don't worry about how the memory for the node is allocated or whether the link to the next node should be a pointer or a reference. Instead, at the implementation level, we have to write code for the data structure, so we choose a programming language and translate the general instructions given by the data structure into code.

These three levels are a hierarchy of abstraction of the way in which we can describe data structures in computer software. The relationship between the levels in this hierarchy are, going from top to bottom, always one-to-many: an ADT can be further specified by many DSs, and a DS can have many implementations (some of which may be equivalent), even in different programming languages. The same DS can also be used to implement several ADTs: we'll see in this and the next few chapters how a dynamic array or a linked list can implement very different ADTs.

Table 7.1 Examples of abstraction versus implementation

Abstraction (ADT)	Implementation (DS)
Vehicle	Car Truck Motorbike
Seat	Chair Sofa Armchair Beanbag chair
List	Dynamic array Linked list
Stack	Dynamic array Linked list
Queue	Dynamic array Linked list

Arrays and linked lists: ADT or DS?

So much for the definitions. Let's discuss a few examples to help you get an idea: What better place to start than with arrays, which we discussed at length in the early chapters of this book?

Hopefully this won't come as a surprise, but arrays can fit into any of the following three levels:

- *Arrays as ADT*—Here we define an array as a high-level abstraction of a sequence of elements. Each element has an intrinsic order and a position (index) associated with it. It must be possible to access each element by its index.

- *Arrays as DS*—In addition to what is specified by the ADT, we enforce that accessing any element in the array must be a constant-time operation. Note that this is one of many possible data structure definitions for arrays—in another definition, we could, for example, force all the elements to be of the same type.

- *Array implementation*—At this level, we consider arrays as language features (for those languages that provide them natively). An array must be allocated in a single, contiguous block of memory, and all its elements must use the same memory and be of the same type. For those languages that don't provide arrays, we can write our own implementation, like I did here: https://mng.bz/Ad9K.

For *linked lists*, the definitions I gave in chapter 6 are already at the data structure level. Here, we specify how the data is organized internally using nodes, how these nodes are designed, and how the operations performed on linked lists work. We also moved toward the implementation level with Python code.

What about the ADT level? We can, of course, define an ADT that is refined by the linked list data structure.

We can call it a *list*—a sequence of elements that can be traversed in some order (the ordering criterion is not important at this level). The elements can be accessed sequentially.

Do you know which other data structure is a refinement of the *list* ADT? If you said arrays, bingo! Linked lists and arrays are two refinements, two data structures, stemming from the same abstract data type.

Table 7.2 A comparison of the running time of arrays and linked lists

	Insert front	Insert back	Insert middle	Delete	Search
Array	O(n)	O(1)	O(n)	O(1)*	O(n)
Singly linked list	O(1)	O(n)	O(n)	O(n)	O(n)
Doubly linked list	O(1)	O(1)	O(n)	O(1)**	O(n)

* If we can change the order of the elements, switching the element to be deleted with the last element. Otherwise, it's O(n).

** If we have a link to the node to be deleted. Otherwise, if we have to find the node first, it's O(n).

You should keep this in mind because it will be an important topic in the next few chapters: we will define some abstract data types and discuss how they can be implemented with both arrays and linked lists.

One more example: The light switch

Before wrapping up the discussion, let's look at another example, from a different angle: the light switch.

Yes, you read that right! We are leaving computer science aside for a minute to show you how this hierarchy of abstractions can be applied to a broader area of science and engineering and hopefully make the differences between these levels of abstraction even clearer. But this is also a useful exercise because a light switch is similar to a very common ADT—the Boolean ADT.

A light switch as an abstract data type

At the highest level of abstraction, a light switch is a device that has two states, on and off, and two methods:

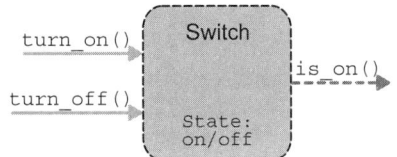

- One to turn (the light) on

- The other one, to turn (the light) off

That's it! That's all we need to specify. We can model an even more generic switch by abstracting its purpose, but for this example, let's keep it tied to the state of the light.

The goal of defining an ADT is to specify an *interface*, a contract with users. As long as we stick to the interface, it doesn't matter how we implement it, and we can even switch between different implementations without breaking any of the applications using our ADT.

A light switch as a data structure

As we move to the data structure level, we need to define more details about how we can interact with our device. Without going into the details of electrical engineering, we can design a few concepts for a light switch.

This is similar to designing different DSs that implement the same ADT: just like we can implement a list using arrays or linked lists, we can implement the switch abstraction using different physical designs.

The first alternative we have is the classic switch with a small toggle that moves up and down.

Turn on: move the lever up.

Turn off: move the lever down.

Internal state:
the position of the level

An equivalent design has two buttons that can be pressed, one for off and one for on. Pressing one button disengages the other.

Turn on: press the "on" button.

Turn off: press the "off" button.

Internal state:
which button is pressed

A variant of this design has a single pressure button, that switches between the two states without any visible change to the device. But we can imagine many more variants, for example, a digital switch, why not?

Turn on: press the "on" button.

Turn off: press the "off" button.

Internal state:
a Boolean variable

All these designs have something in common: we are describing, still at a fairly high level, how the internal state is maintained and how we can interact to change the state. While at the ADT level we only defined the interface of the device (there must be two methods to turn it on and off), for the DSs we describe here, we also need to specify how these methods work (that is, which button to press, and what happens when we do).

Implementing a light switch

When it comes to building a functioning switch, we can take any of the data-structure-level specifications from the previous section and develop it further. How far? Right down to the smallest detail.

Take the two-button switch, for example. At the implementation level, we need to decide the dimensions of the switch and the buttons, the materials used to build it, whether the buttons will stay pressed or they will move back, the internals of the mechanism that closes/opens the circuit, and so on. We need to clarify everything that is needed to build a working switch.

Similarly, in software, at the implementation level, we need to write code that works in real applications.

Containers

In the next five chapters, we focus on a particular class of data structures called *containers*, so, in this section, we introduce them and explain how this group of data structures is different and important for developers.

What's a container?

A container is an abstract concept, a definition for a large group of data structures with common characteristics. Basically, it is a collection of elements, usually of the same type (but not necessarily; especially in loosely typed languages, this constraint can be relaxed).

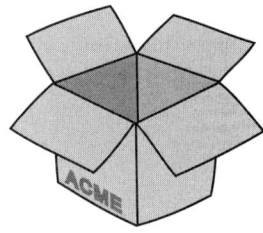

A box is the epitome of a container.

The main feature of containers is to provide a way to organize and store data in a structured way, which allows the efficient implementation of some key operations: accessing, inserting, deleting, and searching the elements a container holds. The purpose of a container is to hold multiple pieces of data as a single entity, allowing developers to work with collections of data more conveniently and efficiently.

Containers abstract away the complexities of data management. Remember back in chapter 2 when we discussed how to model an Advent calendar in software? I mentioned that we could have implemented the calendar as 25 different variables, but that would have been difficult. With an array, we can instead treat the calendar as a single entity, and the data is neatly organized and easily accessible by index.

And in case you were wondering, yes, arrays are containers, and so are linked lists. They are the core containers, the most basic ones, and perhaps the most important ones since they are the foundation for the more complex containers we will discuss in the next chapters.

We know that arrays and linked lists are very different, and they have pros and cons. Similarly, containers can vary in their underlying implementation and capabilities, but they all share the common feature of grouping data elements and a few other characteristics.

What isn't a container?

Are all data structures containers? No, many data structures are not considered containers.

For example, in chapter 13, we discuss *graphs*. While graphs, like containers, are a collection of elements, they are primarily used to represent relationships and connections between those elements and provide various algorithms for exploring those connections. They are not usually regarded as containers because their purpose is different from simply managing data, and their complexity is beyond that of containers.

Another interesting data structure we can use as an example is k–d trees. These special trees have the main purpose of organizing multidimensional data and allowing efficient proximity queries—they go far beyond containers, and they are also not designed to efficiently delete or search elements by value.

Key features of containers

I mentioned that containers have some common characteristics, but what are those? Let's name a few:

- Containers are collections of elements. They hold multiple elements, which can be of the same or different types and can be stored in a particular order or without any order.

- Containers typically provide the same set of basic operations to insert, delete, access, modify, and search elements in the collection.

- Containers can be traversed. All containers offer a way to go through all their elements in sequence. At the implementation level, it's common for containers to provide iterators that allow sequential access to all the elements in the collection and can be used, for example, in `for` loops.

- Containers can maintain the elements they store in a certain order. The order can be based on the sequence of insertion (as we have discussed in lists), or follow specific rules, as we will see in the next three chapters with stacks, queues, and priority queues.

- Containers are designed to provide efficient access to their elements. The complexity of common operations (that is, insert, delete, search) varies depending on the container type.

These features are extremely relevant to software development: any time we need to store elements that will be processed later, we need a container. Most algorithms require us to iterate through elements in a certain order; thus, choosing the right container becomes crucial in these cases, as following the wrong order can break an algorithm or degrade its performance.

Containers, in fact, also have differences, or each wouldn't be considered as a different data structure. Some containers have specific constraints or rules about how elements can be added, accessed, or removed: we will look at many examples in the next three chapters, but we start right here, in the following section, with our first example.

The most basic container: The bag

Can you imagine what the simplest possible container will look like? Meet the bag, the most basic container of all. It's simpler than arrays and linked lists, which is ironic because we have to use either to implement a bag.

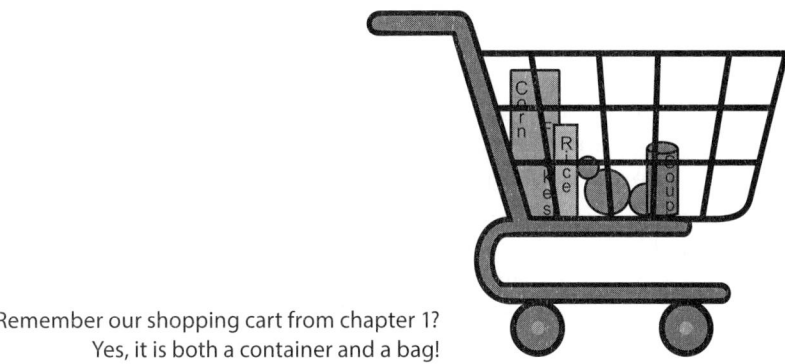

Remember our shopping cart from chapter 1?
Yes, it is both a container and a bag!

Definition of bag

How can a bag be simpler than an array? Well, to begin with, when we add elements to an array, we keep the order of insertion. We can also access a specific element of the array by index, and we can delete elements by value or by index. The thing is, none of these features are strictly required by the definition of containers!

We can insert elements and forget about the order of insertion. We don't have to keep elements indexed either—we would still comply with the definition of container. These are all things that can be simplified, compared to arrays.

Starting with bags, we adopt a more formal way of defining data structures. We will do the same for all data structures in the rest of the book.

The first thing I would like to do is define the *abstract data type* for a bag, and that means specifying its interface: we need to clearly define the methods through which a client can interact with a bag. It's not enough to specify the name, arguments, and return types of all the public methods of an ADT; we must also write in stone the behavior of each method, its *side effects*—the changes it will have on the internal state of the bag, if any—and what the method is expected to accomplish.

Don't worry, following this process for bags will make it clearer.

A bag is a collection of objects with the following methods:

- `insert(x)`—Allows a client to add a single element to the bag. The order of insertion is not important, so an implementation of a bag doesn't need to keep it.

- `iterate()`—Allows a client to go through all the elements in the bag. The order in which elements are iterated is not guaranteed, and it can actually change from one iteration to another.

At this point, we can also add that a bag can store duplicates (no uniqueness constraints, unless they come from the context in which a bag is used). Notice that there are no methods to remove or search elements. These two operations would normally be expected in a container, so bags are kind of borderline—a container with restrictions.

The definitions above fully describe the bag as an abstract data type, and now we can refine the above specifications to define a more concrete data structure. But first, let's look at how we would use bags. After all, as we discussed when defining ADTs, we only need this high-level interface to add bags to the design of our application, while we postpone the definition of the data structure and the implementation.

Bags in action

When will you need to use a bag? Let's look at an example.

Andrea is a backend engineer at the Beanbags company. She recently gave a presentation about how she used a bag container as a cache to collect daily statistics on orders.

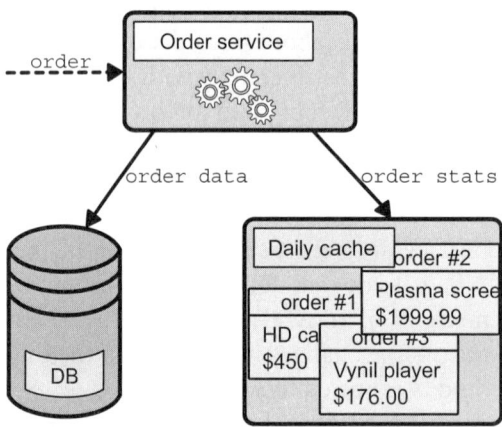

When Sarah from the audience asked Andrea to explain how bags work, she replied, "Did you collect marbles as a kid?"

To better explain how a bag works, she uses an example with marbles. Imagine that our bag data structure can only contain marbles of different colors and patterns. We can add marbles one by one, and they will be inside the bag DS—like with a real bag containing marbles, after a certain number of marbles are added, it's hard to figure out what's inside the bag, and where—it's pure chaos!

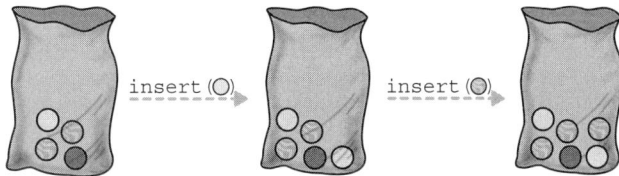

When I was a kid (a long, long time ago!), my friends and I would collect marbles, but, eventually, we also wanted to play, build a marble track, and race. So before starting, everyone had to catalog their treasure (it was also a way to brag to the others!). To count how many marbles one had and how many of each type, there was only one way: pour the marbles on the sand and start counting.

In computer science, the equivalent procedure is iterating through the bag while counting the elements!

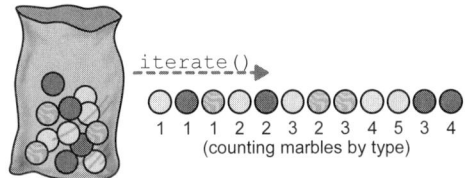

To make sure no one was cheating, sometimes, we would do a second pass to double-check what the other kids were saying. This meant going through a set of marbles again and, of course, the second time you counted them, they wouldn't be in the same order. But if no one cheated or was sloppy, then the order didn't matter, and the totals and breakdowns would match.

This is the same for a bag data structure: to compute statistics about the content of a bag (say, a set of marbles, or our daily orders), we must iterate through its elements. If we iterate twice, we may not get the elements in the same order, but even so, most of the computed statistics will match—all those statistics where the order doesn't matter, like daily total or daily breakdown by type.

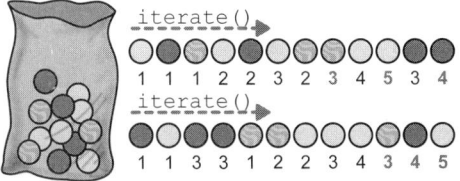

Iterating through the elements of a bag may produce a different order, but statistics that do not depend on the order of the elements, such as sum or total by type, are not affected.

Implementation

Now that we have seen a few examples of how a bag should be used, we are ready to delve into its data structure definition and then its implementation.

The importance of randomness

Let me start with a premise: when defining bags as an ADT, I told you that for bags, we can ignore the order of insertion because the elements can be iterated upon in any order. It's even fine if we don't get the elements in the same order when we iterate through the bag a second time.

But the fact it's possible to iterate through elements in a *random* order doesn't mean that we *must* randomly iterate through elements. In other words, when it comes to building a library that implements a bag, it's fine if we always iterate through elements in the same order—unless, of course, the context requires that we use randomness, for example, because we are performing some operation whose good outcome depends on trying different (and possibly uniformly distributed) sequences.

> **NOTE**   There is an important asymmetry here. While as the implementers of a bag, we could decide to always use a certain order for iterating elements, clients should not rely on that order because the definition of bags clearly states that no order is guaranteed.

There are other data structures where randomness is crucial. We won't see them in this book, but you can find some examples in *Advanced Algorithms and Data Structures* (Manning, 2021). For bags, anyway, and in the absence of domain constraints, we can simplify our lives and just iterate through the elements in the order they are inserted. Again, the definition tells us that we are not forced to follow the order of insertion, but also that we are not forbidden to do so, and in this particular case, following the order of insertion makes our task less difficult.

Bags as a data structure

This consideration regarding the order of the elements frees our hands when it comes to defining a data structure to implement the bag ADT. Because we are not forced to return a random permutation of the elements, a bag becomes a special variant of a list, implementing only a subset of its instructions. It means that we can use any implementation of the *list ADT* (static arrays, dynamic arrays, linked lists) as a basis for our bag DS.

At the data structure level, we can also refine our definitions by adding the desired constraints for the running time and additional space taken by the bag's methods, and the additional space required by the DS to store the elements.

So, let's see the options we have here:

- *Static arrays*–We could add elements in (worst-case) constant time and iterate through the elements in linear time. But the problem with a static array would be that we would have to decide the maximum capacity of a bag at creation. This would be an additional constraint on the ADT definition, and that's a big drawback.

- *Dynamic arrays*—With this solution, we don't have to decide the capacity of the bag in advance. However, the tradeoff is that the insertion becomes `O(n)` in the worst case (although the *amortized* running time to insert n elements would still be `O(n)`, as we discussed in chapter 5).

- *Linked lists*—Since we are allowed to iterate through the elements in reverse order of insertion (and in any order, really), we can use a singly linked list and insert the new elements at the beginning of the list. This way, we can guarantee `O(1)` insertion and `O(n)` traversal, and we have maximum flexibility to grow the list as needed. There will be some extra memory required to store the links, but we will worry about that at the implementation level— asymptotically, both arrays and linked lists require `O(n)` *total* memory to store n elements.

The Bag class

So, the best option to implement a `Bag` class seems to be using a singly linked list to store the elements—we don't need a doubly linked list because we won't be deleting elements, nor will we need to traverse the list from tail to head.

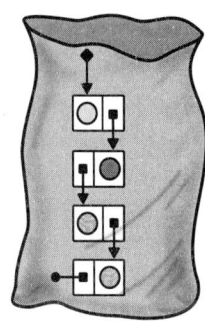

We can use composition and set the linked list as an attribute of the new class. The `Bag` class is just a wrapper around the linked list with the elements. We need this wrapper because we want the `Bag` class to have only two public methods with which clients can interact:

```
class Bag:
    def __init__(self):
        self._data = SinglyLinkedList()
```

The constructor is minimalistic—it simply initializes an empty bag by creating an empty linked list.

Insert

The best advantage of reusing other data structures is that it makes the methods of the `Bag` class clean and short. When adding new elements, as we discussed, we definitely want to insert them at the beginning of the list, not at the end, which would be inefficient for a singly linked list (because, as we discovered in chapter 6, it would require traversal of the entire list to find the last node). What's great about our implementation is that we only need to forward the new element to the insertion method of the linked list:

```
def insert(self, value):
    self._data.insert_in_front(value)
```

Traversal

To allow clients to iterate through the elements of a bag, we could either implement the traverse method or—in languages that allow it—define an iterator. The details of how iterators work in Python are not particularly interesting to us, but you can find an implementation of the iterator for `Bag` in our repo on GitHub: https://mng.bz/ZEWO.

If, instead, you want to define a method `traverse` that returns a Python list with the elements in the bag, here it is:

```
def traverse(self):
    return self._data.traverse()
```

Remember: bags do not guarantee that the elements will be returned in any particular order, so any client code shouldn't count on that. This means that even in tests, you shouldn't impose constraints on the order in which the elements are visited. A good approach in tests is to compare the result and the expected result as sets. Check out the tests I created: https://mng.bz/RZO0.

For instance, I have implemented the `Bag` class with an underlying linked list, and I iterate through the elements in reverse order of insertion. Even though I know in advance the order in which the elements will be returned by the current implementation, if I tested that particular order, I wouldn't be able to switch to a different implementation that uses, for example, arrays to store the elements of the bag and reads them in the order of insertion, because the tests would fail. Similarly, if you write any code that relies on the iteration order of this implementation, replacing it with a different implementation will break your code. And if you are using a `Bag` object from a third-party library over which you have no control, you don't want to find yourself in the position of having to explain to your boss why, all of a sudden, your code was broken when the library owner changed the implementation of a bag without breaking its interface.

Recap

- An *abstract data type* (ADT) is a concept that describes at a high level how data can be organized and what operations can be performed on the data. It provides little or no detail about the internal representation of the data.

- A *data structure* (DS) is a refinement of an ADT definition where we specify how data is organized in memory and the computational complexity of the operations defined by the ADT.

- An *implementation* is a further refinement of the definition of a DS, dealing with a programming-language-specific constraint and producing as output some code, in a chosen language, that fully implements the DS.

- A container is a data structure that belongs to a class that shares some common characteristics:

  - Containers are collections of elements.

  - Containers provide the same set of basic operations to insert, delete, access, modify, and search elements within the collection.

  - All containers provide a way to iterate through all their elements.

  - Containers may or may not keep the elements they store in a particular order.

  - Containers are designed to provide efficient access to their elements. The complexity of common operations (that is, insert, delete, search) varies by container type and is specified at the data structure level of design.

- The bag is the simplest form of container, offering only two methods, one to insert elements and one to iterate through the elements stored in the bag (elements can't be searched or removed).

- A bag can be implemented on top of basic data structures such as arrays and linked lists. The singly linked list implementation guarantees the best running time for both operations defined on a bag. More complex data structures could also be used, depending on specific requirements or constraints.

In this chapter

- introducing the stack abstract data type

- applying the LIFO policy in the real world and
    in computer science

- implementing a stack with arrays and linked lists

- why do we need stacks

In the previous chapter, you familiarized yourself with *containers*, a class of data structures whose main purpose is to hold a collection of objects, and with the simplest of all containers—the *bag*. Bags are simple data structures that require few resources. They can be useful when we want to hold data on which we only need to compute some statistics, but overall, they aren't widely used.

Now it's time to look at containers that are crucial to computer science: we start with the *stack*. You'll find stacks everywhere in computer science, from the low-level software that makes your applications run to the latest graphics software available.

In this chapter, we learn what a stack is, see how stacks work, and look at some of the kinds of applications that use stacks.

Stack as an ADT

As I mentioned for bags, I start our discussion of each container at the abstract data type (ADT) level. So, this is when we define what a stack is, how a stack works at a high level, and the interface a stack provides for us to interact with it.

Stack and LIFO

A stack is a container that allows elements to be added or removed according to precise rules: you can't just add a new element anywhere like with arrays and lists.

The way a stack works is explained by an acronym—*LIFO*—which stands for *last in, first out*. This is a method that is widely used in the real world, outside of computer science. The example used in introductory courses is the proverbial pile of dishes in a restaurant's kitchen: waiters put dirty dishes on the top of the pile, and the kitchen hand takes them in reverse order from the top to wash them. LIFO is also used in cost accounting and inventory management, among other things.

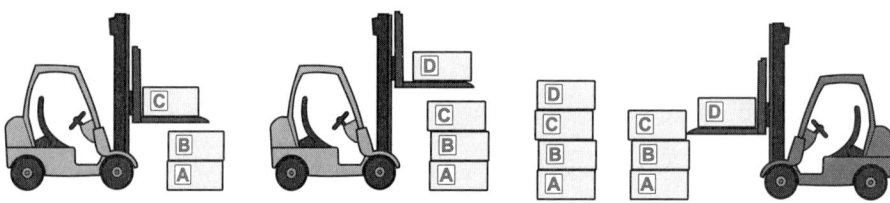

LIFO in stock management

In the context of containers, the LIFO principle requires a data structure in which elements can be inserted and then consumed (or removed) in the reverse order in which they were inserted.

Operations on a stack

To make the stack adhere to the LIFO paradigm, we design its interface with only two methods:

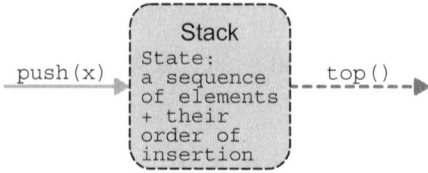

- A *method to insert an element into the stack*—For stacks, we traditionally call this method `push()` instead of just "insert."

- A *method to remove the most recently added element from the stack and return it*—This method is traditionally called `pop()` or sometimes `top()`.

Given the LIFO order constraint, a stack must maintain the order in which elements are inserted. The ADT definition imposes no constraints on how this order must be maintained or how elements must be stored, so, for the sake of an example, we can think of our stack as a pile of elements, not unlike a pile of dishes.

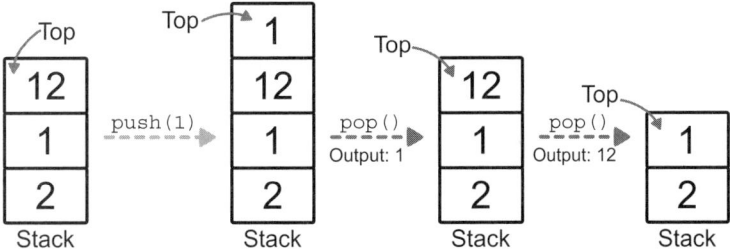

We also need to keep track of the last element that was added to the stack, which (following the pile analogy) is called the *top of the stack*. In practice, what we need to do is to somehow keep a sequence of the elements in the order of insertion, and the top of the stack will be the side of the sequence where we add and remove elements (regardless of how the sequence is stored).

Stacks in action

Carlo runs a small, young startup that ships local gourmet food from Naples to expats around the world. They only ship packages of the same size and weight (20 kilograms), but the customers can partly personalize their order.

Carlo's company is still small, so they have a small space to store the packages ready to be shipped. Carlo bought a tall silo, and the parcels can be only stacked in two columns, leaving just enough room for a forklift to operate. The forklift is also small; it can only lift one parcel at a time. So, from these piles, only the parcel on top can be picked up with the forklift.

Does that ring a bell? Yes, each pile of packages is a stack!

Carlo decides to divide the parcels into two groups. In one pile, he keeps all the standard packages: they are all the same, they have an expiration date far in the future, and once they are prepared, any one of them is equally good to fill a new order. The other pile is used to store custom orders while they sit waiting for the courier to pick them up and ship them.

The "standard" pile works just like a stack—it's not ideal because the desired behavior would be to ship the parcel that was prepared first each time (something we will deal with in the next chapter), but, unfortunately for Carlo, this is the way piling stuff up works.

More interesting is the "custom" pile. This pile also works like a stack, but the problem is that we need to grab specific elements—an operation that stacks' interfaces do not support.

Custom   Standard

Fear not, there is a way to make this work, which is using a second temporary stack. Let's say we have six custom packages stacked up in Carlo's deposit and, for some reason, he needs to take out the third parcel.

What he can do is first grab the package on top, the one marked "6." Then he puts it down next to the unloading area and picks up the next package, labeled "5," and so on. In this way, he builds a temporary stack in the unloading area with the elements above the parcel he needs to ship, the one labeled "3."

Finally, when the target parcel 3 is moved to the courier's truck, Carlo must put the packages in the temporary pile back in their place: again, starting with the one on top, the one marked "4," and so on, until all three parcels are back into the custom pile.

In computer science terms, this is an example of an application that uses two stacks to provide the functionality of an array. If your gut instinct tells you that this must be terribly inefficient, you are right: it requires twice as much memory (two stacks of the same size, one of which is kept empty), and removing/returning a generic element in a stack of size n takes $O(n)$ steps.

But sometimes you might have no choice: when life gives you stacks…

Stack as a data structure

After finalizing the abstract data type for stacks and writing its interface in stone, we need to start thinking about how to implement it.

> **TIP**   Remember that an ADT interface is the only part that should be written in stone. Any change to that interface, or to the intended behavior specified in the ADT phase, will make all data structures built on top of an ADT incompatible.

We discussed this in chapter 7: it is possible to have several alternative DS definitions for a single ADT. At the data structure level, we focus on the details of how the data is stored in a stack, and on the resources required by the operations (which, in turn, are usually determined by the choice of the underlying data structures).

As for bags, we can consider three main alternatives for storing a stack's data:

- A static array

- A dynamic array

- A linked list

Let's take a closer look at each.

Static array for storing a stack's data

If we use a static array to store the elements of a stack, we can push new elements to the end of the array and pop elements from the end of the array. Therefore, a static array guarantees us very good performance for these two operations: they would both require O(1) time and no additional memory.

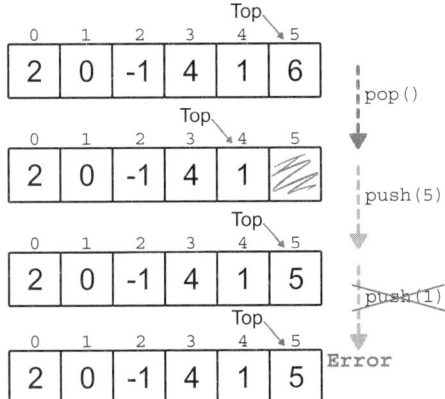

The big concern with static arrays is that their size is fixed. A stack relying on static arrays to store its data would require its maximum capacity to be set when the stack is created, and it wouldn't be possible to resize it. While this is acceptable in some contexts, generally speaking, we don't want this limitation.

Dynamic array

With a dynamic array, the way we push and pop elements wouldn't change—it's still at the end of the array. We would, however, solve the problem of capacity: we could push on the stack as many elements as we wanted—at least until we had enough RAM to allocate a larger array.

The fact that a dynamic array doubles in size when we add a new element to a full array can cause some problems. First, when we grow a dynamic array, we must allocate much more memory than we need—an average of O(n) extra memory. And it gets worse.

If the array is implemented as a contiguous area of memory, as the stack's size grows, it becomes increasingly difficult to find an available chunk of memory large enough to allocate the size of the new underlying array. Furthermore, if the array can't be allocated, we get a runtime error, and our application crashes. Thus, if we expect the stack to grow large, with thousands of elements or more, dynamic arrays might not be the best choice.

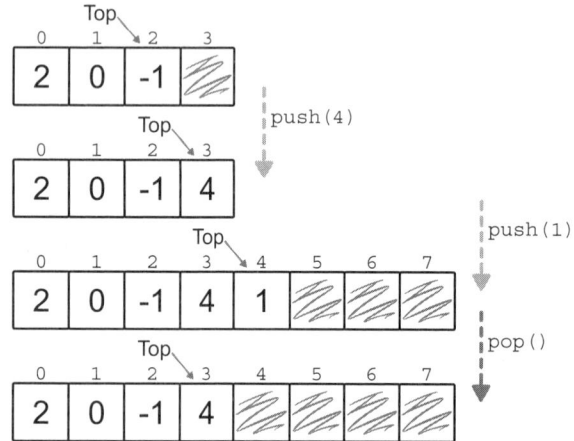

Operations on a stack implemented with a dynamic array. When `push(1)` is called, there is no unused array cell, so the array doubles its size.

Even for smaller stacks, however, we pay a price, compared to static arrays: push and pop becoming $O(n)$ in the worst case for a stack of n elements. If you remember our discussion about dynamic arrays in chapter 5, there is a silver lining. Pushing n elements into an empty stack takes $O(n)$ amortized time; similarly, emptying a stack with n elements takes $O(n)$ amortized time. Both operations require constant additional memory.

Linked lists and stacks

As always, the linked list implementation is the most flexible. For stacks, we only need to make changes to one side of the list, and we can choose to work at the beginning of the list—storing elements in inverse order of insertion is no problem at all as there is no need to iterate through them.

Can you guess why these considerations are important? It's because it means we can use singly linked lists (SLLs). We don't need to traverse the list at all, and inserting and deleting from the front of the list are both $O(1)$ for SLLs, so there is no reason to use doubly linked lists.

The best part? Linked lists, as we know at this point in the book, are inherently flexible, allowing the stack to grow and shrink as needed at no additional cost. In addition, linked lists have fewer constraints on the allocation of the memory they require: a new node can be allocated anywhere (not necessarily next to or near the rest of the nodes). This makes it easier to allocate larger stacks compared to the array implementations.

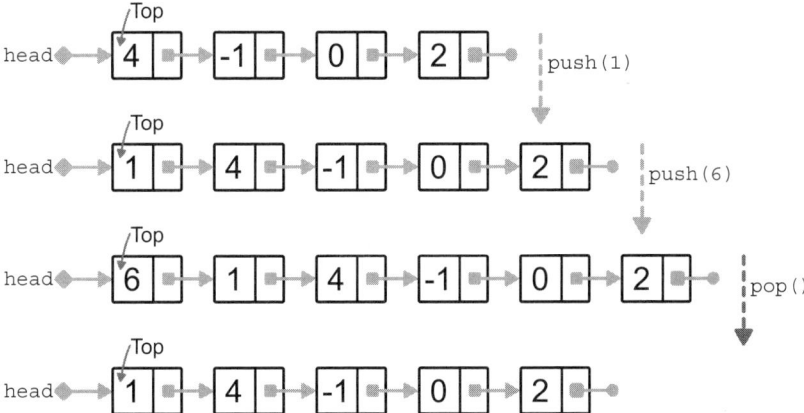

Is all that glitters gold? Well, not always, as you should know. There is the extra memory per element required by linked lists to store the links to the next node. And in the next section, we will look more closely at possible downsides.

But long story short, the implementation with linked lists is your best choice if you need flexibility, and, in theory, it also provides the most efficient implementation of operations on a stack—at least, if the additional memory needed for the node pointers is not a problem. But if you know the size of the stack in advance, the implementation with static arrays can be a better alternative.

Linked list implementation

The analysis at the data structure level suggests that an implementation with an underlying linked list is the alternative that guarantees us the best performance and use of resources for all the stack operations. So, while we'll briefly discuss the dynamic arrays variant later in the section, for now, we will just focus on linked lists, starting with the class definition. You'll notice many similarities with the Bag class we talked about in chapter 7—as with bags, the Stack class is merely a wrapper that restricts the interface of a linked list, allowing only a subset of its methods:

```
class Stack:
    def __init__(self):
        self._data = SinglyLinkedList()
```

And as for bags, the constructor just creates an empty linked list. You can find the full code for stacks in the book's repo on GitHub: https://mng.bz/d6lO.

Technically, in addition to the three options I gave you at the data structure level, there is a fourth alternative: we could implement a stack from scratch, handling the way data is stored without reusing any underlying data structure. But why would we do that? We would gain nothing, and, in exchange, we would have a lot of duplicated code because we would have to implement the details of all the operations.

In the rest of this section, we discuss the operations in the stack's API, push and pop, and a third method, peek, a read-only operation that is sometimes provided outside of the standard API.

Push

Instead of implementing everything from scratch, if we use a linked list to store the stack's data, we can reuse the existing insert_in_front method from linked lists when pushing a new element onto the stack. Assuming that it is already properly tested and consolidated, we can write the push method as a one-liner:

```
def push(self, value):
    self._data.insert_in_front(value)
```

The underlying linked list takes care of all the details; we just have to forward the call to the linked list.

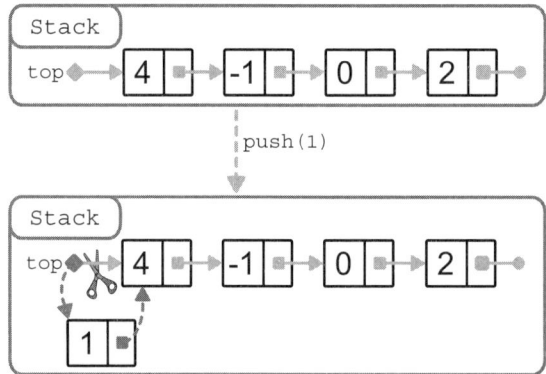

Depending on the context, we can use the push wrapper to perform some checks before actually inserting an element into the list. For example, if there are restrictions on the valid values, we could perform validation at this point: for a stack containing strings, we could check that the value pushed is not the empty string.

Pop

Similar to `push`, the `pop` method relies heavily on the linked list interface. In its simplest form, we could also have a one-liner that simply calls `delete_from_front` on the underlying list.

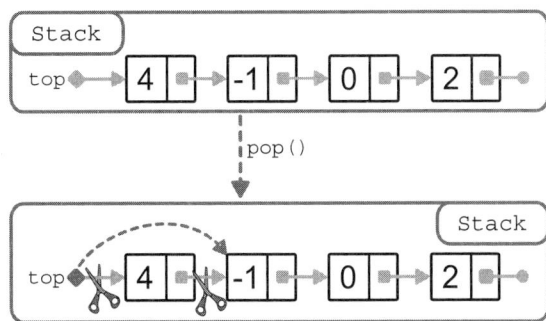

However, if we try to delete from an empty list, an exception will be raised (see chapter 6 for details). This is the expected behavior, but the place where the exception is triggered, and the error message, could be confusing to anyone using a stack, and it would reveal unnecessary internal details to the caller. So, what I believe is best here is to explicitly check the error condition in the stack's method and raise an exception there if the stack is empty. The price to pay for this clarity is, of course, that in the happy case (where no error is triggered), the check is performed twice, once by the stack and once by the linked list:

```
def pop(self):
    if self.is_empty():
        raise ValueError("Cannot pop from an empty stack")
    return self._data.delete_from_front()
```

Alternatively, we can catch the exception raised by the linked list method and raise a different exception.

Peek

The `peek` method should be the easiest one to implement, right? After all, we just need to return the element at the top of the stack without making any structural changes to the stack. And instead, even such a simple method hides some pitfalls! There are some considerations we need to make, and some aspects we need to discuss, to prevent possible future bugs.

The simplest version of this method could also be a one-liner and simply return the data stored at the head of the list (something like this):

```
return self._data._head.data()
```

There are three problems with this approach:

- We don't check if the list is empty before accessing its head.

- It is accessing the private attribute _head of the linked list.

- We would return a reference to the element stored in the head node. If the elements of the list are mutable objects, then whoever gets the reference can change the object at any time.

The first problem can be easily solved the same way we did with pop()—we should just check for the edge case before attempting anything. And for the last one, we can use an existing Python library (https://docs.python.org/3/library/copy.html) to copy the data instead of passing a reference:

```python
import copy
def peek(self):
    if self.is_empty():
        raise ValueError("Cannot peek at an empty stack")
    return copy.deepcopy(self._data._head.data())
```

This is better, but it still accesses a private attribute of the linked list. The only decent solution would be to add a method to the linked list class that returns the element stored in a generic position in the list.

EXERCISES

8.1 Implement a get(i) method for linked lists that returns the i-th element from the head of the list (i≥0). Then, modify the implementation of peek to avoid accessing the _head private attribute of the linked list.

8.2 After implementing get(i), do we still need to call deepcopy in peek? Check your implementation of get and make sure we don't.

8.3 Implement a separate Stack class that uses dynamic arrays to store the stack elements. How does this new implementation compare to the one that uses linked lists?

Theory vs. the real world

In the previous section, when we discussed how to move from the ADT definition of a stack to a more concrete definition of a data structure, I showed you that the implementation of a stack using an underlying linked list is the most efficient. To recap, using an SLL, both push and pop operations can be performed in worst-case constant time, while when using a dynamic array, both methods take linear time in the worst case, but if a large number of operations is performed, their amortized cost can be considered O(1).

Is that it? Should we just implement the linked list version and forget about it?

Well, not really. First, you shouldn't implement your own library unless it's absolutely necessary—either because you can't find an existing implementation that is trustworthy, efficient, and well-tested or because you have to customize your implementation heavily.

Second, if the code where you need to use this library is critical for your application and can become a bottleneck, you should *profile* it.

> **TIP** You shouldn't profile all your code though. Unless you are writing code for a real-time device, that would be time-consuming and mostly useless. The secret is to focus on the critical sections where optimization will improve efficiency the most.

Profiling your code means measuring your application as it runs to see which methods are executed more often and which ones take longer.

In Python, we can do this using *cProfile* https://docs.python.org/3/library/profile.html. So, I implemented a version of the stack, called `StackArray`, that uses a Python `list` to store its elements: https://mng.bz/Bdj8.

Why `list`? First, our version of dynamic arrays has constraints on the type of its elements that would make it incompatible with the linked lists version defined in this section. Second, well, I don't want to spoil it, but it has to do with performance. We'll talk about that in a minute.

So, I wrote a quick script (https://mng.bz/lMB8) that runs millions of operations on both types of stacks (let's call the two classes `Stack` and `StackArray`), with twice as many calls to `push` as to `pop`. The same operations, in the same order, are performed on both versions of the stack, and then we measure how long each version took.

What do you expect as a result? How much would you bet on the linked list version being faster? Well, you might be in for a surprise:

```
 ncalls   tottime  percall  cumtime  percall filename:lineno(function)
3331902    1.919    0.000    2.474    0.000 stack_dynamic_array.py:54(is_empty)
6668098    3.622    0.000    4.858    0.000 stack_dynamic_array.py:67(push)
3331902    3.447    0.000    6.563    0.000 stack_dynamic_array.py:80(pop)
3331902    2.369    0.000    3.248    0.000 stack.py:55(is_empty)
6668098    4.997    0.000   18.379    0.000 stack.py:68(push)
3331902    4.097    0.000   15.871    0.000 stack.py:81(pop)
```

We need to look at the column with the cumulative time, that is, the time spent within a function or any of its sub-calls (this is especially important since we call the linked list methods within all methods in `Stack`).

When implemented with dynamic arrays—as a Python `list`—push is more than four times faster, and `pop` is more than three times faster.

How is this possible? Does that mean we should throw away asymptotic analysis? Of course not. There are a few considerations to make:

- With an implementation based on dynamic arrays, while the worst-case running time for `push` and `pop` is linear, their amortized running time is as good as with linked lists: n operations (push or pop) take `O(n)` time. We have discussed this in chapter 5 for dynamic arrays. Since we are measuring the performance of these methods over a large number of operations, there is no asymptotic advantage to using linked lists.

- Python provides an optimized, extremely efficient implementation for `list`. This code is usually written in C and compiled for use in Python to make sure it's as efficient as possible (https://docs.python.org/3/extending/extending.html). It's hard to write pure Python code that can be nearly as efficient. So, each call to push on an instance of `StackArray` takes a fraction of what it takes on an instance of `Stack`.

- With linked lists, we must allocate a new node on each call to `push` and then destroy a `Node` object on each `pop`. Allocating the memory and creating the objects takes time.

To confirm the third hypothesis, we can look at the stats for the methods in `SinglyLinkedList`:

```
  ncalls  tottime  percall  cumtime  percall  filename:lineno(function)
 3331902    0.759    0.000    0.759    0.000  singly_linked_list.py:86(next)
 3331902    0.795    0.000    0.795    0.000  singly_linked_list.py:72(data)
 6663804    1.591    0.000    1.591    0.000  singly_linked_list.py:228(is_empty)
 6668098    6.545    0.000   13.383    0.000  singly_linked_list.py:242(insert_in_front)
 3331902    6.260    0.000    8.527    0.000  singly_linked_list.py:368(delete_from_front)
 6668098    6.838    0.000    6.838    0.000  singly_linked_list.py:30(__init__)
```

Most of the time taken by `Stack.push` was spent running `SinglyLinkedList.insert_in_front`, and the same is true for `Stack.pop` and `SinglyLinkedList.delete_from_front`.

The last line is also interesting—half of the time taken by `insert_in_front` is spent creating a new `Node` instance.

So, what lessons can we learn from this analysis?

> **TIP** When designing a data structure, choose the implementations that have the best big-O performance. If two solutions have close performance in the asymptotic analysis, consider using profiling to compare the efficiency of their implementations.

That's a good starting point, but, unfortunately, not always enough. There are cases of data structures that are better on paper (their big-O running time is better than the alternatives), but whose implementation turns out to be slower in practice, at least for finite inputs.

One notorious example is Fibonacci heaps, an advanced priority queue that has the best theoretical efficiency. We talk about heaps in chapter 10, but the important point here is that Fibonacci heaps are asymptotically better than regular ones ($O(1)$ amortized time for insertion and extraction of the minimum value, while both are $O(\log(n))$ for regular heaps), but their implementation is much slower for any practical input.

As you gain experience, you will find it easier to identify these edge cases. However, when in doubt, profiling can help you figure out where and how to improve your data structure or application.

More applications of a stack

We have discussed some real-world situations that work like LIFO, but stacks are broadly used in computer science and programming. Let's look briefly at a few applications!

The call stack

A *call stack* is a special kind of stack that stores information about the active functions (or, more in general, subroutines) of a computer program that is being executed. To better illustrate this idea, let's see what a call stack for the `Stack.push` method might look like:

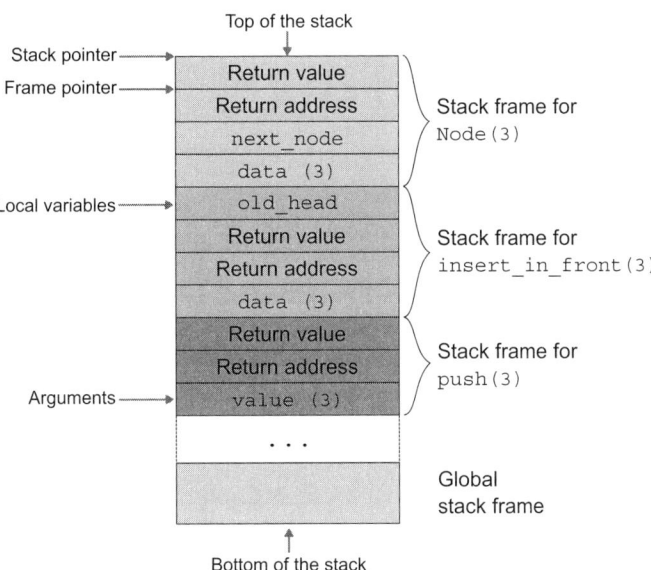

As we discussed in the implementation section, the `push` method calls `SinglyLinkedList.insert_in_front`, which in turn calls the constructor for the `SinglyLinkedList.Node` class:

```
push(3)
... [Stack.push]
    self._data.insert_in_front(3)
    ... [SinglyLinkedList.insert_in_front]
        self._head = Node(3, old_head)
        ... [Node.__init__]
            self._data = 3
```

Execution needs to pass along the element we are pushing to our `Stack` between each call. In code, we do this by using function arguments. At a lower level, function arguments are passed through the call stack: when we call `push`, a stack frame is created for this function call, and an area is allocated for `push` arguments.

The same happens with `insert_in_front`, where the value for the `data` argument is stored (usually at the beginning of the stack frame). There is a similar mechanism for return values, with an area of memory reserved in the stack frame for the values that will be returned to the caller. If the caller saves the return value in a local variable, that's also stored in its stack frame. Finally, each stack frame contains the *return address*: it's the address where the instruction making the function call is stored in memory, and it is used to resume the execution of the calling function when the callee returns.

Stack frames are stacked on top of each other, and the execution rolls back just like a stack: the last function called is the first to return, its stack frame is popped from the call stack (and the return address with it), which allows the execution of the caller to resume, and so on.

Evaluating expressions

Postfix notation is a way of writing arithmetic expressions so that the operator always follows the operands. For example, what is written as 3 + 2 in *infix notation*, becomes 3 2 + in postfix notation. One of the advantages of this notation is that it removes the ambiguities that you have in infix notation.

For example, to compute an expression like 3 + 2 * 4, we need to use the concept of operator priority and agree that multiplication takes precedence over addition so that we actually interpret it as 3 + (2 * 4). If we wanted to do the sum first, we would have to use parentheses and write (3 + 2) * 4. In postfix notation, we don't need parentheses—we can write the two possible combinations as 3 2 4 * + and 3 2 + 4 *, respectively.

The other advantage we have is that we can easily compute the value of a postfix expression by using a stack: when we parse an operand (that is, a value) we push it on the stack, and when instead we parse an operator, we pop the last two values from the stack (for a binary operator), apply the operator, and then push the result on the stack.

Let's look at an example. This is how the parsing of the expression 3 2 4 * + would look like:

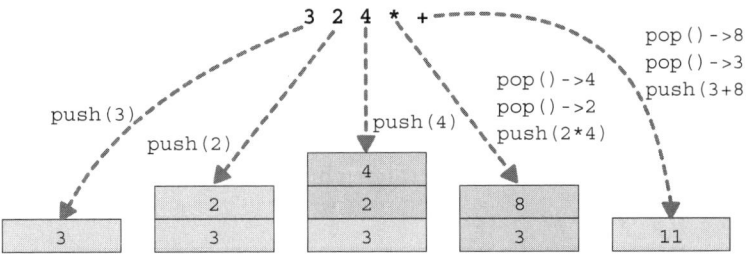

And this is how 3 2 + 4 * is parsed instead:

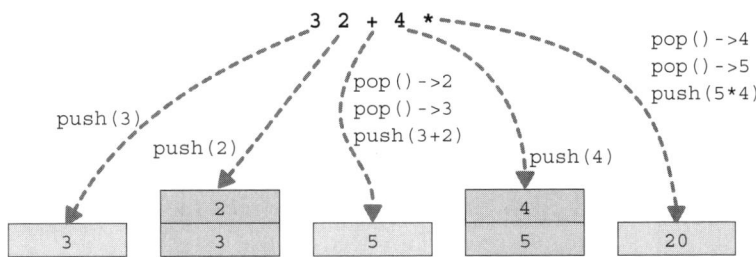

Undo/redo

Have you ever wondered how the *undo* functionality of your IDE or text editor works? It uses a stack (two stacks actually, if you are allowed to revert what you have undone).

The first stack is used to keep track of the changes you make to your documents. This stack is usually limited in size, so older entries will be deleted, and you can only undo a limited number of changes.

When you click undo, the document is restored to the state it was before the last action you performed. But that's not all: the change you have undone gets added to a new stack, the redo stack, so that if you accidentally click undo, or if you change your mind before making any new modification to the document, you can revert it.

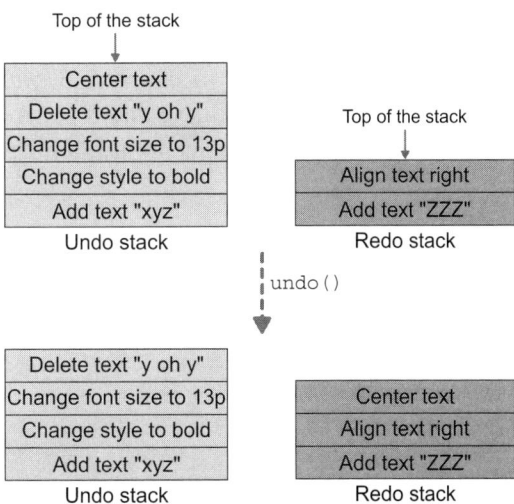

Retracing your steps

Stacks are great when you need to retrace your steps. Remember back in chapter 6 we talked about retracing your steps? We were helping our friend Tim, who was working on a video game and needed to keep a list of the rooms in the game, and how the main character could move between them, from left to right and vice versa.

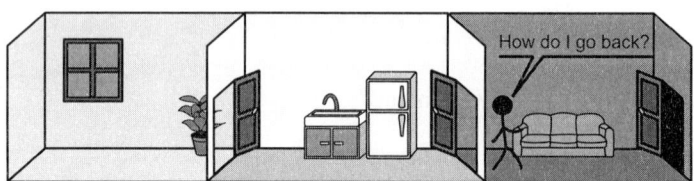

The doubly linked list was perfect for keeping track of the static situation—of the structure of the game. But what if now Tim needs to remember the path that the player has

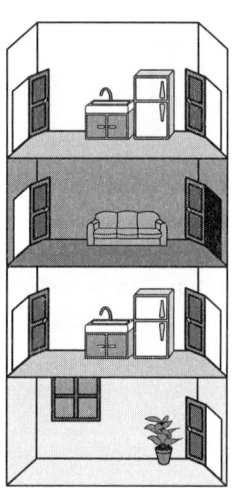

taken from the beginning of the game up to where they are now and allow the character to retrace their steps? Well, you must have guessed it: Tim needs to use a stack!

When the player enters a room, that room is added to a stack. When we need to trace the player's steps, we start to pop rooms from the stack. Note how the same room can be in the stack multiple times if the player re-entered a room after leaving it.

This scenario is an edge case, where our rooms are arranged linearly. In the more general case, we might want to move around a 2D or 3D environment. In the rooms/videogame analogy, we would have more than two doors in some rooms. This kind of environment can't be modeled with a list—we will need a *graph*.

In chapter 13, we discuss graphs, how they can be used to model a city map, and how the *depth-first search* algorithm uses a stack to navigate through the graph.

EXERCISE

8.4 Write a method that reverses an SLL. Hint: How can you use a stack to perform the task? What would be the running time of the operation?

Recap

- A *stack* is a container that abides by the LIFO policy: that is, the *last* element *in* the stack is the *first* element to get *out*. You can picture a stack as a pile of dishes: you can only add or remove dishes at the top.

- Stacks are widely used in computer science and programming, including call stacks, expressions evaluation, the undo/redo functionality, and keeping track of indentation and bracketing in editors. In addition, many algorithms use stacks to keep track of the path taken, such as depth-first search.

- Stacks provide two operations: `push`, to add an element to the top of the stack, and `pop`, to remove and return the element from the top of the stack. There is no other way to insert or delete elements, and search is generally not allowed.

- A third operation can sometimes be provided: `peek`, which returns the element at the top of the stack without removing it.

- A stack can be implemented using either arrays or linked lists to store its elements.

- Using dynamic arrays, `push` and `pop` take $O(n)$ time in the worst case, but $O(1)$ amortized time (over a large number of operations).

- Using SLLs, `push` and `pop` take $O(1)$ time in the worst case.

- The amortized performance of the two implementations is close, and profiling can help you understand which of the two implementations is more efficient in a given programming language.

Queues:
Keeping information
in the same order as it arrives

9

In this chapter

- introducing the queue abstract data type

- understanding FIFO policy

- implementing a queue with arrays and linked lists

- exploring the applications of simple queues

The containers we discuss next are queues, sometimes referred to as simple queues to distinguish them from priority queues, which we describe in chapter 10.

Like stacks, queues are inspired by our everyday experience and are widely used in computer science. They also work similarly to stacks, with a similar underlying mechanism, and they can also be implemented using arrays or linked lists to hold the data. The difference is in details that we will learn about in this chapter.

Queue as an abstract data type

A queue is a container that, similarly to a stack, only allows the insertion and removal of elements in specific positions. What operations are available on a queue? What determines the internal state of a queue, and how does it behave?

Let's first understand how queues work, and then, later in this section, define their interface.

First in, first out

While stacks use the *LIFO* (*last in, first out*) policy, queues abide by a symmetric principle, called *FIFO*, which stands for *first in, first out*. FIFO means that when we consume an element from a queue, the element will always be the one that has been stored the longest, and it is the only one we can remove.

Queues are ubiquitous—the name is self-explanatory (queue being another word for line—and we've all been in a line at some point). FIFO, however, is also a policy that's used with stocked goods, where we remove the oldest units that are likely to have the closest expiration date. The same principle is applied when tackling bugs and tasks from our virtual team board (unless our tasks have priority, in which case, you need to read the next chapter!).

When we apply the FIFO policy to containers, it means creating a data structure in which elements can be inserted and then processed in the same order in which they were inserted.

Operations on a queue

For queues, there are constraints on where you can add and delete elements. There's only one place where a new element is allowed to go: at the *rear* (or tail) of the queue. And elements can only be consumed from the other end of the queue, called the *front* (or head) of the queue.

Therefore, in our interface, we only include the following two methods:

- *A method to insert an element into the queue*—For queues, we traditionally call this method `enqueue()`.

- *A method to remove the least recently added element from the queue and return it*—This method is traditionally called `dequeue()`.

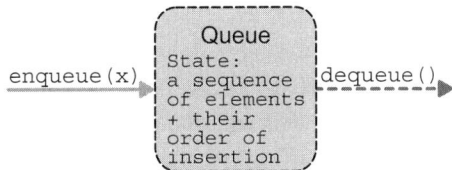

How does a queue work, internally? At the abstract data type (ADT) level, we put no constraint on the internal structure of a queue, but we just define its behavior. Obviously, since we need to consume elements in the same order as they are inserted, we need to save this ordering in the internal state of a queue—but how we do that exactly is something that will be defined only at the data structure level.

At the ADT level, we can imagine a queue in whatever abstract way we find appropriate. Even as the line at the ice cream cart!

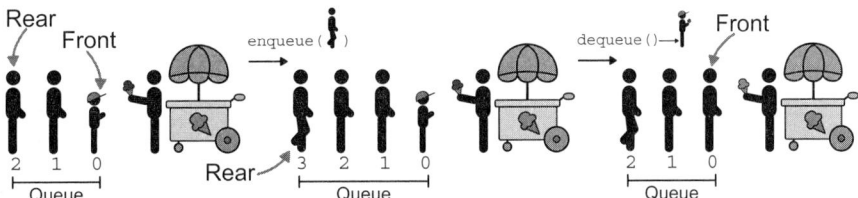

When people queue to get an ice cream cone or to check out, they often stand (or are supposed to stand) in a straight line. When someone joins the queue, they walk to its rear and then stand right behind the last person in line. When the person at the front of the queue gets their ice cream, they walk away, and the person who was standing right behind them takes their place. The positioning, the standing in line, is the structure that keeps the memory of the order of insertion of people in the queue.

We can also use a more computer-science-like example, with boxes and numbers. Compare this to how stacks work, as we showed in chapter 8!

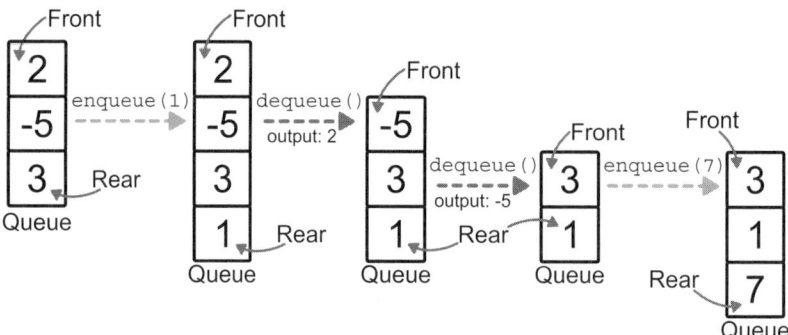

There are at least two notable differences:

- For stacks, we are only interested in holding a reference to their top. For a queue, we need references to both its front and its rear.

- A stack grows and shrinks from the same end, while a queue evolves asymmetrically, with elements added to its rear and removed from its front.

Queues in action

What could be better than picking up a bug from the backlog to start your morning? "Anything," thinks Priyanka as she scrolls through her backlog. (If you have been there, feel free to raise your hand in support!)

Priyanka just started working at a startup that looked so cool from the outside. Their mission resonates with her, and the AI technology the founders developed is fascinating. But what she didn't know was that, besides their core technology, she would find an infrastructural and organizational wasteland. What she didn't realize was that they didn't even have proper task management tools and that their bug backlog would be a bunch of sticky notes left on her desk, screen, and the mini-kitchen table.

So, "scrolling through" her backlog means collecting these sticky notes, hunting them down all over the office, and then trying to interpret the handwriting or finding out who wrote them. In this situation, it's easier to miss and forget a bug than to fix it. After a week of missed fixes and red alerts, Priyanka had enough.

She asked for a problem-tracking product off the shelf, but apparently, there was no budget for it. So, she decided to write one—a simple one of course—as her weekend project.

She tweaked the company's mail server and created a dedicated email address so that when a bug needed to be added to the system, anyone could just send an email. When the email comes in, there is a daemon that picks it up and adds the bug to a queue that's for her to review.

Choosing a queue to manage bugs was crucial for her—each morning she checks the queue, and the system gives her the oldest unresolved bug. If she starts working on that bug, it's all good. If, however, she doesn't think the bug is urgent, she can send it back to the queue, and it will be added to the rear of the queue.

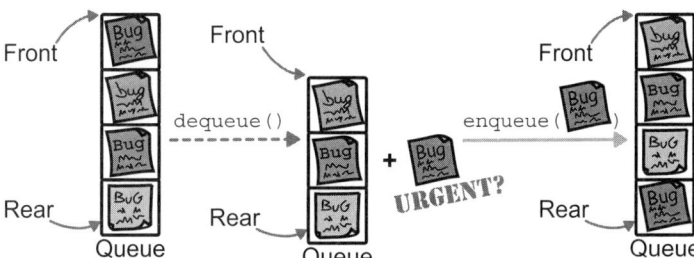

Using a queue for bug tracking ensures she remains organized without misplacing bug reports. Also, the queue implicitly keeps the bugs in chronological order, without having to store a timestamp with them.

This is just one example of how a queue can be part of a real software application, but there could be many more ways to use it. In addition, several algorithms use queues as a fundamental part of their workflow. In chapter 13, we will discuss two graph traversal algorithms: *depth-first search* and *breadth-first search*. They are similar in structure, but to decide which vertex to traverse next, one of them uses a stack, and the other algorithm uses a queue. It's amazing how such a detail can make such a difference in the algorithm's behavior.

Queue as a data structure

Now that we have clarified what interface is needed for a queue, we can take the next step and think about how to implement this data structure. We always have the option of writing a new data structure from scratch, without reusing anything we have already created. This option, however, is only worth considering if none of the alternatives on top of which we can build our new data structure works well. So, the first thing we should always do is check whether we can reuse something and weigh what the benefits and costs are.

Right now, considering what we have discussed in previous chapters, we have the following alternatives:

- Static array
- Dynamic array
- Linked list
- Stack

Let's start from the end—implementing a queue using stacks is possible, but it's just not efficient. Instead of adding elements to the top of the stack by implementing the LIFO policy, we'd need to add to the bottom of the stack. But that's not easy to do with a stack! So, let's cross stacks off our list.

Next, we can also cross off dynamic arrays. While it is possible to implement a queue using dynamic arrays, and there are some advantages to doing so, the complexity and performance cost of a dynamic array implementation is simply not worth it. We'll come back to this topic after we talk about static arrays, and then you'll understand better why we are ruling out dynamic arrays.

This leaves us with two options: linked lists and static arrays. In the rest of this section, let's discuss these two alternatives in detail.

Building on a linked list

A queue is a data structure where the elements are kept in the same order as they are inserted, and all the operations (that is, inserting or deleting elements) happen at either end of the queue. Ring a bell? We add elements to the front (head) of the queue and remove elements from the rear (tail) of the queue. Yes, we have discussed these operations for linked lists.

Can you remember which type of linked list was optimized for removing elements from its tail? Doubly linked lists are perfect for this because we can efficiently add and remove elements to and from both ends.

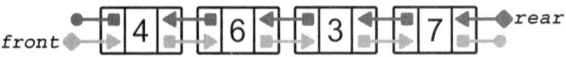

However, if we add new elements only to the tail of the linked list and remove them from the front of the list, we can also use a singly linked list. The only caveat is that we need to slightly adjust our code to keep a pointer to the tail of the list, which can be updated in constant time during these two operations.

Anyway, with doubly linked lists, we can reuse the existing code without any change, which brings us to a cleaner solution: unless we know we have to optimize the memory used, we are going to be fine.

We can have fast implementations of the `enqueue` and `dequeue` methods with almost no effort. We will just reuse the `insert_to_back` and `delete_from_front` methods defined for the linked list.

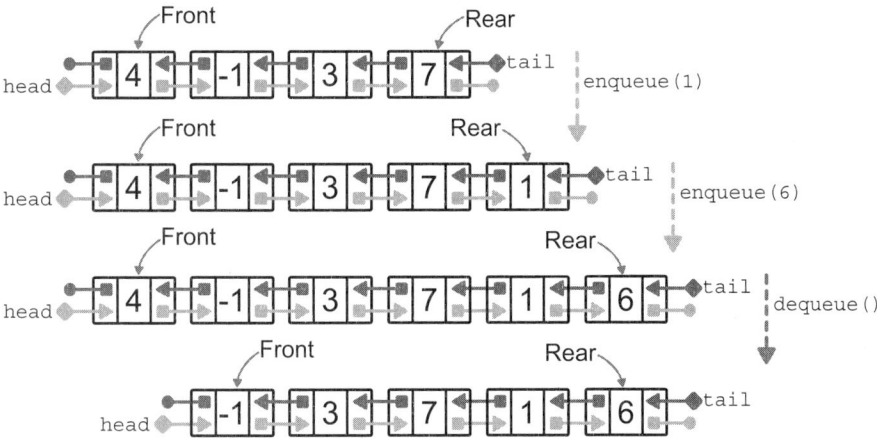

And the best part is that our queue can grow and shrink dynamically without limits or worries. We can rely on the linked list to take care of memory management and resizing.

Storing data in a static array

If we decide to implement a queue using a static array, we have to take into account that the queue size remains fixed upon creation. This is a severe limitation compared to the linked list implementation.

At the data structure level, since we are not going to access elements in the middle of the queue, we are not going to use the best feature that arrays have over linked lists— constant-time access to every element in the array.

There is also another problem. With an array implementation, we keep the front of the queue on the same side as the beginning of the array, while the rear of the queue is on the side of the end of the array. The queue grows toward larger indexes, and we fill the unused array cells after the last element in the array.

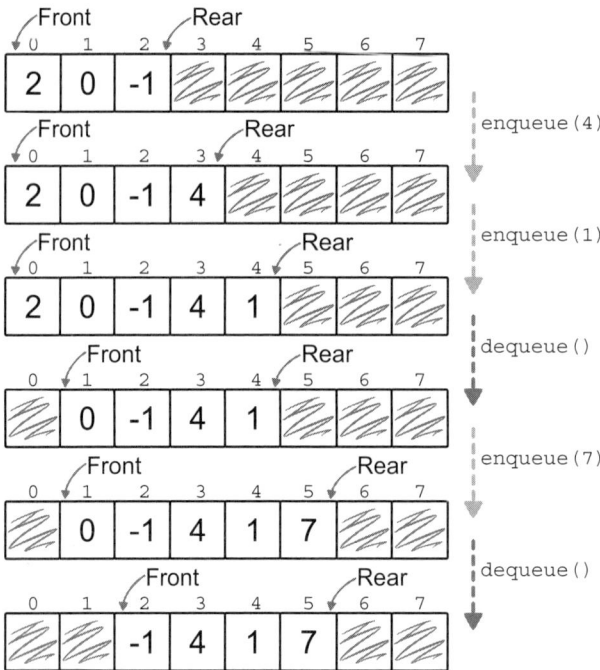

With a stack, the elements stored in the array are naturally kept left justified. If a stack stores n elements, they occupy the indexes from 0 to n-1. But with a queue, when we dequeue an element, we leave a hole between the beginning of the array and the first remaining element. As long as we have enough unused elements after the used ones, we are fine. But what happens when the rear of the queue reaches the end of the array?

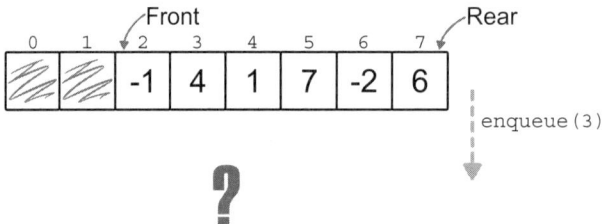

We have two choices. The easiest way is to give up and say that a queue is full when its rear reaches the end of the array. This is called a *linear queue*. But this also means that the capacity of the queue will decrease over time, and we can only perform n insertions on a queue allocated for n elements. Then, after we start dequeuing elements, the actual capacity of the queue gets increasingly smaller. This is not very practical, as you may have guessed.

There is an alternative! We can reuse the space that was freed when elements were dequeued. But how do we do that? Again, we have two options:

- We can move all elements in the queue toward the start of the array so that no empty space is left at the beginning of the array. This means an $O(n)$ overhead every time we move elements, which is far from ideal and unnecessarily inefficient.

- We can get a bit creative with the indexes and use the full array without ever moving an element.

This last option, which is called a *circular queue*, is very interesting. It means no overhead, and it seems too good to be true!

But I guarantee you that it is true. Here is what we do: imagine the elements of our array arranged in a circle instead of a straight line, so that the end of the array touches its beginning. This is where the name, circular queue, comes from.

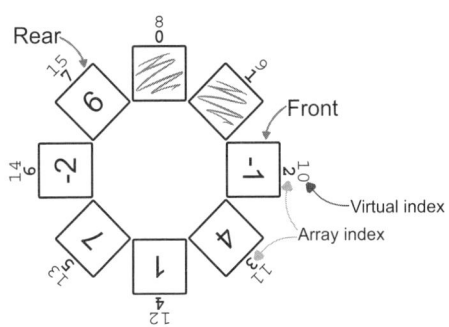

In our example in the figure, we have an array with eight elements, so its indexes go from 0 to 7. What we need to do now is continue indexing as if we could continue after the end of the array. In the circular arrangement, the next element after the one at index 7 is the element at the start of the array, found at index 0. We can write 8 as a secondary index above index 0. Similarly, we write index 9 above index 1, and so on, up to index 15, which is the same element indexed with 7. Let's call these indexes from 8 to 15 *virtual indexes*.

That covers most of the concepts we needed. There is just this tiny piece of math we need to clarify, which is using modular arithmetic. The modulo operator, for positive integers, takes the remainder of the division. For example, 8 % 8 (that is 8 modulo 8, the remainder of 8 when divided by 8) is zero, because that's the remainder of the division operation. Similarly, 9 % 8 == 1, 10 % 8 == 2, and so on. The modulo operator is the way to find out which array index corresponds to a virtual index.

In our example, the rear of the queue has reached index 7, so the next array cell to which we should store a new element is at virtual index 8. Now, if we tried to access index 8 in the array, we would cause an index out-of-boundary error. However, if we keep in mind that 8 % 8 == 0, we realize that 0 is the array index corresponding to virtual index 8. So, we can check whether the array cell at index 0 is empty or already used to store an element. We are in luck: it is empty. How do we know? Well, one way we have is checking where the pointer to the front of the queue is. In our case, it points to index 2, so we are good.

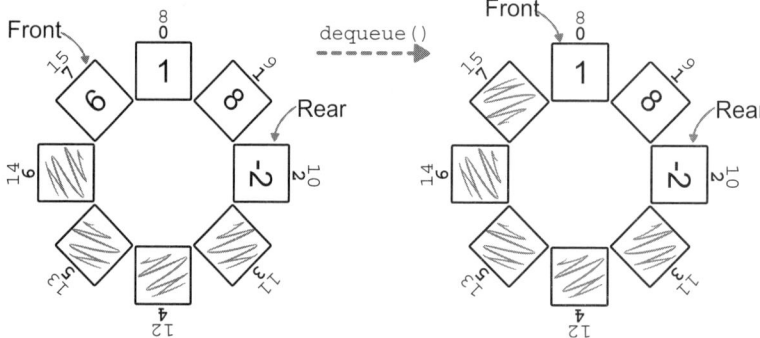

And then, the magic is done! The pointer to the rear of the queue moved past the end of the array and re-entered on the side where it begins. Now it can grow again toward larger indexes, at least until it clashes with the front of the queue (we'll have to check it to avoid clashes).

That settles insertion, but what happens if we dequeue six elements and the front pointer reaches the end of the queue? As you can imagine, we do the same thing as we did for the rear: we use virtual indexes and the modulo operator to let the front pointer wrap around the end of the array.

We'll discuss the details of these operations in the implementation section. For now, instead, let's discuss how the different solutions that we have mentioned compare.

A comparison of the possible implementations

Table 9.1 shows the asymptotic analysis for the running time of different implementations of a queue ADT. We can make some observations.

Table 9.1 Comparison of various implementations of a queue

	`enqueue()`	`dequeue()`	Dynamic size
Static array	$O(1)$	$O(1)$	No
Dynamic array	$O(n)$ worst case $O(1)$ amortized	$O(n)$ worst case $O(1)$ amortized	Yes
Linked list	$O(1)$	$O(1)$	Yes

At the data structure level, there is nothing to suggest that we should prefer an array implementation because the linked list implementation is just as efficient and also flexible, allowing the queue to grow dynamically.

While fast on average, the implementation based on dynamic arrays can't give us guarantees on individual operations. At times, `enqueue` and `dequeue` can be slower because we have to resize the underlying array.

However, we learned in chapter 8 that the real world sometimes behaves surprisingly differently from what the theory tells us. Let's discuss this in the next section.

EXERCISE

9.1 As mentioned, it is also possible to use stacks to store a queue's data. One stack, however, is not enough. Can you find a way to use two stacks to implement a queue? Hint: Either enqueue or dequeue will have to be $O(n)$.

Implementation

The main disadvantage of implementing a queue with an underlying static array is that the queue will have a fixed size, and we have to decide its size the moment we create the queue.

In some situations, this fixed size is a significant problem. However, when a queue's capacity is predetermined, having a fixed size is not a problem.

And, we must say, using arrays also has some advantages:

- *Memory efficiency*—An array will require less memory than a linked list to store the same elements. This is because with an array, besides the space needed for storing the actual elements, there is only a constant-space overhead, regardless of the number of elements in the array.

- *Memory locality*—An array, as we have discussed in chapter 2, is a single chunk of memory where all elements are stored side by side. This characteristic can be used to optimize caching at the processor level.

- *Performance*—Operations on arrays are usually faster than on linked lists.

These three points can make a lot of difference in practice. So, which implementation should we choose?

If you need flexibility in the size of the queue, and clean, minimal code is valuable to you, then go with linked lists. In the implementation based on linked lists, the `enqueue` and `dequeue` methods are just wrappers that call the methods of the underlying linked list: `insert_to_back` for `enqueue` and `delete_from_front` for `dequeue`. Therefore, we won't discuss this implementation in detail here, but you can find the full Python code in the book's repo on GitHub: https://mng.bz/Dd5w.

However, if you can pre-allocate your queue to its maximum capacity or if static size is not a concern, an implementation based on arrays may offer considerable advantages. The code in this case will be more complicated, but it's a tradeoff with improved performance.

In the rest of this section, we will discuss the implementation of a circular queue, the one where the front and rear pointers wrap around the end of the array. The linear queue implementation simply has too many drawbacks to be practical in most situations.

An underlying static array

Let's dive into the details of the array-based implementation: as always, you can find the full code in our repo on GitHub: https://mng.bz/NRa1.

Even before we start with the class definition and the constructor, we must make the first decision. In the implementation using linked lists, the front and rear of the queue were easy to identify—they were just the head and tail of the list. We are not so lucky when we switch to arrays, and we have to decide how to handle these pointers.

Let me stress that this is not the only possible way, but here is what we will do—we will store two indexes, `front` and `rear`:

- `front` will be the index of the next element to be dequeued.

- `rear`, conversly, will be the index of the next array cell where a new element can enqueued.

Initially, we set both `front` and `rear` to 0, the index of the first element in the array.

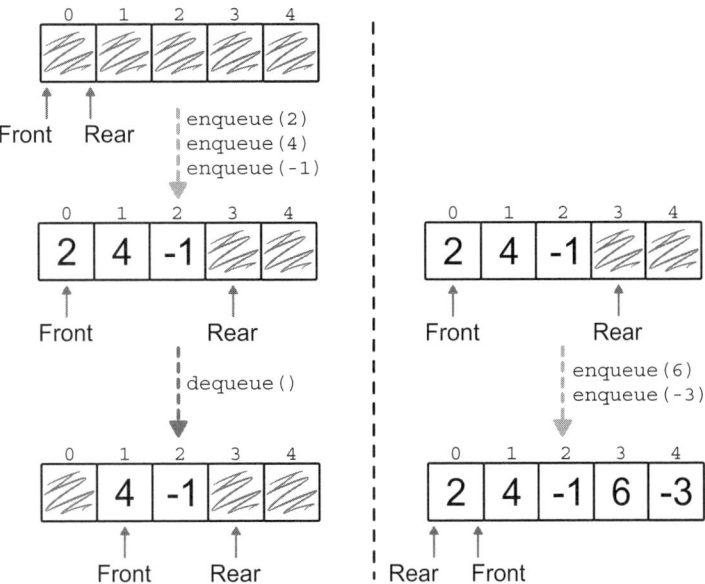

When we enqueue a new element, the `rear` pointer is advanced to the next index. And when we dequeue an element, it's the `front` pointer that is incremented.

All sounds good until we reach the maximum capacity. For example, if our queue has a capacity of five elements, and we enqueue all five elements without dequeuing any, the `rear` pointer will wrap around the array and will point back to the array cell at index 0. So, both when the array is empty, and when it's full, the `front` and `rear` pointers will point to the same index. How can we tell these situations apart?

There are many possible solutions, and here is the simplest one: we store the size of the queue in a variable that is updated on every enqueue and dequeue. This variable will make our life easier and many operations on the queue faster.

So, to recap, when we initialize a queue, we need to set the `front` and `rear` attributes for the class to 0, and we also initialize the size of the queue (that is, the number of elements currently stored in the queue) setting it to 0. We are not done just yet—we also need to initialize the underlying array. Note that I'm using a Python list in these examples although it's actually a dynamic array because it's the most convenient alternative in Python. Not only can it store any object, but we can also initialize it using a one-liner:

```
class Queue:
    def __init__(self):
        if max_size <= 1:
            raise ValueError(f'Invalid size for a queue (must have at
least 2 elements): {max_size}')
```

```
self._data = [None] * max_size
self._max_size = max_size
self._front = 0
self._rear = 0
self._size = 0
```

We simulate a static array of size max_size.
The value we use for the initialization is not
important, but to communicate that we consider
those elements to be empty, we can use None.

The first thing we need to do, however, is store the capacity of the queue, passed through the argument `max_size`. Before accepting it, we need to validate the value passed and make sure that the new queue will be able to host at least two elements. With this setup, checking the queue's size, or whether it's empty or full, becomes trivial:

```
def __len__(self):
    return self._size
def is_empty(self):
    return len(self) == 0
def is_full(self):
    return len(self) == self._max_size
```

Enqueue

Now let's focus on the details of enqueuing a new value to the queue. When we design how this method will work, we need to distinguish between three possible situations (assuming a queue with a capacity of n elements, n>1):

- `front <= rear` and `rear < n-1`: `front` is before `rear`, and `rear` is not at the end of the array.

- `front <= rear` but `rear == n-1`: `front` is before `rear`, and `rear` points to the last element in the array.

- `rear < front`: `front` and `rear` are swapped after `rear` has wrapped around the end of the array.

The initial situation

When the queue is created, both `front` and `rear` are initialized to 0. From that point on, `rear` can only be incremented until it reaches the end of the array. And `front` can also be incremented on dequeue, but it can never get past `rear`.

This is the easiest situation to handle, where we still don't have to worry about virtual indexes and wrapping the `rear` pointer around the end of the array. Before `rear` reaches the end of the array, the queue can't even be full, so all we need to do is store the new value and increment `rear`.

Wrapping around the array

Now we get to the interesting part: `rear` points to the last element in the array. Well, we can start by assigning the new value to the empty cell pointed to by `rear`, nothing changes for this part. At this point, in our example, `rear=4`. If we just incremented it, it would point to index 5, which overruns the boundaries of our array. This is where we remember about virtual indexes, as discussed in the "Queue as a data structure" section.

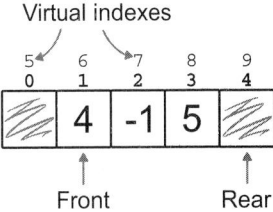

We can extend the regular indexing space of an array with these virtual indexes by imagining that indexes larger than the physical index of the last element will wrap around the array, as if they were arranged in a circle.

Thus, index 5 will point to the same array cell as index 0, and the `rear` pointer will effectively wrap around the array.

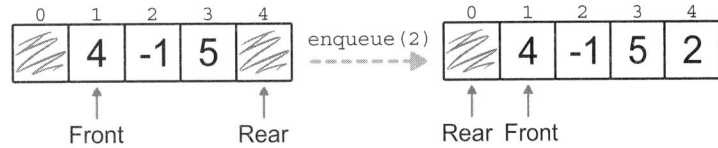

Front and rear swapped

At this point, the queue isn't yet full (because `front` in our example points to index 1, `dequeue` must have been called at some point), but `rear` points to a lower index than `front`. In practice, the two pointers have been swapped.

When we enqueue a new element, we can just increment `rear` as in our first case. But instead of checking for the end of the array, the boundary for the `rear` pointer becomes the `front` pointer instead.

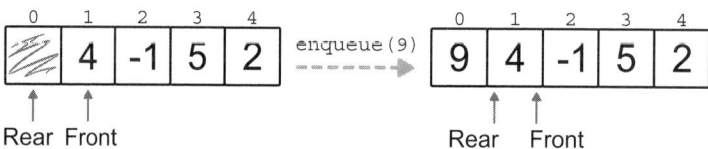

In our example, after enqueuing the value 9, `rear` and `front` both point to the element at index 1, and so `rear` can't advance anymore: the queue is full.

As mentioned at the beginning of the implementation section, there are several ways to translate the checks and increments of the pointer into code, but using a helper variable to remember the size of the queue will make our lives incredibly easier. To understand whether the queue is empty, full, or partially full, we don't have to check where `rear` and `front` are or which of the three cases above we are in. Instead, we just check how many elements are stored.

> **TIP**   Delegate size, emptiness, and fullness checks of a data structure to helper methods that you can reuse in your code. Your code will be cleaner, with less duplication, and thus less prone to error.

To increment `rear`, we could also handle the three cases separately by using conditionals, but I'll go for a cleaner (although arguably less efficient) way—we can use the modulo operator to map virtual indexes into the physical indexes of the array, as explained in the "Queue as a data structure" section.

With these assumptions, the code for `enqueue` becomes as simple as possible:

```
def enqueue(self, value):
    if self.is_full():
        raise ValueError('The queue is already full!')
    self._data[self._rear] = value
    self._rear = (self._rear + 1) % self._max_size
    self._size += 1
```

Dequeue

We've learned how to add elements to the queue. Now let's look at how to remove an element from it.

Similar to what we did for `enqueue`, we need to consider a few cases when designing the `dequeue` method:

- When `front` is before `rear`
- When `front` and `rear` point to the same index
- When `front` and `rear` are swapped after `rear` has wrapped around the end of the array, but `front` is not at the end of the array
- When `front` and `rear` are swapped, and `front` points to the last element in the array

If `front` points to a lower index than `rear`, we can simply increment `front` to dequeue an element.

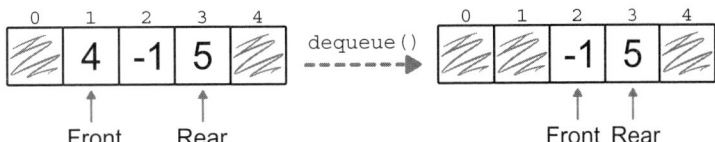

If `front` and `rear` are pointing to the same index, the queue can be either empty or full, and we can only understand which it is by checking the `size` attribute.

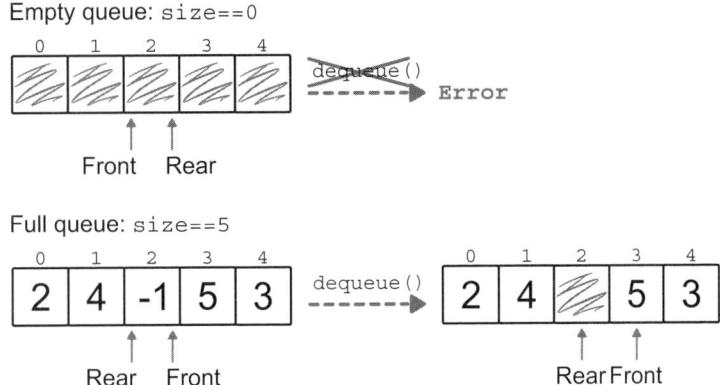

The last two cases are handled similarly to what we did for `rear` when enqueuing a new value. We increment the index that `front` points to, and if `front` is right at the end of the array, we use the virtual index trick and the modulo operator so that `front` can wrap around the end of the array.

Note that when `front` wraps around the end of the array, we go back to the initial configuration where `front` and `rear` are not swapped (that is, `front <= rear`).

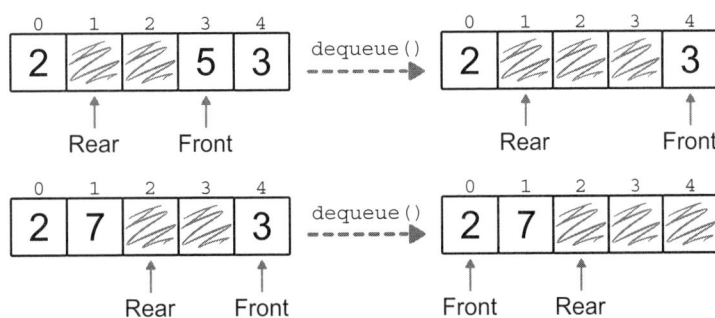

As for enqueue, instead of treating each case separately, we can use the modulo operator and write some cleaner code that doesn't separately address each case:

```
def dequeue(self):
    if self.is_empty():
        raise ValueError("Cannot dequeue from an empty queue")
    value = self._data[self._front]
    self._front = (self._front + 1) % self._max_size
    self._size -= 1
    return value
```

Similar to what we did for stacks, we could define a peek method that returns the element at the front of the queue without removing it. As we saw in the last chapter, however, this method introduces a lot of unnecessary complication, so I wouldn't include it in the queue interface unless it's absolutely necessary.

EXERCISES

9.2 Implement the peek method for the Queue class. What are the main problems we need to be aware of, and how do we solve them? Hint: Check out what we did for stacks.

9.3 Implement an iterator on the queue. Hint: When a queue, or a stack, is used in for loops, the elements are provided in the correct order, but they are also removed from the container.

What about dynamic arrays?

Earlier in the chapter, I mentioned that dynamic arrays are rarely used for queues. Still, it's worth discussing how such a solution works. It helps us better understand how circular queues work. And, although unlikely, in some contexts, dynamic arrays might actually be the best option.

With a static array, even if we use virtual indexes and circular configuration to re-use the array cells freed up on dequeue, at some point, the queue might get full. It happens when the rear pointer reaches the (virtual) index immediately before the front of the queue. If we try to insert another element, we get an error because the queue is full—the rear pointer would walk past the front pointer.

If we were using a dynamic array, instead, this would be the time when we double the capacity of the underlying array—when we try to enqueue an element on a full queue, we can just allocate a new array. The problem is that our new array would have a size of 16, while our old array had a size of 8.

It might not seem like a big deal, but all the virtual indexes, as we had computed them on the old array, would be misplaced, and we couldn't use modulo 8 to compute the array indexes. So, we would need modulo 16.

Even worse, if we copy the array as it is over the new array, we will encounter a big problem: the rear and front pointers will no longer make sense, and there will be a big hole in the middle of the queue. And yet, when we try to enqueue a new element, the rear pointer will still be just before the front pointer! So, because of this, depending on how we implement `is_full`, the method could erroneously consider the queue full. Or, in our implementation, the queue would overwrite existing elements and still stop before it fills the additional space.

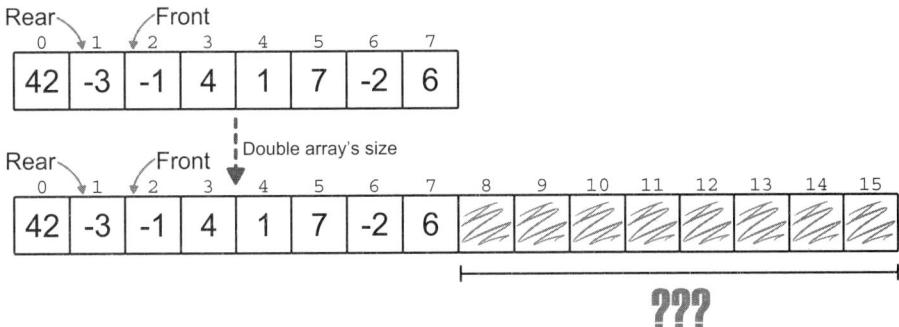

There is a way to work around this. When we copy the elements to the new array, we need to align the front of the queue to index 0, as shown in the following figure.

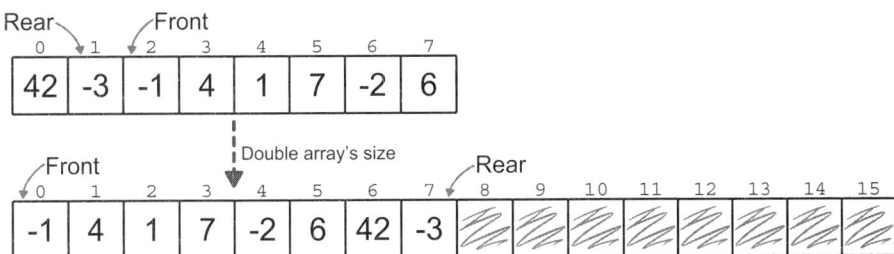

This won't be any slower than copying the elements in the same positions as they were, and it won't affect the asymptotic analysis. But it will make the code more complicated. Add to this the fact that with dynamic arrays the worst case for `insert` and `delete` is `O(n)`, which in turn means that `enqueue` and `dequeue` would also take linear time in the worst case. All in all, if you need a flexible queue whose size can adapt, you are often better off with an implementation based on linked lists.

More applications of a queue

At the beginning of this chapter, we have discussed both real-world situations that work according to the FIFO principle and a software application such as task management that (in its simplest form) uses a queue. There are many other areas where queues are used as a part of a larger system and many algorithms that rely on a queue to work. For example, in chapter 13, we will talk about breadth-first search, an algorithm for traversing a graph and finding the minimum distance (in terms of number of edges) between one vertex of the graph and any (or all) of the other vertices.

Let's discuss some other examples of how queues are used in computer science.

Messaging systems

When building large applications, and especially large web applications, the pace of requests can sometimes get too fast and too hectic to handle properly. When the requesters can afford a slower (non-real-time) response, we can regulate the pace of a web service by using the so-called *pull strategy* and a queue.

Typically, a web service is configured to use the push strategy: when a service or a user client has a request, it directly contacts the service, which then handles the request. A surge of requests, however, can exceed the capacity of the server. Suppose that your service can handle a maximum of 100 requests per minute. If there is a surge of 200 requests within a few seconds, your service will be overloaded, some (in this case, many) requests will be lost and never answered, and your service may even crash.

With a messaging system, instead, requests are pushed to a high-capacity service that simply enqueues them as messages to a buffer like Kafka. Your service then reads (*pulls*) the messages from the queue at its own pace and in the same order they were sent.

If the buffer doesn't support a priority for the messages, then the data structure it uses is exactly the simple queue we are presenting in this chapter. When priority is involved, a different type of queue is used, which we discuss in the next chapter.

Web servers

A similar strategy can be used by web servers to keep track of the requests received from clients. In this case, there may be no messaging service buffer, and the web server may simply use a queue to store the incoming requests before processing them at its own pace.

Operating systems

When it comes to scheduling CPU usage among active processes, disk usage, or printer spooling, your operating system can use a queue to round-robin the processes that need to access the same resource. Modern operating systems (OS) support the concept of process priority so that resources such as CPU or disk are allocated first and more often to high-priority processes. Printer spooling, however, is more likely to be handled more fairly according to the FIFO policy, so you can find a printer queue in your OS.

Recap

- A *queue* is a container that adheres to the FIFO policy: that is, the *first* element *in* the queue is the *first* element *out*. You can picture a queue as a line at the checkout counter: people enter at the back of the queue, and the one person at the front gets served.

- Queues are widely used in computer science and programming, including messaging systems, networking, web servers, and operating systems. In addition, many algorithms use queues to keep track of the order in which elements must be processed, such as breadth-first search.

- Queues provide two operations: enqueue (to add an element to the back of the queue) and dequeue (to remove and return the element from the front of the queue). Similarly to stacks, there is no other way to insert or delete elements, and searching is generally not allowed.

- A queue can be implemented using either arrays or linked lists to store its elements.

- Using linked lists, enqueue and dequeue take $O(1)$ time in the worst case.

- Using static arrays, we can implement a *linear queue*, which can only support a fixed number of enqueue operations. Alternatively, we can implement a *circular queue*, where the array is imagined as a circular container. This requires additional complexity.

- While it is possible to use dynamic arrays, this type of implementation is quite complicated and not very common.

Priority queues and heaps: Handling data according to its priority | 10

In this chapter

- introducing the priority queue abstract data type

- the difference between queue and priority queue

- implementing a priority queue with arrays and
    linked lists

- introducing the heap, a data structure for the priority
    queue abstract data type

- why heaps are implemented as arrays rather
    than trees

- how to efficiently build a heap from an existing array

In chapter 9, we talked about queues, a container that holds your data and returns it in the same order in which it was inserted. This idea can be generalized by introducing the concept of priority, which leads us to priority queues and their most common implementation—heaps. In this chapter, we discuss both, together with some of their applications.

Extending queues with priority

In the previous chapter, we saw some examples of queues in real life, such as the line to get an ice cream. Not all queues, however, have such a linear development. In an emergency room, for example, the next person to see a doctor isn't necessarily the person who has waited the longest, but rather the one who needs the most urgent care. And the order is dynamic, not set in stone.

In this section, we introduce the concept of priority and derive from that a variant of the plain queue called *priority queue*.

Handling bugs (revised)

Remember Priyanka, our software engineer who handles bugs at an early-stage startup? We met her in chapter 9. She has re-engineered the way bugs are handled at her company, making sure no bugs get lost.

The new system works well, so well that she is overwhelmed with work. To manage this, Priyanka has decided to bring in a small team specifically dedicated to addressing and fixing bugs. But that alone is not enough. There is a step in the protocol she created that makes her waste a lot of time.

If you remember, the process was largely automated: engineers would send an email with the bug they found, and a daemon would extract the bug from the email and add it to a bug queue. At this point, however, it was up to Priyanka to look at the bug and decide whether it was urgent. If the bug was urgent, it had to be fixed immediately. Otherwise, it was enqueued back to the rear of the queue.

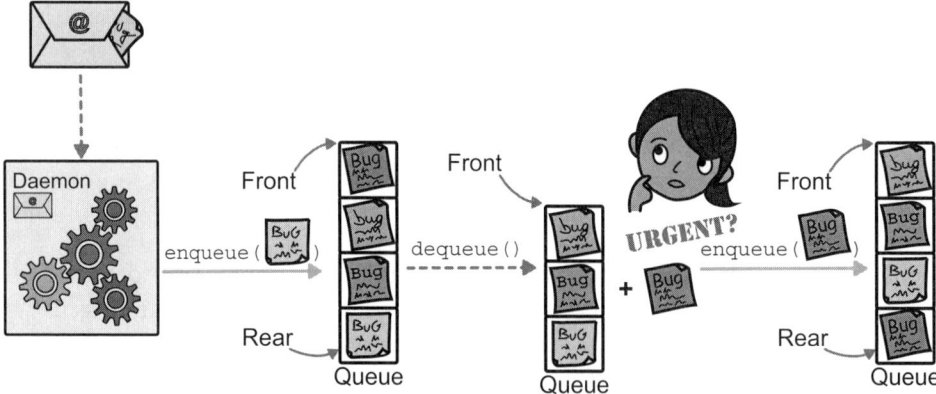

Deciding whether a bug is urgent is expensive in terms of Priyanka's time. To assess the urgency of a bug, Priyanka often has to reach out to the engineer who filed the bug or to the team who owns the area affected by the bug to understand the context and the impact of the bug.

It takes her a long time to process each bug. It also requires commitment from other engineers, and the effort may be wasted if they agree that the bug is not urgent.

To turn the situation around, Priyanka has an idea: What if it's up to the person filing the bug to say whether it is urgent or not? She and her team may still have to talk to the owners of the affected code to fix the bug, but they will do so only after someone else has determined that a bug is urgent and needs to be fixed right away. This modification requires a change in the queue. Now, when Priyanka asks for the next bug, the system doesn't return the oldest bug, but the most urgent one.

To allow for some more flexibility, Priyanka creates a system with four levels of urgency: desired, needed, urgent, and critical. "Critical" is for those bugs that should have been fixed yesterday because they affect the end users. At the other end of the scale, "desired" fixes can wait. They usually are tech debt—improvements that you want to add even if they don't really affect the end user.

To handle the bugs according to their priority, a regular queue is not enough. It must be replaced with a priority queue.

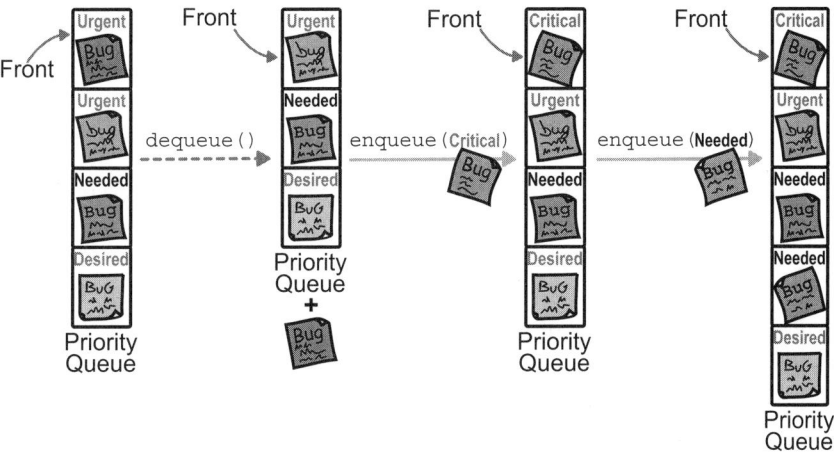

You'll notice that in a priority queue, we no longer need to keep track of the rear of the queue. That's because when a new element enters the queue, it's not placed last, but its position is determined by its priority.

The abstract data type for priority queue

As with plain queues, there are two important methods that we need to include in the interface of a priority queue: one to add a new element to the queue and one to get the element with the highest priority. Traditionally, we use a different nomenclature for these methods. The one that adds a new element is just called `insert`. There is less consensus about the one that pulls and removes the highest-priority item. It is sometimes called `pull_highest_priority_element` (sometimes shortened as `pull`), `extract_max`, or just `top`. I'll go with the latter, for personal preference and brevity.

The contract that a priority queue establishes with its clients is that the queue will always return the element with the highest priority. How this is done is not something we need to specify at the abstract data type (ADT) level: as always, we'll talk about it when we get to the data structure level.

EXERCISES

10.1 Priority queues are based on the notion of priority. But they also are still queues. What choice for the priority of an element would make a priority queue behave like a simple queue?

10.2 What could be a possible choice for the priority of an element that would make a priority queue behave like a stack?

Priority queues as data structures

How can we store the data of a priority queue? We have two alternatives: we can keep the elements sorted by priority, or we can search for the current highest-priority element every time we have to return it.

Let's discuss the former option first. Throughout this section, we will show examples with integers, where higher numbers mean higher priority.

Sorted linked lists and sorted arrays

Maintaining the elements sorted by priority simplifies the `top` method. In fact, for this method, we only need to return the element at the front of the queue. The `insert` method, however, has to deal with new elements, adding them to the existing data and making sure that the order is maintained. Two data structures are good candidates to implement this behavior: sorted linked lists and sorted arrays.

For linked lists, the singly linked variant is sufficient because we can simply remove elements from the head of the list, while insertion takes linear time anyway. We keep the elements sorted from highest (head) to lowest (tail) priority, and when we add a new element, we must scan the list until we find the right place for it, just as we discussed in chapter 6. Deleting an element from the front, however, is a constant-time operation, as you should know by now.

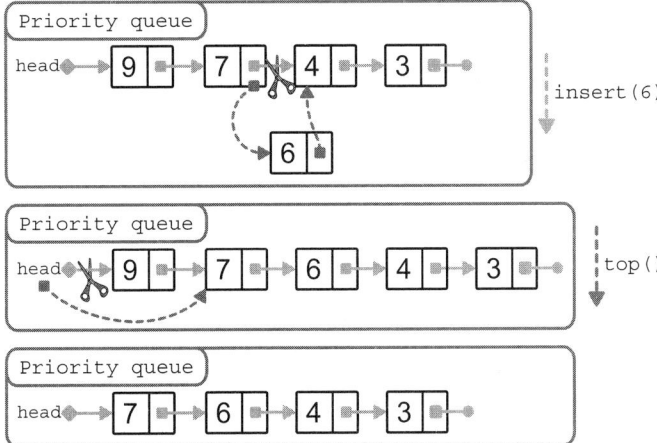

With arrays, we can use a similar strategy, but we have to be smart to keep the running time of `top` as fast as possible. We have two options for the order of elements: we can sort them from highest to lowest priority, or vice versa. In the first case, to remove the element with the highest priority, we would have to move all the other elements in the array. So, the right way is to have the highest priority at the end of the array.

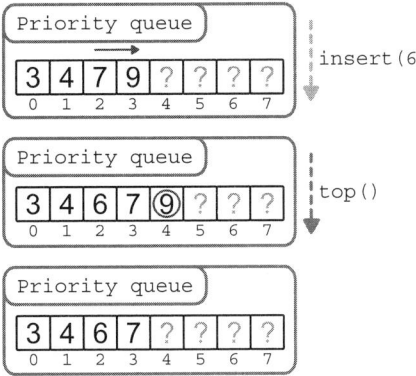

Unsorted linked lists and unsorted arrays

The opposite alternative is to use the unsorted version of these two data structures. Insertion becomes easy and constant-time in both cases, because we can just append a new element wherever it's more convenient. This means at the front of a linked list and at the end of an array.

Conversely, extracting the highest priority element becomes complicated because no information about the elements is available. We have no choice but to go through the whole list, element by element, keeping track of the highest priority found.

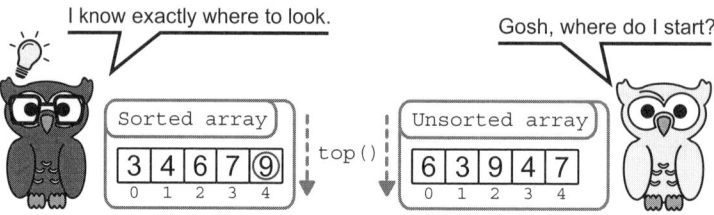

Performance overview

Table 10.1 recaps what we have learned so far.

Table 10.1 An initial comparison of various implementations of a priority queue

	`insert()`	`top()`	Dynamic size
Sorted static array	O(n)	O(1)	No
Unsorted static array	O(1)	O(n)	No
Sorted linked list	O(n)	O(1)	Yes
Unsorted linked list	O(1)	O(n)	Yes

Linked lists and arrays behave similarly. If we keep them sorted, insertion is slow, and getting the top element is fast. For the unsorted variants, the opposite is true.

These are two extremes, completely sorted sequences and completely unsorted ones, with opposite extreme behaviors. Wouldn't it be nice if there was an intermediate solution that allows us to do better than O(n) for both operations?

Partial ordering

For a sorted array A, if we pick two indices i and j, with i < j, we immediately know that A[i] ≤ A[j]. That's because a sorted array is totally ordered, so given two elements, we can immediately know how they compare based on their position. We know where to find the largest element in the array, and if we remove it, we also know which element will take its place. At the opposite extreme, in unsorted arrays we have no information at all.

The more information we have, the more expensive it is to build and maintain the data structure. Trivially, we have to compare more elements to fully sort an array.

The key to better performance is to share the load between these two operations and balance the minimal information required with the maximal elements accessed per operation. The balance is achieved by ordering the elements only partially. This idea stems from the consideration that, as mentioned earlier, we don't need to know, at all times, the exact order in which the elements will be returned—we just need the next one.

Heap

In the previous chapters, when discussing the data structures for implementing an ADT, I often mentioned that it is always possible to design a new data structure from scratch, but that this is usually not the best alternative. Now it's time to discuss an exception to the rule.

The best data structure to implement a priority queue is neither an array nor a linked list. We can't reuse a stack or a queue for this task. Instead, we introduce a new type of data structure that we haven't met before.

In the rest of this section, we will discuss the *heap* and how we can use it to implement priority queues.

A special tree

A heap is a special kind of tree. If you are not familiar with tree data structures, don't worry. I'm going to explain what we need here, but you can also refer to chapter 11 to get the basics.

In this chapter, we restrict ourselves to binary heaps, which means that we will use binary trees. And, in fact, property 1 of a binary heap is that each node of the tree can have at most two children.

This is not strictly necessary for heaps—they can be ternary trees, quaternary trees, and so on. However, binary heaps are the simplest, and they are enough to fulfill our needs in most cases. If you'd like to learn more about d-way heaps (heaps where nodes have more than two children), you can read a detailed description in chapter 2 of *Advanced Algorithms and Data Structures* (La Rocca, 2021, Manning).

You might have noticed that the nodes in a tree are organized into levels. In the following example, the root of the tree, a node labeled with the letter M, is the only node at level 0. At level 1, we have two nodes, the two children of node M, labeled with B and Z, and so on.

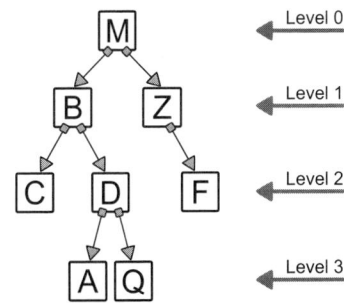

But a heap is not just any binary tree. To be a binary heap, a tree must satisfy two additional properties.

Property 2 is a structural property. The heap tree is "almost complete," which means that every level of the tree, except possibly the last level, is complete; furthermore, the nodes on the last level are as far left as possible.

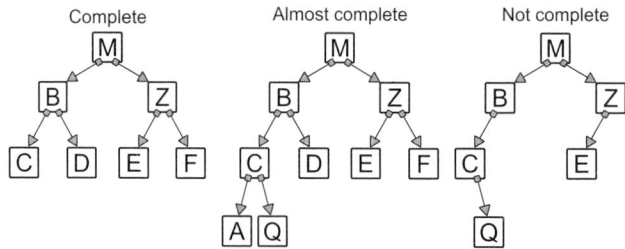

Finally, property 3 is about the data in the heap. In a heap, each node holds the highest priority element in the subtree rooted at that node.

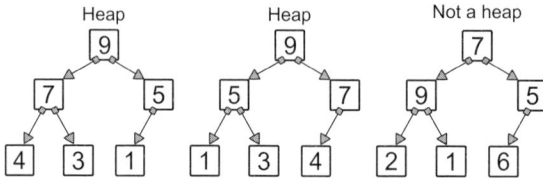

This last property guarantees that the element with the highest priority is always at the root of the heap. The problem now, of course, is that we need to restore these properties when a new element is added to or when the root is extracted from the heap. We'll explain how to do this in the next section when we discuss the implementation layer for heaps.

Some properties of a heap

From the foundational properties of heaps, there follow some other very interesting properties. From property 3, we can infer that all paths from the root to any leaf of the tree are sorted.

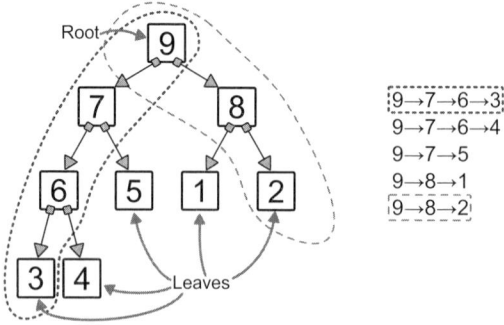

Incidentally, this is a possible partial sorting of an array—it's the tradeoff we talked about in the last section, where we don't have all the information about how each pair of elements compares, but we do have some information.

From properties 1 and 2, instead, we can infer some interesting structural properties. First, we know exactly how many nodes there will be at each level.

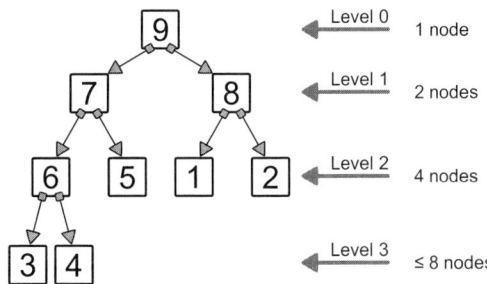

At the first level, level 0, there can only be the root. Since each node can have at most two children, level 1, where the children of the root are, can have at most two nodes. Iterating, we can say that the next level has four nodes, and in general, each level i can have at most 2^i nodes (and it will have exactly 2^i nodes, unless it's the last level). The index i of the levels is their height, that is, their distance from the root.

From all these properties, we derive that the heap's height (that is, the length of the longest root-to-leaf path) is as small as `log(n)` for a heap with n elements. Don't worry, I won't go into the math. I'll leave that to you as an exercise!

Performance of a heap

The reason why having a bound on the height of the heap is so important is that we can implement `insert` and `top` operations so that they only walk a path from the root to a leaf or vice versa. This, in turn, means that their running time is proportional to the height of the heap.

So, if `insert` and `top` on a heap take time proportional to the height of the heap (and they do—I'll show you this in the next section), then we can update Table 10.1 to Table 10.2, which shows that heaps provide a more balanced performance for the operations on a priority queue.

Table 10.2 An updated comparison of various implementations of a priority queue

	`insert()`	`top()`
Sorted array/linked list	O(n)	O(1)
Unsorted array/linked list	O(1)	O(n)
Heap	O(log(n))	O(log(n))

Max-heap and min-heap

Before we get into how to implement a heap, I'd like to make a clarification. You can often find the heaps that we have shown in the examples described as max-heaps: a max-heap is a heap where each parent has a value no smaller than its children. Consequently, the root of a max-heap contains its largest element.

What if we need to have the smallest elements at the root (because we want to extract the next smallest element in a sequence)? In this case, you can often see a min-heap being used—a heap where each parent has a value no larger than its children.

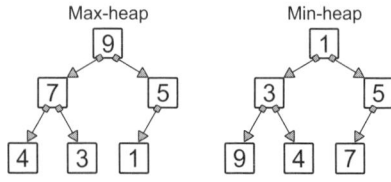

Using the idea of a min-heap can be confusing and complicate heap implementation as it inverts parent–child comparisons and the necessary checks. I believe the correct way to handle heaps is through the concept of priority—a heap always has the highest priority element at the root, and for each parent–child pair, we guarantee that `priority(P)` ≥ `priority(C)`. Then, for example, if we want to have smaller numbers at the top of the heap, we can define the priority of a number x as -x, the opposite of x.

This requires defining and applying a function to get the priority of an element, but it removes all ambiguity and gives us more flexibility.

EXERCISE

10.3 Can you prove that the height of a heap with n elements is `log(n)`? Hint: Remember, the heap is an almost complete tree.

Implementing a heap

Now that we have established that we need a new data structure for priority queues, it's time to look at how to implement it. I also postponed the discussion of the main operations on a heap, which would normally be part of the DS layer. There is a reason for this: they are heavily influenced by how we implement a heap, and there is a plot twist that we need to unveil before we can talk about implementation. But we need to follow a certain order to explain everything.

How to store a heap

We could certainly store a heap as a tree, similarly to what we do with linked lists and what we will see in chapter 11. However, we don't usually do this because there is a better way. To explain why, we need to go back to the second property of a heap. Because a heap is an almost complete binary tree, we know exactly how many nodes we have at each level.

Let's try to add an incremental index to each node, starting with 0 for the root, and traversing the tree from top to bottom and from left to right.

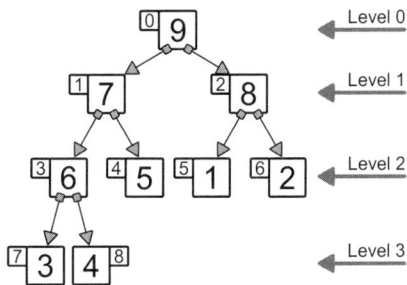

There are a few things we can infer from this figure. Take, for example, the node with index 3. We know that its parent has index 1, and its children have indexes 7 and 8. Similarly, for the node with index 2, its parent's index is 0, and its children's indexes are 5 and 6.

We can devise a rule: given a node with an index $i > 0$, its parent's index is given by the integer division $(i - 1) / 2$, and its children have indexes $2 * i + 1$ and $2 * i + 2$. That's interesting, but what can we do with this information?

Here is another consideration that will help us figure that out: we assigned the indexes so that all the nodes at level 1 come before the nodes at level 2, which come before the nodes at level 3, and so on. An almost complete tree is left justified, which means that there is no "hole" in our indexing, and even at the last level, we know exactly where in the tree the node with index 8 is.

We saw this idea earlier when we talked about arrays: elements in a static array are (usually) kept left justified, with no gaps between the first and last element. And indeed, there is a parallel between this tree and arrays.

If we reorganize the elements of the tree linearly, placing each level side-by-side, the indexing we assign to the nodes will perfectly match the indexing of an array with the same elements.

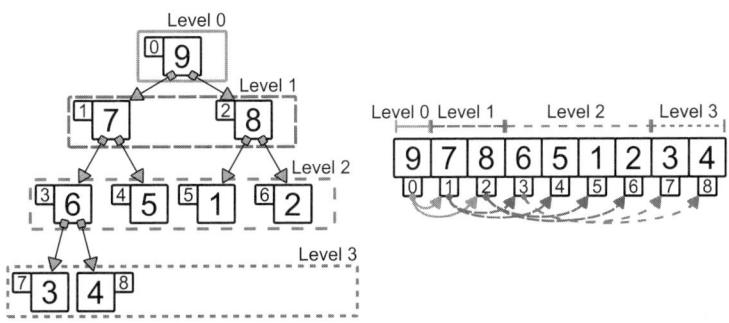

And here is the plot twist—we end up using an array to store the heap's data! Well, it's a special array with some constraints and some useful properties, but nonetheless, it's an array. In the rest of this section, we'll assume the array has enough space to store the elements we add, and so we'll treat it as a static array for the purposes of analyzing the operations on the heap. By now, you know that if you need a dynamic array instead, the bounds on the running time are not meant as worst case, but rather as amortized.

Constructor, priority, and helper methods

Given all that you have learned in the previous subsection, you can imagine that we will define a `Heap` class that uses an array (a Python list) as an internal attribute. As discussed earlier, I prefer passing a function to extract element priority, ensuring the highest priority is always on top of the heap:

```
class Heap:
    def __init__(self, elements=None, element_priority=lambda x: x):
        self._priority = element_priority
        if elements is not None and len(elements) > 0:
            self._heapify(elements)
        else:
            self._elements = []
```

I also strongly encourage you to always develop some helper methods that take care of the details of comparing the priority of two elements, finding an element's parent, and finding its children. Besides giving you cleaner code, abstracting these operations into their own methods will help you reason about more complex operations without having to check each time if you need to use < or >, or if you got the formula to get the index of the parent node right:

```
def _has_lower_priority(self, element_1, element_2):
    return self._priority(element_1) < self._priority(element_2)
def _has_higher_priority(self, element_1, element_2):
    return self._priority(element_1) > self._priority(element_2)
def _left_child_index(self, index):
    return index * 2 + 1
def _parent_index(self, index):
    return (index - 1) // 2
```

There is one more helper method, `_heapify`, which builds a heap from an existing array. However, we'll talk about it at the end of this section.

Once we have defined these methods, we are ready to discuss the main operations on a heap. For the examples in this chapter, we will use the bug queue example we discussed at the beginning of the chapter, with one change: priorities are decimal numbers instead of classes. A higher number indicates a higher priority.

Insert

Let's start with insertion. To help you visualize what we are doing, I'll show you the tree and array representations of the heap side by side. We will use this heap/bug queue as the starting state.

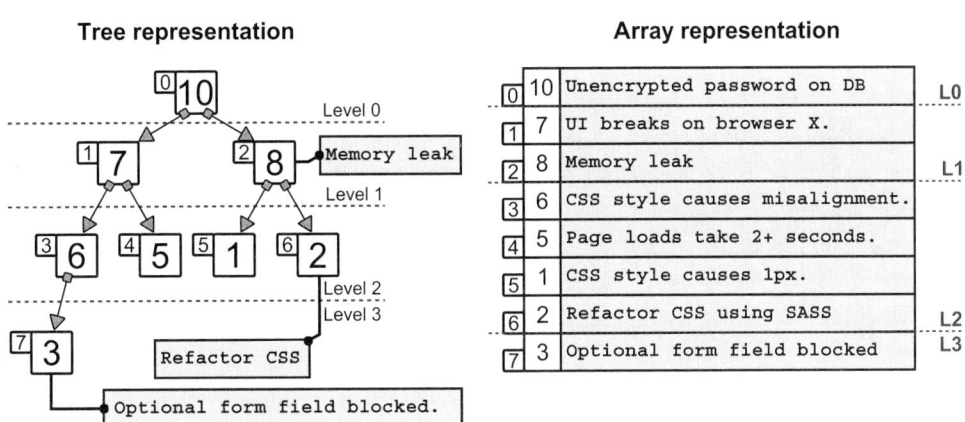

Each element is a pair with the bug description and its priority. In the tree representation, most of the descriptions are omitted due to space limitations. For the same reason, going forward, I'll only display the descriptions in the array representation.

Now, suppose we want to add a new element. Like we said, we assume that the array has been allocated with enough space to append new elements, and we only show the portion of the array that is actually populated, leaving out the empty cells.

We want to add the tuple (`"Broken Login"`, 9). First, we add the new element to the end of the array. But then we notice that the new element breaks the third property of heaps because its priority is higher than its parent!

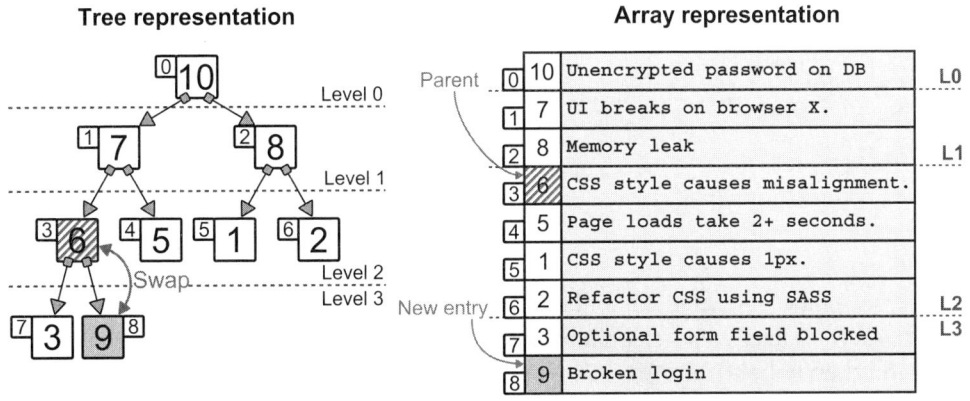

What can we do to fix this? Here is an idea: swap the child and parent nodes! This will fix the priority hierarchy for both of them, and it will also be fine with the sibling node (the one with index 7) because it was already not greater than the old parent, which, in turn, is smaller than the new element.

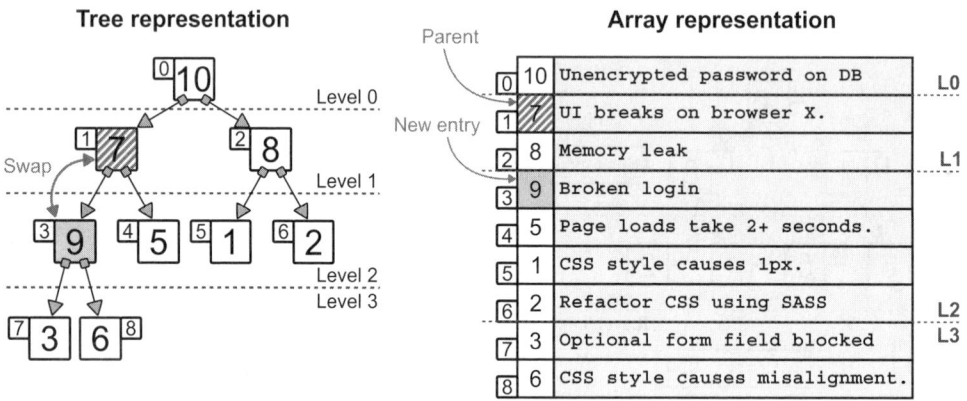

But we are not done yet. The new element, even in its new position, can still break the heap's properties. And indeed, it does because its priority is higher than its new parent, the node with index 1. To restore the heap's properties, we *bubble up* the new element until it either reaches the root of the heap or we find a parent with higher priority. In our case, this means just one more hop and we are done.

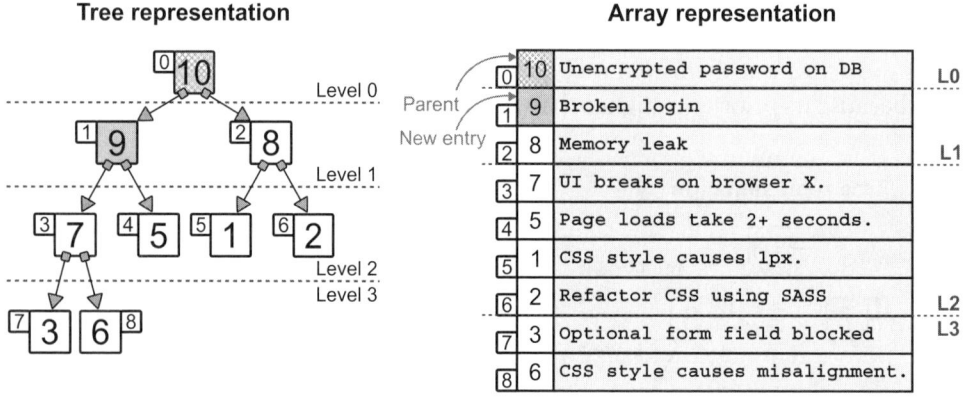

Code-wise, I have extracted the bubble-up part into its own helper method so that the `insert` method itself looks clean and short. Just append a new element to the end of the array, and then bubble it up:

```
def insert(self, element):
    self._elements.append(element)
    self._bubble_up(len(self._elements) - 1)
```

Of course, the complexity is all in the helper method. This method contains an optimization. Instead of repeatedly swapping the same element with its current parent, we trickle down those parents that should be swapped and finally store the new element in its final position:

```
def _bubble_up(self, index):
    element = self._elements[index]
    while index > 0:
        parent_index = self._parent_index(index)
        parent = self._elements[parent_index]
        if self._has_higher_priority(element, parent):
            self._elements[index] = parent
            index = parent_index
        else:
            break
    self._elements[index] = element
```

There is a violation of the heap's properties, and we need to swap the new element with its parent.

The new element and its parent don't violate the heap's properties, so we have found the final place to insert the new element.

How many elements do we have to swap? We can only bubble up the new element on a path from a leaf to the root, so the number of swaps is at most equal to the height of the heap. Therefore, as I promised, insertion on a heap takes `O(log(n))` steps.

Top

Now let's start with the heap of nine elements we obtained after inserting ("Broken Login", 9) and remove its highest priority element, the root of the heap. Just removing the element from the heap leaves us with a broken tree. There are two subtrees, each of which is a valid heap, but their array representation is broken, that is, without a common root.

Tree representation   **Array representation**

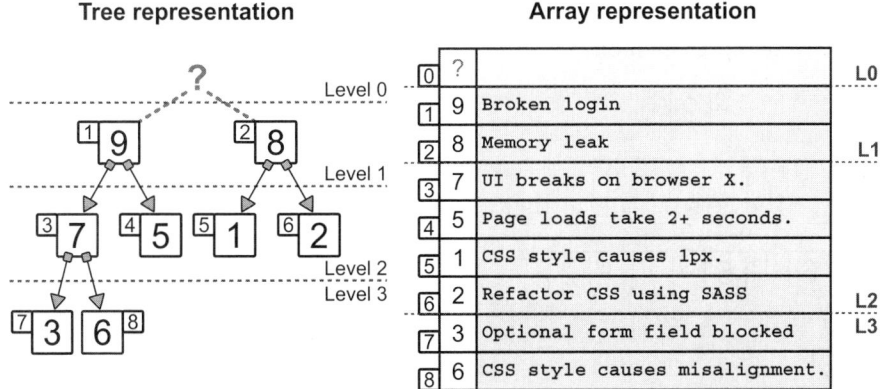

Shifting the remaining elements would mess up the heap's indexing and structure. Similarly, bubbling up one of the former root's children (like in `insert`) won't work because, first, we'd be moving to one of the subtrees the hole left by the former root. And second, we would have to bubble up the largest of the children. Depending on which one is the largest and on the structure of the heap, we might end up with a hole at the leaf level, breaking the "almost complete" property.

Here is a better option: How about we take the last element of the heap (in this case, the one with index 8) and move it to the root of the heap, replacing the former highest priority element? This will permanently fix the structural problem and restore the second property of the heap, making it an almost complete tree.

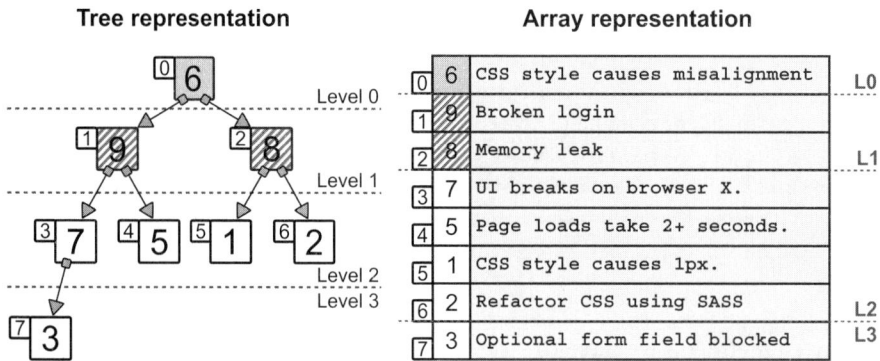

Not all the properties of the heap, however, are now restored: the third property is still violated because the root of the heap is smaller than at least one of its children (this was likely to happen since we took a leaf, likely one of the smallest elements in the heap, and moved it to the root).

To reinstate all the heap's properties, we need to *push down* the new root, down toward the leaves, swapping it with the smallest of its children until we find a place where it no longer violates the third property of the heap. Here is the final position that we found for element 6, with the path of nodes swapped to get there highlighted.

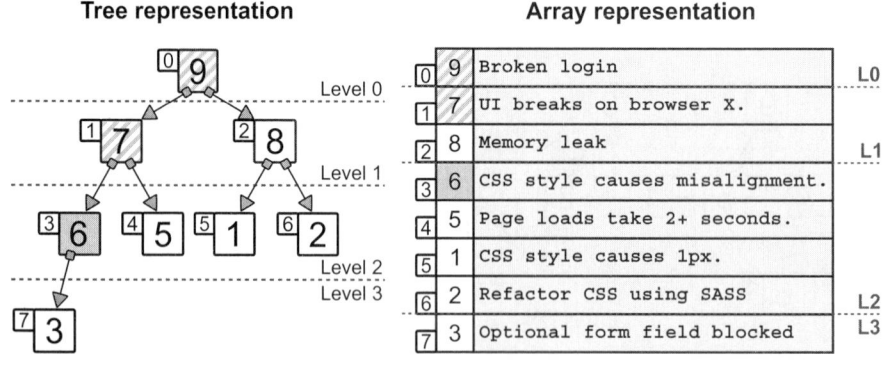

Similar to what we did with `insert`, we have a short method body for `top`, handling edge cases and the first step, where we move the last element of the array to the root of the heap:

```
def top(self):
    if self.is_empty():
        raise ValueError('Method top called on an empty heap.')
    if len(self) == 1:
        element = self._elements.pop()    ◄──────  If the heap has a single element,
    else:                                          we just need to pop its root.
        element = self._elements[0]
        self._elements[0] = self._elements.pop()
        self._push_down(0)
    return element
```

Most of the work is done by a helper method, `_push_down`.

We need an extra helper method to find out which of a node's children has the highest priority. The method returns `None` if the current node is a leaf (this will help us later):

```
def _highest_priority_child_index(self, index):          The current node
    first_index = self._left_child_index(index)          has no children.
    if first_index >= len(self):
        return None    ◄──────                            The current node
    if first_index + 1 >= len(self):                      only has one child.
        return first_index    ◄──────
    if self._has_higher_priority(self._elements[first_index], self._
elements[first_index + 1]):
        return first_index
    else:
        return first_index + 1
```

Once we have this method, `_push_down` becomes easier. What we have to do is, given a node, check whether it is a leaf (we'll get `None` from the call to `_highest_priority_child_index`), and if so, we are done.

Otherwise, we compare the current element with the one of its children that has the highest priority. If they don't violate the third heap property, we are also done. If they do, we have to swap them and repeat the process:

```
def _push_down(self, index):
    element = self._elements[index]
    current_index = index
    while True:
        child_index = self._highest_priority_child_index(current_index)
        if child_index is None:
            break
```

```
      if self._has_lower_priority(element, self._elements[child_
index]):
          self._elements[current_index] = self._elements[child_index]
          current_index = child_index
      else:
          break
  self._elements[current_index] = element
```

As with insert, we optimize the method by avoiding explicit swapping. But how many swaps would we have to do? Again, we can only go along a path from the root to a leaf, so it's a number at most equal to the height of the heap.

This time, we have another aspect we need to check. We are swapping the element pushed down and the smallest of its children, so we need to find that first. How many comparisons do we need to find out which child is the smallest and if we need to swap it with the pushed-down element? We need at most two comparisons for each swap, so we are still good because we have $O(log(n))$ swaps and $O(2*log(n)) = O(log(n))$ comparisons.

So, this shows that the logarithmic bound I have anticipated for this method is indeed correct.

Heapify

One more heap operation to discuss is the *heapification* of a set of elements—creating a valid heap from an initial set of elements. This operation is not part of the priority queue interface because it's specific to heaps. The context is as follows: we have an initial array with n elements (no assumptions can be made about their order), and we need to build a heap containing them. There are at least two trivial ways of doing this:

- We can sort the elements—a sorted array is a valid heap.

- We can create an empty heap and call insert n times.

Both operations take $O(n*log(n))$ time and possibly some (up to linear) extra space.

But heaps allow us to do better. In fact, it's possible to create a heap from an array of elements in linear time, $O(n)$. This is another advantage compared to using sorted arrays to implement a priority queue.

We start with two considerations: every subtree of a heap is a valid subheap, and every leaf of a tree is a valid subheap of height 0. If we start with an arbitrary array and represent it as a binary, almost complete tree, its internal nodes may violate the third property of heaps, but its leaves are certainly valid subheaps. Our goal is to build larger subheaps iteratively, using smaller building blocks.

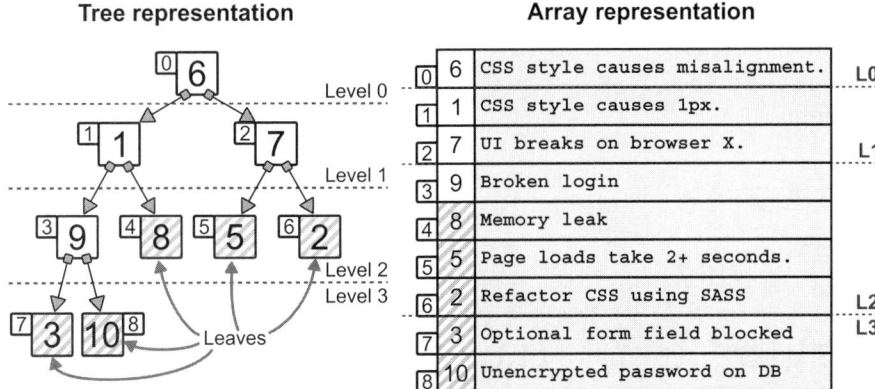

In a binary heap, at least half (plus/minus 1) of the nodes are leaves, so only the other half of the nodes, the internal nodes, can violate the heap properties. If we take any of the internal nodes at the second-to-last level, level 2 in the example, it will have one or two children, both of which are leaves and therefore valid heaps. Now we have a heap with a root that might violate the third property and two valid subheaps as children—exactly what we have discussed for the top method, after replacing the root with the last element in the array. So, we can fix the subheap by pushing down its current root.

In the example, the only internal node of level 2 is the one at index 3, which violates the heap properties. After pushing it down, the subtree rooted at index 3 becomes a valid heap.

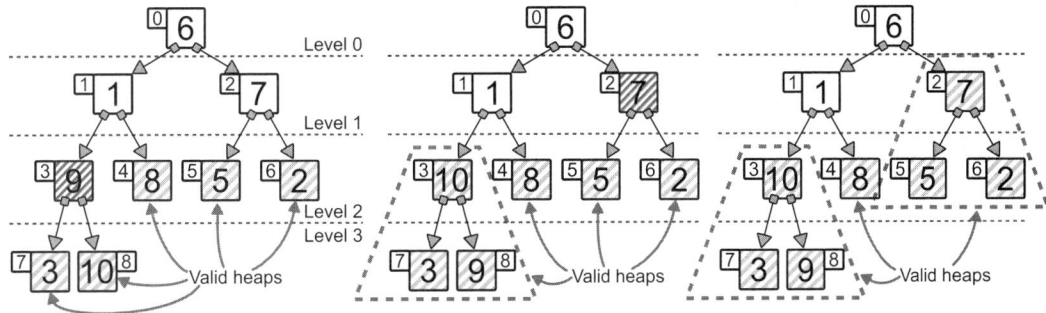

Next, we go to level 1, where the only other node whose children are leaves is the one at index 2. Note that, if there are n/2 leaves, then there are n/4 internal nodes whose children are only leaves. In this example, there are only two of them, for five leaves (here, the division is assumed to be an integer division).

We try to push down the root of the subtree, but in this case, there is nothing else to do. Now, all the subheaps of height 1 are valid. We can move to the subheaps of height 2 (there is only one of them) and then to the subheaps of height 3, which is the whole heap in this example.

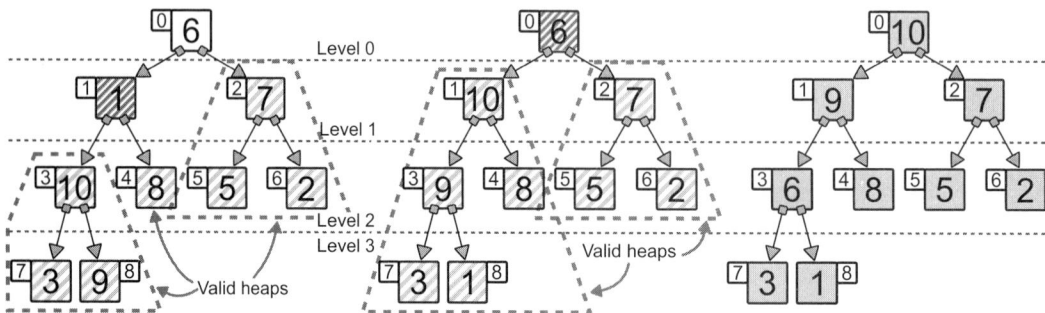

It's easier to code it than to explain or understand it. The body of _heapify is just a few lines: it copies the collection in input to a new array, then computes the index of the last internal node of the heap (using a helper function that returns the index of the first leaf) and finally iterates over the internal nodes, pushing each of them down. It's important to go through the internal nodes from the last (the deepest in the tree) to the first (the root) because this is the only way to guarantee that the children of each node we push down are valid heaps:

```
def _heapify(self, elements):
    self._elements = elements[:]
    last_inner_node_index = self._first_leaf_index() - 1
    for index in range(last_inner_node_index, -1, -1):
        self._push_down(index)
def _first_leaf_index(self):
    return len(self) // 2
```

How long does it take to heapify an array? It takes O(n) comparison and assignments. For a mathematical proof, you can take a look at section 2.6.7 of *Advanced Algorithms and Data Structures* (Manning, 2021) available at https://mng.bz/KZX0.

I'll give you some idea here. For $n/2$ nodes, the heap leaves, we don't do anything. For $n/4$ nodes, the parents of the leaves, _push_down will do at most one swap. The pattern continues, with at most two swaps for $n/8$ nodes (the parents of the $n/4$ ones in the previous step, and so on, for $\log(n)$ of such terms). The sum of these numbers of operations is O(n).

Priority queues in action

Now that we understand how a heap works, let's see it in action! In this section, we'll discuss a nontrivial example of how we can use a heap. And we'll meet some old friends!

Find the k largest entries

After breaking the ice with programming and arrays, Mario is on a roll. In chapter 2, we saw him using an array to store the statistics of a die to find out if the die was fair. Now he wants to reuse those skills to win the lottery.

His idea is simple (and statistically unsound, but Mario is in seventh grade, so he can't know that yet). He wants to keep track of which numbers are drawn most frequently in the national lottery and play the lottery with the six most frequent numbers. His assumption that these are the most likely numbers to be drawn is, as we know, wrong, but his parents encourage him to go ahead with his project to develop some analytical and programming skills.

So, they find Mario the records of the weekly lottery drawing for the last 30 years and set him up with a computer and a Python interpreter. They also help him code the I/O part so that he can assume that the numbers drawn can be inserted one at a time. Mario's application doesn't remember when a number was last drawn. It just counts how many times it appears among the winning six.

He reuses the program he wrote for the dice to store the number of occurrences of each of the 90 numbers that can be drafted in the lottery. Eventually, after hours of typing and entering all 30 years of data, he gets an array with 90 entries, where `drawn[i]` is the number of times the number `i` has been drawn in the last 30 years. (For the sake of simplicity, the array is allocated for 91 elements, and he just ignores the first entry.)

To find out what the most frequently drawn numbers are, Mario plans to sort the array and take the first six entries. But when he talks to his friend Kim about his plan, she challenges him: "I can write a more efficient solution." Kim is really good at coding, and in their class, they just studied priority queues. So, Mario accepts the challenge and takes a swing at a better solution: "How about using `heapify` to create a heap with 90 elements and then extract the six largest ones?"

Kim grins: "That's better, but I can still improve it!"

"See," she adds, "if we had to pick the k largest out of n elements, sorting all of them would take `O(n*log(n) + k)` steps. Your solution would take `O(n + k*log(n))` steps and `O(n)` extra space. But I can do it in `O(n*log(k) + k)` steps and with only `O(k)` additional space."

When Mario gasps in surprise, Kim cheers and explains to him how the better solution works. She will create a heap, inserting elements as tuples `(number, frequency)`. But she won't use a regular heap—this heap will only store k elements, in this case the six largest elements found so far.

Here is the crucial bit: the heap must be a min-heap. Or rather, in terms of priority, the priority of an element must be the opposite of its frequency, so that the root of the heap will hold the one element with the lower frequency.

She will then look at the lottery numbers one by one and compare them to the root of the heap. If the root of the heap is smaller, she will extract it and then insert the new entry. Eventually, only the six more frequently drawn entries will be in the queue.

Here is some code that does the job:

```
def k_largest_elements(arr, k):
    heap = Heap(element_priority=lambda x: -x[1])
    for i in range(len(arr)):
        if len(heap) >= k:
            if heap.peek()[1] < arr[i]:
                heap.top()
                heap.insert((i, arr[i]))
        else:
            heap.insert((i, arr[i]))
    return [heap.top() for _ in range(k)]

print(k_largest_elements(drawn, 6))
```

When we remove the smallest element, we don't need the value. We just discard it.

Now Mario has only one question tormenting him: Should he share the money with Kim if they win?

Recap

- Priority queues generalize regular queues, allowing us to use criteria other than the insertion order to determine which element should be extracted next.

- A *priority queue* is an abstract data type that provides two operations: `insert`, to add a new element, and `top`, to remove and return the element with the highest priority.

- Priority queues can be implemented using different data structures, but the maximally efficient implementation is achieved using heaps.

- A *binary heap* is a special type of tree. It's a binary, almost complete tree, where each node has a priority higher than or equal to its children's. The root of the heap is the element with the highest priority in the heap.

- Heaps have another characteristic. They are a tree that is better implemented as an array. This is possible because a heap is an almost complete tree.

- With the array implementation of a heap, we can build a priority queue where `insert` and `top` take logarithmic time.

- Additionally, it's possible to transform an array of n elements into a heap in linear time, using the `heapify` method.

In this chapter

- modeling hierarchical relationships with trees

- binary, ternary, and n-ary trees

- introducing data constraints into binary trees: binary
  search trees

- evaluating the performance of binary search trees

- discovering how balanced trees provide better
  guarantees

This chapter marks a shift from the previous few chapters, where we focused on containers. Here, we discuss trees, which is a data structure—or rather a class of data structures! Trees can be used to implement several abstract data types, so unlike the other chapters, we won't have an ADT section here. We'll go straight to the point, describing trees, and then focus on one particular kind of tree—the binary search tree (BST). We'll describe what trees do well and how we can make them work even better.

What makes a tree?

In chapter 6, we discussed linked lists, our first composite data structure. The elements of a linked list, its nodes, are themselves a minimal data structure. Linked lists are based on the idea that each node has a single successor and a single predecessor—except for the head of the list, which has no predecessor, and the tail of the list, which has no successor.

However, things are not always so simple, and the relationships are more intricate. Sometimes, instead of a linear sequence, we need to represent some kind of hierarchy, with a single, clear starting point, but then with different paths branching out from each node.

Definition of a tree

A generic tree is a composite data structure that consists of nodes connected by links. Each node contains a value and a variable number of links to other nodes, from zero to some number k (the branching number of a k-ary tree, that is, the maximum number of links a node can have).

There is a special node in each tree, called the root of the tree. Its peculiarity is that no other node in the tree points to the root.

If a node P has a link to another node C, then P is called the parent of C, and C is a child of P. In the figure, the root of the tree has two children, with values 2 and 8. Some trees also have explicit links from children to parents, to make traversing of the tree easier.

When a node has no links to children, it's called a leaf. The other nodes, which do have children, are called internal nodes. In the figures in this section, there are six leaves with values 5, 1, 2, 3, 4, and 7.

For a tree to be well-formed, every node must have exactly one parent, except for the root, which has none. This means that if C is a child of P, the only path from the root to C goes through P. It also means that all paths from the root to a leaf are simple, that is, there is no loop in a tree. In other words, in any path from the root to a leaf, you will never see the same node twice. Let's get a few more definitions before moving on.

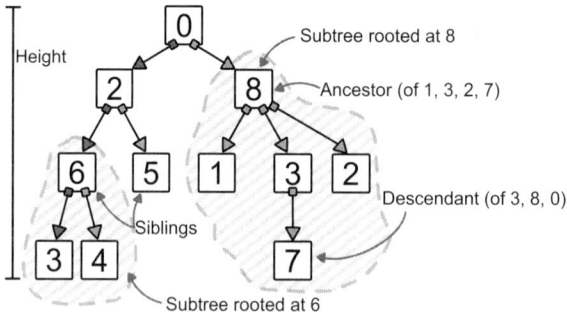

A node N is an ancestor of a node M if N is in the path between the root and M. In that case, M is called a descendant of N. In other words, a descendant of a node N is either one of the children of N or the descendant of one of the children of N. Of course, the root is the one ancestor that all the other nodes have in common. In the figure, we can also see that node 8 is an ancestor of node 7.

All children of the same node are siblings. There is no direct link between siblings, so the only way to get from one sibling to another is through their common parent.

A subtree is a portion of the tree containing a node R (called the root of the subtree) and all the descendants of R. Each child of a node is the root of its own subtree.

The height of a tree is the length of the longest path from the root to a leaf. The height of the tree in the figure is 3 because there are multiple paths with three links, such as 0→2→6→3. The subtree rooted at the node with value 8 has a height of 2.

From linked lists to trees

Linked lists model perfectly linear relationships, where we have defined a total order on the elements in the list: the first element goes before the second, which goes right before the third, and so on. However, a tree can easily represent a partial relation, where there are elements that are comparable and ordered and others that are not comparable or have no relationship between them.

To visualize this difference, how about considering two different approaches to break-fast? I'm talking, of course, about the European continental breakfast, which is usually more sweet than savory.

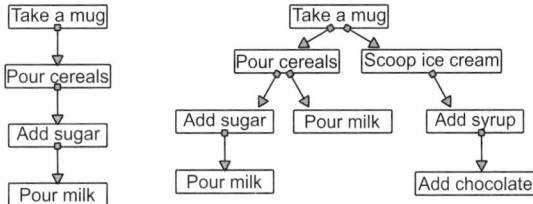

Anyway, food aside, let's consider two approaches. The first approach is the methodical approach. Let's take as an example someone who always eats their cereal in the morning and repeats the same gestures in the same order. This linear approach can be modeled using a linked list.

Our second option is what I would call the inspirational approach. Most mornings, I'll stick to my diet and eat cereal without adding sugar. Some other mornings, I feel a little down, and I add sugar to my cereal to sweeten up my day. And sometimes, when I'm feeling mopey, I skip the cereal altogether and go straight for the ice cream bucket! This approach, involving choices and multiple options, could not be represented by a linked list—we need a tree for that.

Table 11.1 summarizes additional differences and similarities between linked lists and trees.

Table 11.1   A comparison between linked lists and trees

Linked list	Tree
A single node has no predecessor (the head).	A single node has no parent (the root).
A single node has no successor (the tail).	Many nodes don't have children (the leaves).
Each node has exactly one outgoing link to its successor.	Each node has zero, one, or many links to its children.
Doubly linked lists: each node has exactly one link to its predecessor.	In some trees, nodes have links to their parents. If they do, each node has exactly one link to its only parent.

Binary trees

Binary trees are defined by restricting each node to a maximum of two children. Thus, in a binary tree, a node may have zero, one, or two child links. We usually label these two links: we have the left and right children of a node, and thus its left and right subtrees. The order of the children, however, isn't always important for all binary trees.

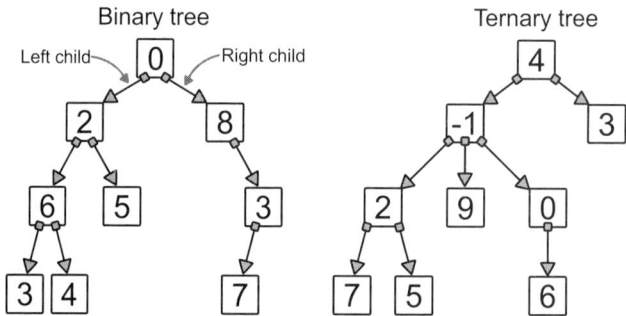

Some applications of trees

The number of areas where trees are used is impressive. Whenever we need to represent hierarchical relationships, trees are the answer. Trees are used in machine learning, and decision trees and random forests are some of the best nonneural network classification tools. We have discussed the heap in chapter 10, which is a special tree that efficiently implements priority queues. There are many more specialized trees, such as b-trees, which are used to store data efficiently (like in databases), or kd-trees, which allow the indexing of multidimensional data. But these are just the tip of the iceberg: trees are a very large class of extremely versatile data structures.

Binary search trees

Besides modeling relationships, we can also use trees as containers. We did so with heaps, whose scope is narrow. But we can have a more general-purpose container, which we discuss in the rest of this chapter—the *binary search tree* (BST). Its name gives away some of its properties: it's a tree, it's binary, so each node has (optionally) a left and a right child, and it's used for searching.

These trees are designed to make search fast, potentially as fast as binary search on a sorted array. And they have one important advantage over sorted arrays: insertion and deletion can be faster on a BST. What's the catch, and what's the tradeoff? Like linked lists, trees require more memory to implement, and their code is more complex, especially if we want to guarantee that these operations are faster than on arrays.

In this section, we will describe the BSTs as data structures and discuss their implementation.

Order matters

Similarly to heaps, where we have constraints on the structure and data of the tree, to go from a binary tree to a BST, we have to add a property on the data stored in the nodes.

> **DEFINITION** All BSTs abide by the *BST property*: for any node N that stores
> a value v, all nodes in the left subtree of N will have values less than or equal
> to v, and all nodes in the right subtree of N will have values greater than v.

Bear in mind that there is an asymmetry between the two subtrees: if there are duplicates, we need a way to break the tie so that we always know where to find possible duplicates of a node's value. The choice of the left subtree is completely arbitrary, based only on convention.

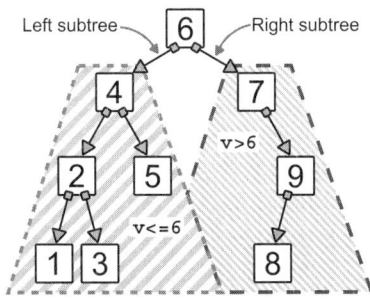

Class definition and constructor

This is a good time to discuss the implementation of the class for BSTs. Since we are dealing with a composite data structure, we need to implement an outer class for the public interface, shared with the clients, and an inner, private class for the node representation. I implemented a lean version of the Node class, and most of the action will happen in the outer class. Just know that the other way around is also possible:

```
class Node:
    def __init__(self, value, left=None, right=None):
        self._value = value
        self._left = left
        self._right = right
    def set_left(self, node):
        self._left = node
    def set_right(self, node):
        self._right = node
```

Here I have left out the getter methods, which just return references to the private fields of a Node (you can find them in the full code in the book's repo). While the left and right children of a node can be later changed using the setter methods shown here, I won't allow a node's value to be changed. If you want to change the value of a node in the tree, you'll have to create a new Node instance and set its children.

The constructor for the outer class is even simpler. We just need to initialize the root to the empty node:

```
class BinarySearchTree:
    def __init__(self):
        self._root = None
```

Search

If we look more closely at the data property on a BST, we can learn some interesting things. Given a node in the tree, we can associate a range of possible values to its subtrees and to the edges of its left and right children.

Each node N containing a value v partitions the possible values in its subtree so that if we traverse the tree using the left link, we can only find values x≤v, while if we go right, we can only find values x>v.

But we actually know more than that, because the constraints of the ancestors of a node are also valid for its children. In the example shown in the figure, if we traverse the left branch from the root, we know that we can only find

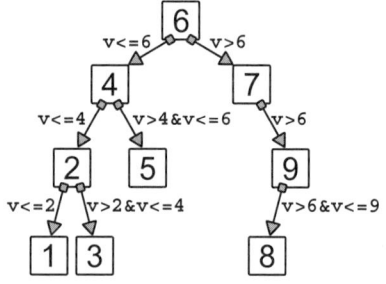

values x≤6. Then, we find a node with value 4. Its right subtree can only have values >4, but because of its parent, in the whole subtree rooted at 4, there can't be any value >6, so for any x in the right subtree of the node 4, we know that 4<x≤6.

That's a lot of information: How can we use it?

The answer is, in searching. If we search our example tree for a certain value, say 100, the moment we look at the root, we realize that our target can only be in the right subtree of the root. This means that we don't need to look at the left subtree at all! Similarly, if the value is less than (or equal to) the root's, we don't need to look at the right subtree.

What happens with the next node, the one that, in our example, stores the value 7? The same principle applies—we either go left or right (in this case, if we are still looking for 100, we go right). At each node, we can only go left or right. We never climb up the tree, toward the root. At some point, if we haven't found our target yet, we will try to follow a null link. Either we are at a leaf or we have reached an intermediate node with a single child (a left child when we want to go right, or vice versa). There we know that our search is unsuccessful because our target couldn't be in any other path in the tree. And why is that? Because at every turn, at every node, the two (possible) subtrees are mutually exclusive, and so we followed the only path where the target value could have been stored.

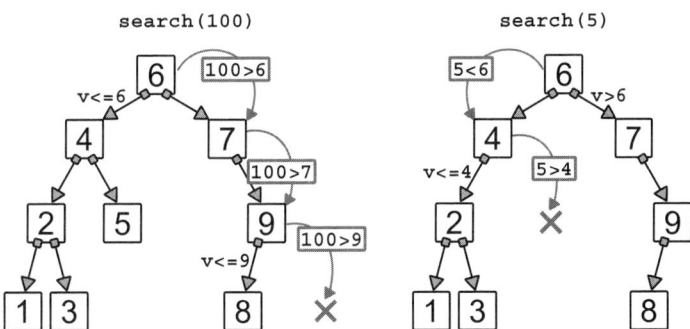

The fact that the search method follows a single path, from the root to (possibly) a leaf, means that it will take no more steps than the height of the tree—it needs O(h) comparisons, where h is the height of the tree.

Now let's look at the implementation. The search method takes a value and returns the node of the tree that contains that value, or None if no such value is stored in the tree. Similar to what we did with linked lists, this method is provided as a private method because we don't want to expose the internal structure of the tree to clients. We can easily provide a public contains method that checks whether a search returned None.

Now, I'm going to show you a variant of the search method that returns a tuple—together with the node found, we return its parent. The reason is that if we don't store a reference to the parent of the node, we are in a situation similar to that of a singly linked list, where we have to remember the predecessor of a node while scanning the list, otherwise, we won't be able to retrieve the predecessor later:

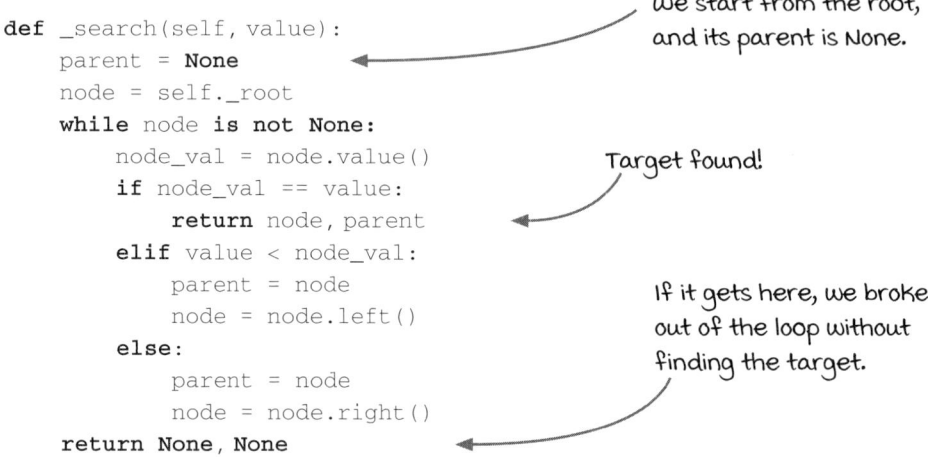

```
def _search(self, value):
    parent = None
    node = self._root
    while node is not None:
        node_val = node.value()
        if node_val == value:
            return node, parent
        elif value < node_val:
            parent = node
            node = node.left()
        else:
            parent = node
            node = node.right()
    return None, None
```

We start from the root, and its parent is None.

Target found!

If it gets here, we broke out of the loop without finding the target.

Find the minimum and maximum

Before moving on to the methods that modify a BST, I'd like to discuss a special kind of search: finding the maximum and minimum elements in a tree. This is a simpler task than a generic search. In fact, we know exactly where these two elements will be in the tree.

For example, to get the maximum element, we start at the root and follow the links to the right children until we reach a node that has no right child. This node (which could be the root itself, of course) stores the maximum value in the tree. Why is that? Because if we ever turn left at some point, even after we reach a node with no right child, then the values we could find in the left subtree could be at most the same as the value stored in the current node.

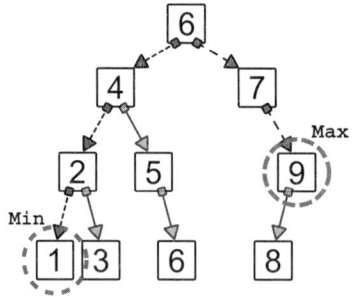

It works similarly for the minimum, except we always go left instead of right. Now, let's take a look at the implementation for the method to find the maximum—we will use it again soon.

A key BST feature is its recursive structure—each subtree is also a valid BST. This also means that we can find the maximum and minimum of any subtree of the main tree. So, let's implement in the `Node` class the method that finds the maximum of the subtree rooted at the given node:

```python
def find_max_in_subtree(self):
    parent = None
    node = self
    while node.right() is not None:
        parent = node
        node = node.right()
    return node, parent
```

Note that, as with `_search`, we also need to return the parent of the node that was found.

Insert

Now that we know how to search a BST and how to create an empty BST, we need to learn how to populate it! The insertion method is very similar to the way we do search. That's no coincidence. When we insert a new element, we are actually searching for the position that this new element would have in the tree if it was already inserted.

Of course, there are some differences with the search method. We can't stop when we find the same value that we want to insert (unless we don't allow duplicates, but that's an edge case). Instead, if we find another occurrence of the value we want to insert, we keep traversing the tree by making a left turn.

In general, when we get to a node, we first check the value it stores to understand which branch we need to traverse and whether we need to go left or right. Suppose we figure out that we need to go left. If the node has no left child, we have found the place where we have to add the new element. All we have to do is create a new node and attach it as a left child of the current node. The case where we need to go right is treated symmetrically.

Let's look at a few examples to clarify how insertion works.

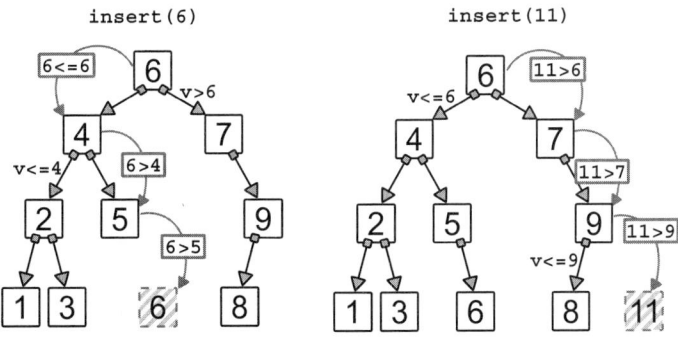

In the first example, we add a duplicate of the value at the root of the tree, 6. At the root, we go left, as we always do when we find the same value as the one stored in a node. We traverse this branch until we reach the leaf with the value 5, and we know we can add our new node there.

I've always found it curious how two occurrences of the same value can end up so far apart in a BST. In a sorted array, they would be adjacent, but not in a BST. Keep this in mind as we will talk about it again.

In the other case presented, we add the largest value yet in the tree, so we traverse a path to the far right of the tree, and there we add a new node for the value 11.

The code for the insert method isn't much different from the search method:

```python
def insert(self, value):
    node = self._root
    if node is None:
        self._root = BinarySearchTree.Node(value)      # The tree is empty.
    else:
        while node is not None:
            if value <= node.value():
                if node.left() is None:                # We have found the right place for the new value.
                    node.set_left(BinarySearchTree.Node(value))
                    break
                else:                                  # We need to keep traversing the left branch of this subtree.
                    node = node.left()
            elif node.right() is None:                 # Here as well, we have found the right place for the new value.
                node.set_right(BinarySearchTree.Node(value))
                break
            else:                                      # We need to keep traversing the right branch of this subtree.
                node = node.right()
```

Since insertion in a BST is equivalent to an unsuccessful search, its running time is also O(h), where h is the height of the tree.

Delete

While adding an element is relatively straightforward, deleting one is much more complicated. But again, this method relies heavily on search since what we need to do is find the value we want to delete and get a reference to the node that contains it. This is preferable to directly passing the node to be deleted to the delete method. Among other things, we also need a reference to the parent of this node to be deleted.

When we delete a node, we have to distinguish between the following three situations:

- We are deleting a leaf.
- We are deleting a node with only one child.
- The node we want to delete has both children.

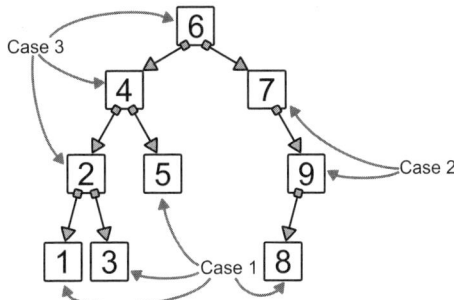

For each of these cases, we have a slightly different workflow when the node to be deleted is the root. In all these situations, we assume that we have already performed a search and found the node N to be deleted and its parent P.

Deleting a leaf

This is the simplest case—a leaf by definition has no children, so there are no loose ends to tie up. The only thing we need to do is sever the link between the parent node and the one we want to remove from the tree. This is why we need to return the parent node in a successful search.

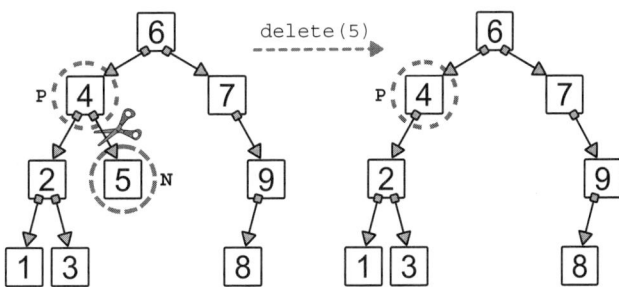

What happens if the node to be deleted is the root and has no parent? If the root is a leaf, then removing it will leave us with an empty tree.

Deleting a node with only one child

If the node we want to delete has exactly one child, the process is still simpler compared to nodes with two children. We can directly link the child to the parent of the deleted node.

Here, we have four cases. The node N can have a left or right child, and N itself can be the left or right child of P. The four cases can be treated in the same way, and the only thing that changes is which pointers are used.

To clarify, let's consider the case where the child C of node N is a right child. In our example, we want to delete the value 7 from the tree.

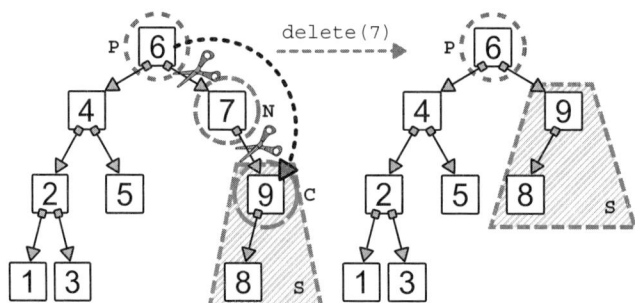

What we need to do is cut the links between P and N and N and C, and create a new direct link between P and C. In this example, since N was also a right child of P, C is set as the new right child of P. This way S, the former right subtree of N, is moved up and is now the right subtree of P.

What if N was the root of the tree? Well, in that case, all we would have to do is update the root, and we would be done.

Deleting a node with both of its children

This is the most complicated case. Suppose we want to delete node 4 in the BST we used as an example throughout this section. (We'll actually use a slightly different tree for clarity.)

Once we find it, we realize that the node N we want to delete has both children. So, we can't just short-circuit the link from its parent P to one of its children because we wouldn't know how to fix the other subtree of N. We can't even bubble up values like we did in the heap!

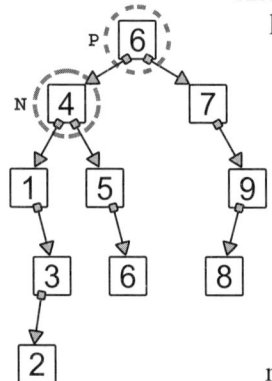

Instead, to replace the node we delete, we would need a value that is smaller than any element in the right subtree of N and not smaller than any other value in the left subtree of N. This value v is the predecessor of N in the subtree rooted at N. It's the one value that, if we sorted all the values in the subtree rooted at N, would be just before `value(N)`.

In our example, this value is 3, which happens to be the maximum of the left subtree of node 4! Well, that's not a coincidence. The value v we are looking for is *always* the maximum of the left subtree of N. And even better for us, the node M that contains this maximum can't have a right subtree.

In fact, if M had a right subtree, it would mean that there was a node in the left subtree of N that has a value greater than v, which is a contradiction. So, this means that if we were to delete M, we would be in either case 1 or case 2 of the delete method. In other words, it's easy to delete node M, and that's great for us!

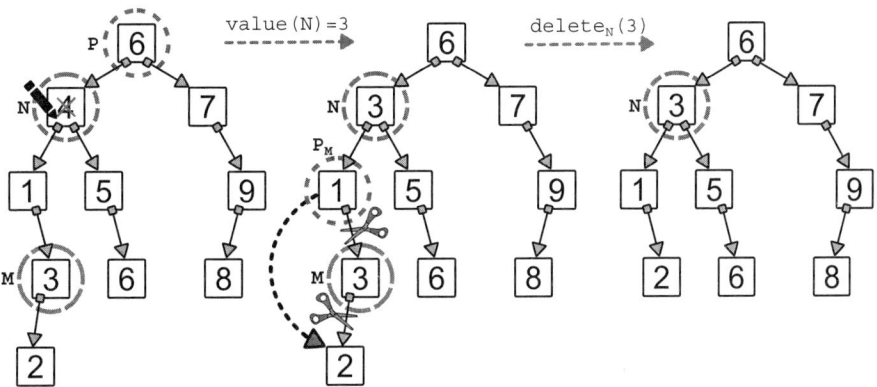

So, here is the plan to delete node 4: we replace the value of the node with its predecessor in the subtree rooted at 4, which is node 3. Then we delete node 3 in the left subtree of 4, knowing that this node, being the maximum of left(4), will be easy to delete. And then, we are done.

Putting it all together

Now that we have discussed how to solve all the possible cases for deleting a node, let's put it all together and write a method for the BST class. This is going to be the most complicated method we have written so far.

The main differences with what we have discussed in the previous subsections are implementation details, like the fact that we won't just replace the value in the node to be deleted, but rather replace the whole node.

```
def delete(self, value):
    if self._root is None:
        raise ValueError('Delete on an empty tree')
    node, parent = self._search(value)
    if node is None:
        raise ValueError('Value not found')
    if node.left() is None or node.right() is None:
        maybe_child = node.right() if node.left() is None
            ↪else node.left()
```

This branch covers cases 1 and 2.

This instruction allows us to later use the same code for both variants of case 2, and also for case 1 when both children are None.

```
        if parent is None:
            self._root = maybe_child
        elif value <= parent.value():
            parent.set_left(maybe_child)
        else:
            parent.set_right(maybe_child)
    else:
        max_node, max_node_parent = node.left().find_max_in_subtree()
        if max_node_parent is None:
            new_node = BinarySearchTree.Node(max_node.value(), None,
node.right())
        else:
            new_node = BinarySearchTree.Node(
                max_node.value(),
                node.left(),
                node.right())
            max_node_parent.set_right(max_node.left())
        if parent is None:
            self._root = new_node
        elif value <= parent.value():
            parent.set_left(new_node)
        else:
            parent.set_right(new_node)
```

If parent is None, then node is the root. Otherwise, check whether node is a left or right child.

Find the max in the left subtree of the node to be deleted.

In this case, it means the max of the left subtree is exactly the left child of node.

In none of the three cases we ever climb up the tree, but we always follow a path from the root to a leaf. Therefore, `delete` also takes at most `O(h)` steps.

Traversing a BST

Traversal is one of the fundamental operations of data structures. For some of the data structures we have discussed so far, the way to traverse them was obvious. For arrays and linked lists, you start at the beginning and proceed linearly. For other data structures, traversal was disabled. The elements in stacks, queues, and priority queues can only be iterated by being removed from the container.

For BSTs, we are stepping on to uncharted territory in our journey. This data structure is inherently nonlinear, so how do we traverse it?

For a generic binary tree, there are three ways to traverse it:

- Pre-order, where we visit each node before its subtrees.

- Post-order, where we visit the subtrees of a node before visiting it.

- In-order, where, given a node N, we first visit its left subtree, then N, then its right subtree.

For a BST, the option that makes more sense is in-order.

To understand why, let's consider a mini-BST, with a root and two children, and check in what order the nodes would be visited: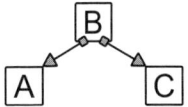

- Pre-order: B A C

- Post-order: A C B

- In-order: A B C

In-order is the only way to get the sorted sequence of elements in a BST. You can find the code for the in-order traversal on the book's GitHub repo: https://mng.bz/9de1.

Predecessor and Successor

Exceptionally, for BSTs, we describe two additional operations: finding the predecessor and successor of a node. Formally, given a collection C without duplicates, the successor of an element x is the element s, which is the minimum among the elements in C that are greater than x. Similarly, the predecessor of x is the maximum among the elements that are less than x.

These operations are trivial in a sorted array and in a sorted doubly linked list—the predecessor and successor of an element x are (if present) adjacent to x, literally the element before and after x in the data structure.

In the unsorted versions of these DSs, the operations are still not complicated, but they become expensive—we have to scan the whole container to find a successor.

What about BSTs? We know that elements in a BST follow a certain order, but getting predecessor and successor is not a constant-time operation.

When discussing the `delete` method, we discovered that, given a node N, the predecessor of N limited to the subtree rooted at N is the maximum of N's left subtree (if it exists). However, when it comes to finding the predecessor of a node N in the whole tree, it's not so simple:

- If N has a left subtree, then yes, its predecessor is the maximum of that subtree.

- If N does *not* have a left subtree and it's a right child, then its parent is also its predecessor.

- If N does *not* have a left subtree and it's a left child, we have to climb up the tree until we find node M that is a right child—its parent is the predecessor of N.

- If we reach the root before finding such a node, then it means that N is the minimum of the tree, and it has no predecessor.

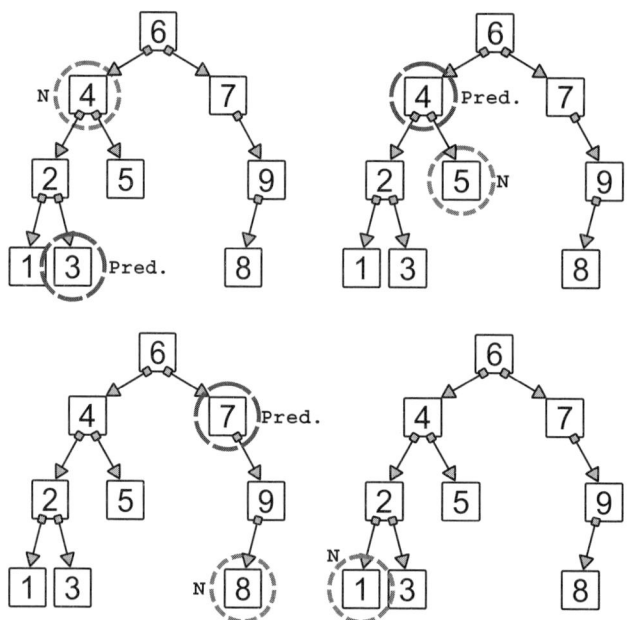

To implement this method in a BST that doesn't store links to the nodes' parents we would have to use a technique called *backtracking*, which is beyond the scope of this book. You can read more about these methods in *Introduction to Algorithms* (Cormen, Leiserson, Rivest, Stein, 2022, MIT Press), chapter 12, page 258.

The two important things I want you to remember are that these two operations are harder than you might think and that they take O(h) time in a BST.

EXERCISES

11.1 Implement a BST class where nodes contain a link to their parent, and then add the predecessor and successor methods.

11.2 Can you find an example among the BSTs shown in the previous sections where the predecessor method described above would fail? Hint: Refer to the next exercise.

11.3 When a BST contains duplicates, then getting the predecessor of a node is a bit more complicated, while the successor method can work as it is. Can you explain why?

11.4 How can we fix the predecessor method to deal with duplicates?

Balanced trees

All the operations we have seen on BSTs take time proportional to the height of the tree. Is that a good thing? This question translates to, given a BST with n nodes and height h, is O(h) better than O(n)? It certainly can't be worse, but the question is, could it be O(h) = O(n)?

Binary search trees in action

Mario, our little friend who's learning computer science, got burned when he challenged his mother. If you remember, in chapter 3, he bet—and lost—that he was faster at finding baseball cards from a deck. Mario knows he can't trick his mother that easily, but he wants to use what he learned to pull a fast one on someone else. So, he decides to try his mother's trick against his classmate Kim. But Mario wants more than just to win. He wants to impress Kim, so he plans to use BSTs (which he just learned about from his parents' computer science textbooks) instead of a sorted array.

The challenge is the same. They are each given half of Mario's deck of cards, and each of them prepares a list of cards to find in the shortest time possible.

The only problem for Mario is that Kim knows BSTs better, and when she hears that he wants to go that way, she quickly arranges her half of the cards deck so that the cards are almost sorted (descending, in reverse order).

When Mario starts to build his BST on the floor of his room, he realizes that she played him. The tree won't fit in his room, and Mario has to continue building a long, long branch out in the hallway.

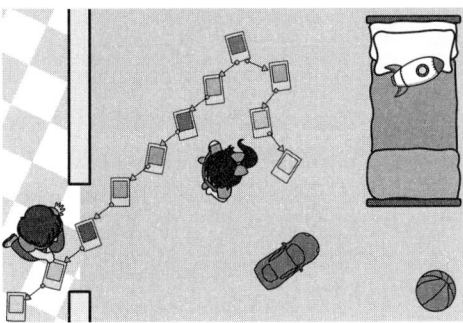

By the time he gets back to his room, Kim has already found her five cards, leaving Mario mopey and defeated. Finally, he asks her, "I know you tricked me, but what happened here?"

Adversary insertion sequences

What Kim did was select a carefully crafted sequence that is known to cause trouble to BSTs. If we insert the elements of a BST from the smallest to the largest (or vice versa), we get completely skewed trees that look like linked lists.

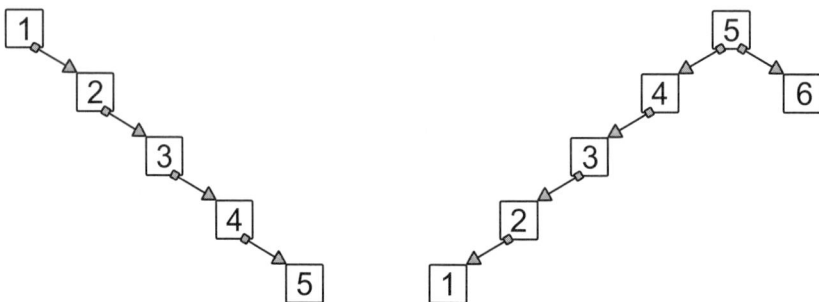

In these extreme cases, the height of the tree is exactly n. If you think about it, it's ironic how we get the worst performance from sequences that were already sorted!

To prove that for generic BSTs, $O(h) = O(n)$ in the worst case, that single example of a worst-case scenario would be enough. Unfortunately, it's not the only one. We don't have to be so unlucky as to have all the elements inserted in their final order to get a skewed tree. If we can find in the insertion sequence a (nonadjacent) subsequence of half, or say a quarter, or a fifth (and so on) of the sorted elements, then the height of the tree will be at least $n/2$, $n/4$, or $n/5$. And we know that $O(n/5) = O(n)$.

Deletions make your tree skewed

There are two other sources of imbalance for the BSTs. First, when we have duplicates, as you know, we break ties by always going left. This means that the left branches will be slightly larger on average than the right branches.

Second, and worse, when we delete values from a BST, we always take the maximum of the left branch of the node to be deleted. It means we make the left branch increasingly smaller, and after many deletions, the tree will be fairly skewed, with the right branches sensibly larger than the left branches.

Tree balancing

From what we have discussed so far, things don't look good for BSTs. If we choose the wrong insertion order, we get a skewed tree. And if we perform a lot of deletions on the tree, we also get a skewed tree. So, are we doomed?

There are some tricks we can use that might help. If we have some control over the insertion sequence, we can shuffle the order of the input sequence to reduce the proba-bility of having an even partially sorted sequence. And one way to deal with the imbalance caused by `delete` is to randomly alternate between the predecessor and successor of the value to be deleted to replace it.

But often, we don't have control over the insertion sequence, which could be dynamic and "just in time." And anyway, none of these tricks can give us a guaranteed upper bound on the height of the tree.

However, in chapter 10, we discussed the heap, whose height is guaranteed to be `O(log(n))` for n elements: Can we get something similar for BST? Of course, the structure of the heap is different—for a heap, we don't store a total ordering of the nodes, and this makes it easier to keep its height logarithmic.

But there are also ways to force a BST to be *balanced*. A binary tree is said to be *height-balanced* if, for any node, the difference in height between its left and right subtrees is at most 1, and both of its subtrees are also balanced.

There are data structures, evolutions of the BST, which can guarantee this condition. One of these structures uses the properties of the heap to achieve balance: randomized heaps are a nondeterministically balanced binary search tree. You can read more about them in chapter 3 of *Advanced Algorithms and Data Structures* (La Rocca, 2021, Manning).

The most used balanced search trees are, however, red–black trees and 2–3 trees. You can read more about them in the same chapter of *Advanced Algorithms and Data Structures*, or in chapter 13 of *Introduction to Algorithms* (Cormen, Leiserson, Rivest, Stein, 2022, MIT Press), and in section 3.3 of *Algorithms 4th Edition* (Sedgewick, Wayne, 2020, Pearson), respectively.

With a *balanced binary search tree* (BBST), operations such as search, insertion, and deletion can be performed on the tree in `O(log(n))` time. This makes BBSTs the data structure with the best average performance across the full range of operations: there are some operations where a sorted array or a linked list might be faster, but the average over all operations favors BBSTs.

And that also answers the question, What do I need BSTs for? You can use them to do the same things as a sorted array, but overall faster.

Recap

- Trees are recursive data structures consisting of nodes. Each node stores a value and a certain number of links to children. Each child is the root of a valid subtree.

- Trees are perfect for modeling hierarchical relationships and any situation with paths branching out of intersections.

- In binary trees, each node can have zero, one, or two children. Nodes without children are called leaves. The other nodes, called internal nodes, have one or two children.

- Links to children in a binary tree are usually labeled "left" and "right." In some, but not all, binary trees, this distinction may have a meaning.

- In a *binary search tree* (BST), for any node N, the left subtree of N can only contain values not greater than N's, and the right subtree can only contain values greater than N's.

- BSTs are good for search—if the tree is balanced, search can be completed by comparing at most $O(\log(n))$ elements.

- In general, for a BST with n nodes and height h, all operations (insertion, deletion, search, predecessor and successor, maximum and minimum) take $O(h)$ time.

- For *balanced binary search trees* (BBST), the height h of the tree is guaranteed to be $O(\log(n))$, and so all the above operations take logarithmic time.

Dictionaries and hash tables: How to build and use associative arrays | 12

In this chapter

- discovering how the dictionary ADT improves indexing

- implementing a dictionary with the data structures we already know

- introducing a new data structure that is a game changer for dictionaries—the hash table

- how hashing works

- comparing chaining and open addressing, two strategies for resolving conflicts

So far, we have discussed data structures that allow us to retrieve stored data based on the position of elements. For arrays and linked lists, we can retrieve elements based on their position in the data structure. For stacks and queues, the next element that can be retrieved is at a specific position.

Now we introduce key-based data structures, sometimes called *associative arrays*. This chapter also introduces the dictionary, the epitome of key-based abstract data types, followed by a discussion of efficient implementation strategies for retrieving elements by key.

The dictionary problem

Our little friend Mario is getting really serious about collecting baseball cards. Do you know what his favorite part is? Trading cards with his friends!

Mario has a good memory, but now that he has hundreds of cards, it's hard for him to remember all the cards he already owns and the ones he's missing. This is especially so because when he trades cards with his friends, he only has a few moments to claim a card before someone else takes it. To stay ahead of the competition, Mario could use a mobile app that scans cards with the camera and checks in a split second whether that card is already in his collection and how many copies he has.

This, the core of the app (besides the UX and the object recognition), is what a dictionary does. It stores data by some key (in the case of baseball cards, we could use the player's name or even the photo of the card) and lets you search data by key. In our example, keys can be associated with attributes such as the number of copies of a card you own or specific details about the card (team info, stats, and so on).

Removing duplicates

Another common use case for dictionaries is to remove duplicates from a collection.

Suppose that we want to remove duplicates from an array. With what we have learned so far, we would normally sort the array and then find duplicates next to each other as we scan the sorted array. The main cost of this method comes from sorting, which has a running time of $O(n*log(N))$.

Let's imagine we have this magical black box, a dictionary D, that can tell us if we have seen a certain object before. Then we can use it to filter out duplicates from a collection C.

The idea is that we can start with an empty dictionary and then go through the list of elements and add each item c simultaneously to D and a support collection tmp, unless we find out that c is already in the dictionary. If it is, we know we have a duplicate:

```
tmp = []
for c in C:
    if not c in D:
        D.add(c)
        tmp.append(c)
C = tmp
```

In Python, we can use a `set` for this purpose, which is a special kind of dictionary that stores only elements without associating a value to them. A similar example would be counting the number of occurrences of each element in a collection:

```
counters = {}
for c in C:
    counters[c] = counters.get(c, 0) + 1
```

This is a shorter syntax that's allowed by Python, but it's equivalent to checking whether the dictionary contains a key `c`, and then retrieving and incrementing its associated value or initializing the value associated with a new key to `1`.

Here is the question I expect you to ask: Is using a dictionary better than sorting when removing duplicates? Well, it mainly depends on how expensive it is to check a dictionary for an element and to add new entries to it. If either operation costs more than `O(log(n))`, then the dictionary version is more expensive. If both are less than logarithmic, then it's a great deal. The performance of a dictionary depends on its implementation, and we'll talk about that later in this chapter.

For now, let's focus on the abstract data type—what we can do with a dictionary and not how we do it.

The ADT for dictionaries

When we describe the interface of a dictionary, we need to include the following three methods:

- To insert a new value

- To retrieve the value associated with a key, if any

- To delete a value, or the value associated with a key

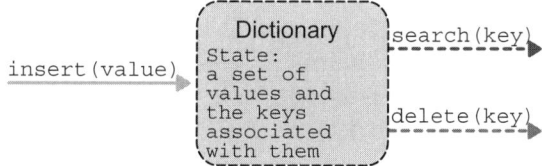

In the most common definition of the dictionary interface, we store values to which we can associate keys. For some types of values, such as integers, the associated key is the value itself. Keys can be computed from values by applying a free function to them. In Python, the built-in `hash` function is the perfect candidate for the job. Or, if we are dealing with objects, an object would have its own method to return a key.

With these assumptions, the `insert` method takes the full value to add to the dictionary, while `search` takes only the key (which is supposed to be smaller than the value) and retrieves the associated value. The `delete` method, however, can take either the key, the full value, or a reference to the full value to be deleted.

A variant of this API is also possible, where we explicitly associate keys and values by passing two distinct values and storing them separately. For example, Python's dictionary works this way.

Dictionaries can also provide more methods. For example, methods to retrieve the minimum and maximum keys stored or, given a key, to retrieve its predecessor and successor. These methods, however, are not part of the core interface for dictionaries, so you won't always find them. The reason is that they are usually only provided with some implementations of the dictionary ADT for which they are easy to implement and fast to run.

Data structures implementing a dictionary

Which of the data structures we have already discussed can be used to implement a dictionary? Take a moment to think about this, and then let's review the answer together.

So, we need to be able to insert new elements, but also to retrieve and delete any element stored in the dictionary. These requirements disqualify stacks, queues, and priority queues, because what they can retrieve and delete depends on the order of insertion or priority. So, we are left with arrays, linked lists, and binary search trees, all of which support the three operations. For all these options, we assume that we store both keys and values explicitly as pairs.

Array

Insertion works right out of the box. We create a `(key, value)` pair and store it in the array using the plain `array.insert` method. What happens if we insert two pairs with the same key but different values? Normally, a dictionary allows only one value to be associated with each unique key. However, if we allow only one value per unique key, then we must tweak insertion to first check whether the key already exists.

To delete a key, we must first perform a special search to find a pair whose key matches the argument.

Similarly, when it comes to `search`, we just pass the key as an argument, and we must scan the array to find a pair whose first value matches the key.

We can use sorted or unsorted arrays. The former makes search fast but insertion linear time, and the latter allows constant-time insertion (if we don't have to check for duplicates) but makes search slow.

Linked List

Most of the principles discussed for arrays also apply to linked lists. We usually want to use doubly linked lists to make `delete` more efficient. Again, we can choose between sorted and unsorted lists, except that lists, if you remember, don't support binary search, so we don't really have an advantage using the sorted version.

Balanced Binary Search Tree

We have just discovered balanced binary search trees in the previous chapter, but they are actually a good option in this case! All the operations we need to perform on a dictionary (including the accessory ones such as `max`) can be run in logarithmic time on a balanced tree. We must be as careful with duplicates as with the other two data structures, but this option guarantees the most balanced performance at the cost of some extra memory.

Summary

Table 12.1 lists the time each of the implementations discussed in this chapter takes for the main operations on dictionaries. I included a column for the time needed to create each data structure from a collection of n elements. This is a cost that needs to be taken into consideration, and it isn't always the same as the cost of n insertions (remember `heapify` in chapter 10?).

Table 12.1   Running time for various implementations of the dictionary

	Insert	Delete	Search	Init with n elements
Unsorted array	O(1)	O(n)	O(n)	O(n)
Sorted array	O(n)	O(n)	O(log(n))	O(n*log(n))
Unsorted doubly linked list	O(1)	O(n)	O(n)	O(n)
Sorted doubly linked list	O(n)	O(n)	O(n)	O(n²)
Balanced binary search tree	O(log(n))	O(log(n))	O(log(n))	O(n*log(n))

In the analysis for table 12.1, I assumed that no checks on the keys to add are performed (otherwise the running time of `insert` can never be lower than the one of `search`) and that `delete` takes the key to be removed as an argument and as such needs to find it first.

As anticipated, balanced binary search trees have the best average performance considering all the operations.

Hash tables

The previous section summarized known alternatives and offered a recap of some key takeaways from the previous chapters. Now it's time to take another step and think about something completely new that changes the rules of the game. This section describes a new data structure and discusses how it works when implementing the dictionary ADT. You think $O(\log(n))$ is good? Think again! You won't believe what we're about to accomplish.

A new way of indexing

Arrays don't guarantee great performance for dictionary operations because, with key-based indexing, we lose their main advantage: constant-time access by index. So, how could we exploit this huge advantage of arrays? Let's go back to Mario and his baseball card collection.

Let's imagine that his collection of cards is static, with a fixed number of cards, and, to keep things simple, there are no duplicates. If there are n cards and the collection of cards never changes, we could in theory associate an integer between 0 and n-1 to each card. Ring a bell? We could use this integer as the index of an array. But how can we associate this index with each card? For now, let's imagine that we have an oracle function, a black box that spits out the right index when we feed it with a card.

We can ask this oracle, for example, what's the index associated with Joe Di Maggio's card, and the oracle answers 3. So, we know that we can store the card in the array's fourth cell (at index 3), and we can use the same index to retrieve that card when we search for it.

Note that we would have to use the array in a different way than what we have discussed in chapter 2. The elements stored in the array wouldn't be left justified, and their positions wouldn't be determined by the order in which they were inserted.

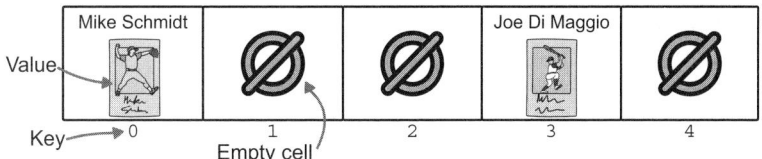

This data structure is called a *direct-access table*. The stored elements would be scattered over the entire capacity of the array, and we might find empty cells between the elements. For this reason, we also need a way to keep track of which cells are used and which ones are empty. Nothing complicated: we can just store None, null, or whatever special value your programming language offers to encode the absence of a value.

Under certain conditions, which we'll describe later in this section, we call this oracle function an indexing function.

Of course, what I'm describing here is a better-than-ideal situation, and we'll soon discuss all its limitations. But if we could use this solution, its performance would be orders of magnitude better than anything we have discussed in the previous section. Once we have the index provided by the oracle function, all operations, such as searching, inserting, or deleting an element, would take constant time!

Is it too good to be true? Well yes, unfortunately, it is.

The cost of indexing

First, there is an important detail that we have skipped: What's the cost of the indexing function? To understand this, let's further break down the operation of getting from a card to its index in the array.

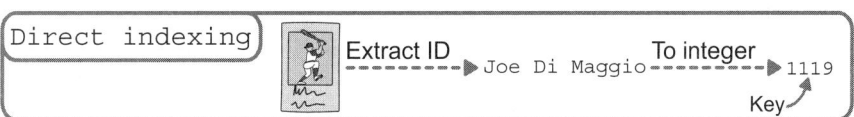

With direct-access tables, the key of an object is its index in the array. But we still need to compute this key.

We start with the full object, a baseball card (or its digital representation), and extract from it a unique identifier. This ID may be an integer, in which case we are done. More often, however, the ID will be some sort of string, and we need an extra step to convert it to an integer. This is not difficult at all. One way would be to convert each letter to an integer by taking its ASCII or Unicode value and then adding up all the values. That's what is shown in the figure. But this formula has a big problem: all anagrams of a sentence produce the same value because we don't take into account the position of the letters. So, goodbye to unique IDs.

A better formula multiplies the value of each letter by a number determined by its position. For example,

```
id = 0
for c in 'Joe Di Maggio':
    id = id  + ord(c)
    id *= 256
```

This code treats an ASCII string as a base-256 number. Here we just convert the base-256 "number" `'Joe Di Maggio'` to a base-10 integer.

As you can see, to get from the element we want to store to its index in the array, there are intermediate steps that may require some extra cost, for example, iterating over a string. We can factor this out by assuming that the indexing function takes `O(k)` time, where `k` is some value that depends on the elements we want to store. This value `k` is usually independent of the number of elements we are storing, and if it can be bounded by a constant (for example, if all names are at most 50 characters long), then we can treat it as a constant-time operation. But don't forget that there is a cost to extract keys.

Problems with the ideal model

The cost of the indexing function is just the tip of an iceberg. Our assumption that the collection of cards is static and immutable is a bigger problem. As you can imagine, that's not future proof: new baseball cards are released every year. And if we replace baseball cards with books in an online bookstore, the situation gets even worse because the catalog changes at random times.

To deal with this, we should create an array large enough to hold all possible keys for all possible products. If we compute the index from the names of the players interpreted as base-256 numbers, with `'Joe Di Maggio'`, we get an index in the order of 10^{29}. Even if it was possible to create an array that large, we would have a huge array that would be left mostly empty. Let's crunch some numbers to illustrate this. Suppose that all the possible name combinations for baseball cards are in the order of 2^{64}, which is more or less 20 billion billions. The number of all-time Major League players is in the order of 20,000, and so, considering that a player can have a 20-year career, we can assume that less than 400,000 unique baseball cards have ever been printed.

Even if Marco managed to buy one copy of every baseball card ever printed, it would just fill less than 0.000000000002% of an array with a capacity of 2^{64} elements, and around 0.009% of a more somber array allocated for 2^{32} elements.

In other words, that's a huge waste of memory. Using an array as a direct-access table is only possible in very particular situations, where we can put constraints on the size and composition of the set of elements to store.

However, there is some good in this idea. Maybe not everything has to go down the drain.

Hashing

We need to introduce something new to make it work. Our biggest problem with direct-access tables is that the indexing space is usually too large, and we can't afford to allocate such large arrays.

What we want is to allocate an array of size $m \ll |keys|$, a container that can store the number of elements we expect to have, not all possible elements that could ever exist. In our example, Marco wants to create an array of about a thousand elements to store his baseball cards, not one with a capacity of billions.

But if the capacity of the array we are using is less than the number of possible keys, then we can no longer use keys as indexes. We need to rethink the process of computing an index from an object, and we need to add an intermediate step that will always produce a valid index.

This step is what we call *hashing*, and the array we use to store elements indexed by hashing is called a *hash table*. Broadly speaking, hashing can describe the entire process of getting from an object to its index. In other words, a hash function can take the entire object as input and return a valid index.

But the crucial step where hashing takes place is to go from an arbitrary integer identifier to a valid index for our hash table.

Hash functions

What are the properties of a hash function? And what makes a good hash function?

These are key questions that we must answer to implement a hash table. The requirements for hash functions depend on the context, specifically the possible values to store and the size of the hash table:

- The domain of a hash function must be the set of all possible keys. Of course, the possible values for the input depend on the context. But we can always convert the elements to be stored to integers, so we can say that the domain for a general-purpose hash function is the set of all integers.

- A hash function must return a valid index. If our hash table has size m, then the output of the hash function associated with the table must be an integer between 0 and $m-1$.

Understanding what makes a good hash function is somewhat more complicated. In theory, a desirable property of hash functions is uniformity: each element should be equally likely to be hashed to any of the m slots in the hash table, regardless of where any other element has been or will be hashed. Unfortunately, uniformity is hard to obtain (elements are often not drawn independently) and hard to verify (because we usually don't know the distribution of the keys).

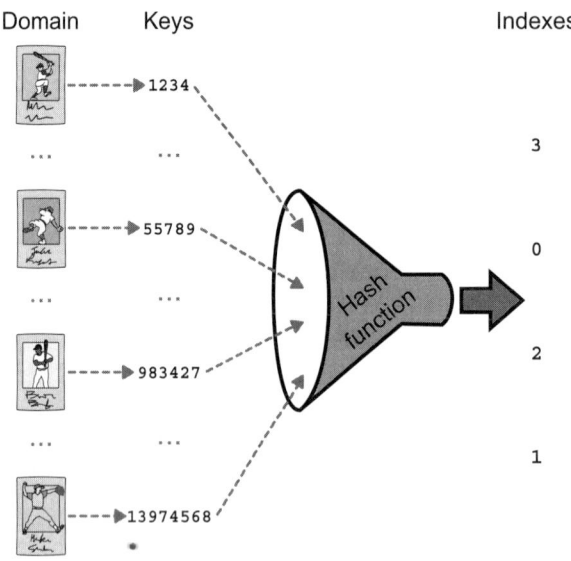

In these cases, the best we can do is design heuristics that perform well enough even without coming close to uniformity. A rule of thumb when designing these heuristics is to make sure that the output is independent of any patterns that might be present in the data.

The division method

In chapter 9, when we discussed circular queues, we introduced the concept of virtual address space and discussed how to wrap around the end of the queue when either the front or rear pointers exceed the end of the array.

The division method works the same way. Given a hash table of size m, for any integer key k, we compute the index where we store k using a hash function h(k) = k % m, which is the remainder of the division of k by m.

The method is simple, but this apparent simplicity hides some challenges. For example, if we choose m to be a power of two, $m = 2^p$ for some positive integer p, we are in trouble. The problem is that the result $k \% 2^p$ is exactly the p least significant bits of k. If we aren't sure that the distribution of the least p bits of the keys is uniform, then we should be careful about the value we choose for m—the size of the table.

As a rule of thumb, whenever we use the division method, the best choice for m is a prime number that is not too close to a power of two. Finding prime numbers is not the easiest operation, so we might be open to alternatives.

The multiplication method

If we want to have more freedom in choosing the size of the hash table, or if we don't have a say in the choice, we can resort to a different method to compute the hash function. The multiplication method is an effective alternative, but it's also more complex to compute.

The first thing we need to do is choose a real number, a constant A, to multiply by our input key k. The second step is to take the fractional part of this product, so we compute (k*A) % 1.

From this step, we can deduce that not all choices of A are equally good. For example, integers are a terrible choice because the resulting value would always be 0.

The hard part is that the best value for A depends on the characteristics of the data to be hashed. Nevertheless, we can always follow Donald Knuth's advice and use A = (math .sqrt(5)-1)/2, which should work well in most situations.

However, we are not done yet! We still need to multiply the resulting real number by m, the size of the table, and then take the integer part of the result (which will be an integer between 0 and m − 1).

The Python version of function h is

```
h = lambda k: math.floor(m * ((A * k) % 1))
```

As I mentioned, the choice of m is not critical for this method. Unlike the division method, a power of two is often used because it allows some optimization in the calculation of h.

This method has another desirable property, in comparison to the division method: keys that are close to each other end up on indexes that are far apart. This is important for spreading the load evenly across the table, and in the next section, we'll discuss why this is critical.

There are, of course, other ways to compute our hash function, but these will do for our purposes, and now it's time to address the "elephant in the table."

Conflict resolution

When I introduced hash tables, I told you that the capacity of the array we are using is less than the number of possible keys, and therefore, we can no longer use keys as indexes because a key could be larger than the largest index of the hash table.

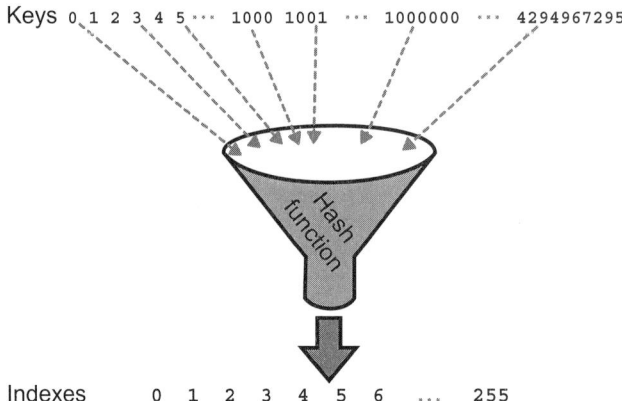

There is another consequence of this size difference that I have glossed over—the hash function will map at least two keys to the same index. This follows from the so-called pigeonhole principle.

If we have five pigeons and four holes, there will be at least one hole with two pigeons. There might also be more than one hole with two pigeons, or holes with more than two pigeons.

So, in a hash table, at some point, we will have two keys mapped to the same array cell. When this happens, we say we have a *conflict*. What can we do in these situations? How do we handle conflicts?

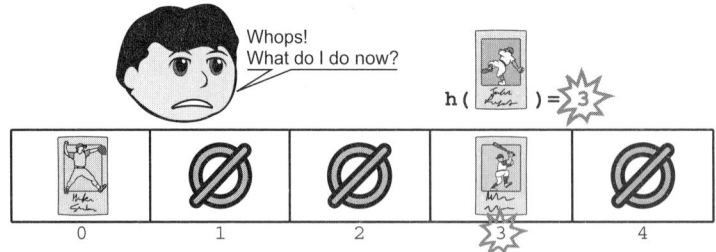

There are two main strategies: *chaining* and *open addressing*. They are radically different approaches, with pros and cons. We discuss them in detail next.

Chaining

The first way we can resolve a conflict is by allowing multiple items to be stored in the same cell. Of course, we can't make an array cell larger and store more than one value in it. So, we need to be creative.

Instead of storing values directly in the array's cells, each cell stores the head of a linked list, called a *hash chain*. When a new element x is hashed into the i-th cell, we retrieve the hash chain pointed to by that cell and insert x at its front. If we want to avoid duplicates, we can instead add new elements to the tail of the list, after traversing the entire list and checking that x is not there.

Which type of linked list should we use? As we discussed in chapter 5, doubly linked lists are the best option when we need to delete elements at random positions. However, we won't have a reference to the node to be deleted, so the only difference with singly linked lists will be the complexity of the code to delete an element.

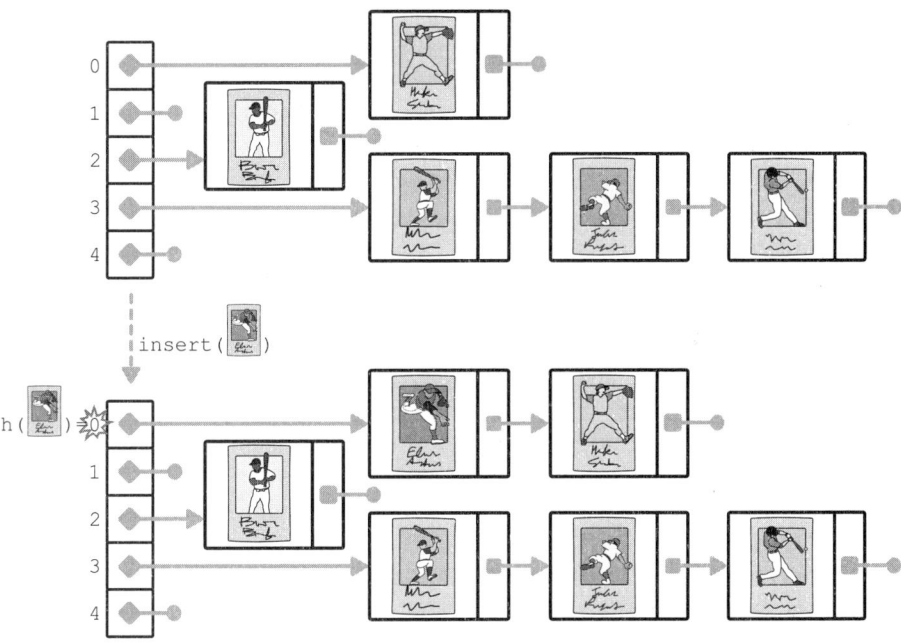

Since we already have both types of lists implemented, I used singly linked lists and the multiplication method for the hash function. To compute the index of a value, we apply the multiplication method to the key associated with the value. Internally, the class uses the built-in hash method by default to extract a key from any object. However, it is possible to customize the way we extract keys when the class is initialized:

```
class HashTable:
    __A__ = Decimal((sqrt(5) - 1) / 2)        ← The constant for the multiplication
    def __init__(self, buckets, extract_key=hash):   method, defined as a class property
        self._m = buckets
        self._data = [SinglyLinkedList() for _ in range(buckets)]
        self._extract_key = extract_key
    def _hash(self, key):
        return floor(self._m*((Decimal(key) * HashTable.__A__)%1))
```

This is the bulk of the code we need to write to implement a hash table. Later, I'll show you that its methods take only a couple of lines each because we can use the methods of class `SinglyLinkedList` to do the hard work.

So how efficient is a hash table with chaining? To understand this, we need to take a different approach to asymptotic analysis than we have done so far. Let's assume we have a hash table with m buckets in which we have already stored n elements. We also assume that computing the hash of a key takes $O(1)$ and that we don't care about duplicates.

For our analysis, the key factor is the size of the hash chains. But if we don't know the exact distribution of the keys in advance, we can only reason in terms of averages. We can hypothesize that, *on average*, each array cell will have n/m keys mapped to it.

For insert, we are in luck: if we insert new elements at the front of the lists, then the `insert` method is particularly efficient, taking only constant time, regardless of the values of m and n:

```
def insert(self, value):
    index = self._hash(self._extract_key(value))
    self._data[index].insert_in_front(value)
```

What about the `search` method? As we said, the average list has n/m elements, and we can only use linear search, so the average running time for `search` is $O(1 + n/m)$. However, if we are particularly unlucky (or not careful enough, as we'll see), all the keys could be mapped to the same bucket. The worst-case running time for search is, therefore, $O(n)$:

```
def _search(self, value):
    index = self._hash(key)
    value_matches_key = lambda v: self._extract_key(v) == key
    return self._data[index].search(value_matches_key)
```

In the code for `search`, we use a special search method for linked lists that takes a predicate as its only argument and returns the first element for which the predicate returns `True`. Remember, for this whole class to work, keys must be unique identifiers for values.

Deleting an element can take constant time on doubly linked lists, but only if we have a reference to the list node to be deleted. Otherwise, it takes the same time as searching.

Although it is common in the literature for the `delete` method to take a reference to where the value to be deleted is stored, my advice is to avoid this version because it's neither clean nor safe. We can thus choose between deleting by key or deleting by value. For the sake of space, we only present the delete-by-value version, but both of them require a search to be performed first and take $O(1 + n/m)$ on average:

```
def delete(self, value):
    index = self._hash(self._extract_key(value))
    self._data[index].delete(value)
```

You can find the full code for class `HashTable` on GitHub: https://mng.bz/jXRP.

In general, iterating through all the elements of a hash table takes $O(n+m)$ steps because we have to go through at least all the array cells, even if the linked lists they point to are empty.

What if we are interested in finding the minimum or maximum of the table? In that case, we must scan the whole table, so the running time is also $O(n+m)$. The same reasoning applies if we want to find the successor or predecessor of an element.

Table 12.2 summarizes the running time of the main methods of a hash table with chaining.

Table 12.2 Running time for a hash table implementation of the dictionary ADT (with duplicates)

	Insert	Delete	Search	Init with n elements
Chaining (average)	$O(1)$	$O(1+n/m)$	$O(1+n/m)$	$O(m+n)$
Chaining (worst case)	$O(1)$	$O(n)$	$O(n)$	$O(m+n)$

Open addressing

Chaining isn't the only way to resolve hashing conflicts. If we want to avoid composite data structures and store elements directly in the table, we can take a different approach. In open addressing, for each key, we can *probe* all m array cells, in some order, until we either find what we were looking for (an element or an empty cell), or we probed all cells. In a way, after a conflict we get a retry, a second chance (and a third chance, and so on).

To allow probing, we extend the hash function to take two arguments: the key to be hashed and the number of attempts already made. Let me explain how this works. Suppose we want to insert a new element, whose integer key is 714. We compute p(714,0)=3, and then we check cell 3 and find that another element whose key is (say) 423 is already stored at index 3.

But we don't give up! Instead, we compute p(714,1)=1 and probe another cell, at index 1: unfortunately, it's still not available. Let's try again: p(714,2) = 6, and at index 6, we find an empty cell. We can then store our element, and we are done.

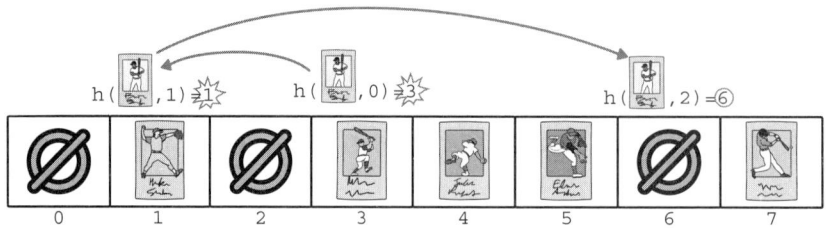

Search works similarly, with one important caveat: the moment we are hashed to an empty cell, we know the search is unsuccessful. Otherwise, we check the value we found, and if it matches the target of the search, we are successful. Otherwise, we know we need to try again.

Of course, the hash function must be designed in such a way that, for any possible key k, [p(k,i) **for** i **in** range(0,m)] contains all possible indexes of the hash table. In other words, <p(k,0), p(k,1),…,p(k,m-1)> should be a permutation of the sequence <0,…,m-1> for any k.

Given a valid hash function h, two of the most commonly used options for the probing function are *linear probing*, with p(k,i) = (h(k) + i) % m, and *quadratic probing*, where p(k,i) = (h(k) + a*i + b*i²) % m for some constants a, b.

Problems with open addressing

Compared to chaining, open addressing has one main advantage—you don't waste memory for the linked lists, and you need only minimal overhead for the array.

However, there are many drawbacks:

- Chaining allows unlimited element storage, whereas open addressing uses a static array, fixing hash tables' capacity at initialization ($n \leq m$).

- Linear and quadratic probing often produce element clusters, long chains that must be traversed during search and insertion, thus slowing down these operations. Quadratic probing works a little better but, for a given size of the table m, not all combinations of a and b are valid (the formula must return a valid permutation of the indexes).

- With open addressing, deleting an element becomes complicated. If we just left a position empty, then we would break search. Going back to our example, if after inserting an element x at index 6 we deleted the element at index 1 leaving an empty cell, new searches for x might stop prematurely upon encountering the empty cell at index 1.

We could use a special value for deleted elements, but then in a search, we would visit more elements than are actually stored, making it slow. Otherwise, we need to disable element removal, but then we fill up the table quickly, and we have to allocate a larger table even if not needed.

Long story short, if you need to delete items, you should use chaining.

Risks with hashing

Hash tables offer a noticeable improvement over any other implementation of the dictionary ADT. It almost seems too good to be true. But you must remember that in data structures, as in life, there is no rose without a thorn (but many a thorn without a rose).

The first thing to remember is that while `insert`, `search`, and `delete` can be maximally efficient with a hash table, other operations such as `maximum`, `minimum`, `successor`, and `predecessor` are faster when a BST is used instead.

However, there are bigger potential problems that can arise if we are not careful. A premise: the version of chaining I presented inserts elements at the front of linked lists and ignores duplicates for maximum efficiency. If we need to check for duplicates or if we want to keep the linked lists sorted for some reason, then insertion becomes linear time, as summarized in table 12.3.

Table 12.3 Running times for a hash table, when duplicates are not allowed

	Insert	Delete	Search	Init with n elements
Chaining (average)	$O(1+n/m)$	$O(1+n/m)$	$O(1+n/m)$	$O(m+(n/m)^2)$
Chaining (worst case)	$O(n)$	$O(n)$	$O(n)$	$O(m+n^2)$

There are situations where we can't allow duplicates, and this exacerbates the problem we'll describe next. In particular, note how building the table becomes a quadratic operation.

Half of the problem with hash tables is that, while the average performance is very good, the worst-case performance is on the side of bad (worse than an implementation using BSTs).

The other half of the problem is that, unless we take countermeasures, a client can deliberately make a hash table perform poorly. In particular, if the hash function is fixed and known (or if it's possible to reverse engineer it), a client can find sequences of keys that all map to the same hash chain. This has been exploited for an attack that targets the hash table used by servers to store the HTTP parameters sent with POST requests.

Sending millions of form parameters, all known to hash to the same bucket in the table, slowed down the processing of a request to about a minute—a minute during which one processor core was busy with this task. You can imagine how sending hundreds or thousands of these requests could bring a server to a halt.

You can read more about the exploit at https://lwn.net/Articles/474912/, and you can find the original paper explaining the vulnerability in detail at https://mng.bz/WEK1.

Note that the vulnerability wasn't caused by the server code, but it was inherent in programming languages such as Perl, PHP, Python, Ruby, Java, and JavaScript. So, how can we prevent this attack?

This vulnerability stems from the deterministic nature of the hash function. Of course, the function must be deterministic for a given table, and it can't change with every operation. Otherwise, the table would be broken. However, creating a hash function with a random element initialized along with the hash table can prevent the key bucket mapping from being exploited by attackers. This might not be enough as an attacker may still be able to guess the hash function used, but more complex solutions have been developed to address this risk.

For this reason, it's so important that you understand how hash tables (and the other data structures in this book) work. Only by understanding their internals can you wisely choose the libraries you use, verify their specifics, and make sure they don't have such vulnerabilities.

Recap

- The *dictionary* is an abstract data type for a container that stores elements that can later be searched (or deleted) by key. Dictionaries are used everywhere, from routers to key-value databases.

- We can use several of the data structures discussed in this book to implement a dictionary ADT, but balanced binary search trees are the ones that guarantee the best performance over all operations.

- An implementation using *hash tables* offers the best average performance for `insert`, `search`, and `delete`.

- A *direct-access table* is an array where each key (integer element) `k` is stored at index `k`, making search-by-value as fast as constant time. Non-integer elements are first converted to integers by extracting a unique ID. Direct-access tables are impractically large.

- A *hash table* is a special version of an array, where the index of an (integer) element is returned by a special function called a hash function. Hash tables can be much smaller than the range of values stored, making them more practical than direct-access tables.

- Since the range of keys of a hash table can be larger than the number of cells in the table, we can't avoid *conflicts*, that is, two keys mapping to the same array cell.

- Conflicts can be resolved through *chaining* or *open addressing*.

- In chaining, each table cell references a linked list where the elements are stored. These tables can grow indefinitely.

- In open addressing, a different permutation of the table's indexes corresponds to each key. If on insert we find that the first index is already taken, then we try the second one, and so on—similarly with search.

- Hash tables with open addressing can't store more elements than the number of cells. They make deleting elements complicated, and their performance degrades with the filling ratio. Thus, they are rarely used.

- The average running time of insertion, search, and deletion for hash tables is constant time. The worst-case performance, however, is linear time.

- If the hash function used is deterministic or easily guessed by an attacker, it is possible to design a sequence of keys that will cause the hash table to perform very poorly. This originated a vulnerability in servers written in several programming languages, including Perl, PHP, Python, Ruby, Java, and JavaScript.

Graphs: Learning how to model complex relationships in data | 13

. . . .

In this chapter

- defining graphs

- discussing the basic properties of graphs

- evaluating graph implementation strategies:
  adjacency list and adjacency matrix

- exploring graph traversal: breadth-first search and
  depth-first search

. . . .

In our final chapter, we discuss another data structure that exceeds the characteristics of a container—graphs. They can be used to store elements, but that would be an understatement as graphs have a much broader range of applications.

This chapter defines what graphs are and discusses some of their most important properties. After covering the basics, we move on to their implementation. Finally, we briefly discuss two methods for traversing a graph.

What's a graph?

Not surprisingly, the first question we want to answer is, "What is a graph?" There are many ways to define graphs, ranging from informal definitions to rigid theory. I'll start with this definition: graphs are a generalization of trees. When I introduced trees in chapter 11, I told you that they can be used to model hierarchical relationships. Graphs allow you to model more general relationships. For example, the structure of your file system or an arithmetic expression can be represented using trees, but trees are not suitable to represent a friendship graph or the flow of a computer program. For these kinds of relationships, we need graphs.

Definition

We'll return to the differences between graphs and trees later in this section. For now, it's time for a more formal definition of a graph.

We can define a graph G as a pair of sets:

- *A set of vertices* V—These are entities that are independent of each other and unique. The set of vertices can be arbitrarily large (it can even be empty).

- *A set of edges* E *connecting the vertices*—An edge is identified by a pair of vertices. The first one is called the *source* vertex, and the second one is called the *destination* vertex.

We can write $G = (V, E)$ to make it clear that the graph has a set of vertices V and a set of edges E.

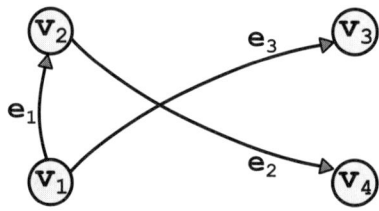

Considering the example in the illustration, we can write the following:

$$G = ([v_1, v_2, v_3, v_4], [(v_1, v_2), (v_1, v_3), (v_2, v_4)])$$

Let's look at some more basic definitions:

- An edge whose source and destination are the same is called a *loop*.

- *Simple graphs* are graphs without loops, with at most one edge between any two vertices. For any couple of vertices u, v, where $u \neq v$, there can only be (at most) one edge from u to v.

- *Multigraphs*, in contrast, can have any number of edges between two given vertices. Both simple graphs and multigraphs can be extended to allow loops.

- An edge can have a numerical value associated with it. Such a value is called its *weight*, and the edge is then called a *weighted edge*.

- A graph is *sparse* if the number of edges is relatively small. For reference, we can consider a graph with n vertices to be sparse if its number of edges is $O(n)$ or less.

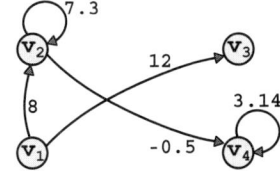

- A graph is *dense* if the number of edges is close to the maximum possible, which can be at most $O(n^2)$ for a simple graph with n vertices.

Friendship graph

In this section, we meet again a group of friends we made in the first chapter.

The animal farm is abuzz! A new social network has recently been introduced, and everyone is constantly looking at their phones. The Lion and the Tiger have been feuding for a long time, and now their rivalry has moved into the digital world. There is an election coming up at the animal farm, and the Tiger wants to take over the position of King of the Farm from the Lion. To that end, she and her staff are trying to use social networks by mapping a friendship graph to make sense of their respective connections. They want to understand who has the larger following—the Tiger or the Lion—and identify which animals to focus on in the Tiger's campaign to sway their vote.

The vertices of this graph will be the animals on the farm. The edges of the graph will represent friendship relationships in social networks. Because we have to start somewhere, in the first version of the friendship graph, the vertices are the Tiger and her campaign advisor and best friend, the Monkey.

Directed vs. undirected

After adding the Monkey to the graph, the next honor goes to the Crocodile, the IT director of Tiger's campaign. As a software developer, Croc raises a good technical question: Should they use a directed or an undirected graph?

In a *directed graph*, edges have a direction: they only go from the source vertex to the destination vertex. This means that if two vertices u and v are connected (only) by an edge (u,v), we can go from u to v, but it's not possible to go from v directly to vertex u.

Social networks such as Twitter or Instagram, where you can follow other users even without being followed back, are better represented by directed graphs. Other applications best modeled by directed graphs include maps (some roads are one-way), workflows, and processes (any state machine really).

On Twitter, everyone in her campaign follows the Tiger, who doesn't follow anyone back. The Crocodile follows the Monkey because he is the campaign manager.

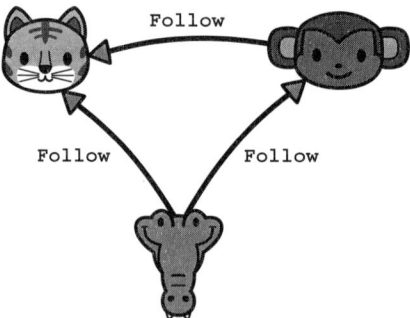

In an *undirected graph*, instead, edges can be traversed in both directions. So if an undirected graph has an edge (u,v), we can also go from v to u. The LinkedIn connection and Facebook friendship are two-way (symmetrical) relationships that should be represented by undirected graphs.

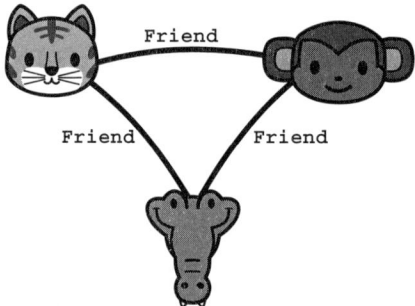

You may have noticed that edges can have descriptive text next to them. These labels should not be confused with the weight of the edge. In this case, they are just decorative, but (especially in multigraphs) labels can have meaning (for example, specify conditions that must apply to take a certain edge or actions to perform when traversing it).

Is it possible to transform a directed graph into an undirected graph, and vice versa? An undirected edge (u,v) is equivalent to two directed edges (u,v) and (v,u). So, it's always possible to represent an undirected graph with directed edges. The opposite is not true: for example, the directed graph in this section is not equivalent to any undirected graph.

For this reason, it's usually more practical to use directed edges in computer representations of graphs, regardless of the actual type of graph, to ensure greater flexibility.

Cyclic versus acyclic

At the Tiger campaign headquarters, the animals are working hard to expand their follower graph. They've just added the Zebra and the Giraffe, and they've noticed that the latter isn't following the Tiger yet (they'll have a little chat with the Giraffe later!).

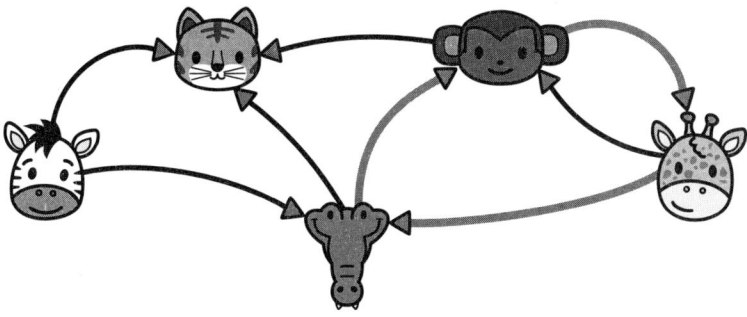

There is something else interesting in this graph: I have highlighted three edges, making them a little thicker. They go from the Giraffe to the Crocodile, from the Crocodile to the Monkey, and from the Monkey to the Giraffe. That, as you may already know, is a cycle.

Let's take a small step back. We define a *path* in the graph as a sequence of one or more edges (v_1, v_2), $(v_2, v_3)...(v_{n-1}, v_n)$, where for each adjacent pair of edges in the sequence, the destination of the first edge is the same as the source of the next. In simpler words, a path is a sorted sequence of edges that allows traversing the graph from a vertex v_1 to a vertex v_n.

A *cycle* is a path that starts and ends at the same vertex—in a cycle, $v_1 = v_n$. If you look closely at the graph, you may notice that Crocodile→Monkey→Giraffe isn't its only cycle. There is, in fact, a smaller cycle between the Monkey and the Giraffe.

A graph that has no cycles is called *acyclic*.

Connected graphs and connected components

To get a better idea of the competition, it's time to add the Lion and his friends to the graph. After including just a few of the Lion's connections, something is already apparent: the Lion has a different style than the Tiger. He follows back his connections, probably trying to make them feel closer.

However, the most interesting aspect of this graph is the presence of two different large areas, two clusters centered around the Tiger and the Lion, with no connection between those two parts.

Each of the two regions is a *connected component*, that is, a subgraph where all vertices are connected.

Let me give you some definitions. Given a graph G = (V,E),

- A *subgraph* G' = (V',E') consists of a subset V' of the vertices of the original graph and a subset E' of the edges between the vertices in V'.

- Two vertices u and v are *connected* if there is a path from u to v.

- An undirected graph is *connected* if all its vertices are connected. A connected graph has only one connected component.

A directed graph is *weakly connected* if the undirected graph obtained by replacing directed edges with undirected ones is connected. But there is a stricter definition of connectivity. Two vertices u and v are *strongly connected* if there is at least one path in the graph that goes from u to v and one that goes from v to u.

In an undirected graph, two connected vertices are also strongly connected. In a directed graph, instead, this is no longer true, and it's usually important to identify its *strongly connected components,* that is, the maximal subgraphs whose vertices are all strongly connected to each other.

In our example, when the team adds the Chicken to the graph, we notice that it becomes a weakly connected graph (the Chicken follows the Crocodile and is followed by the Cow), but it's not a strongly connected graph. We can, instead, identify five strongly connected components in the graph.

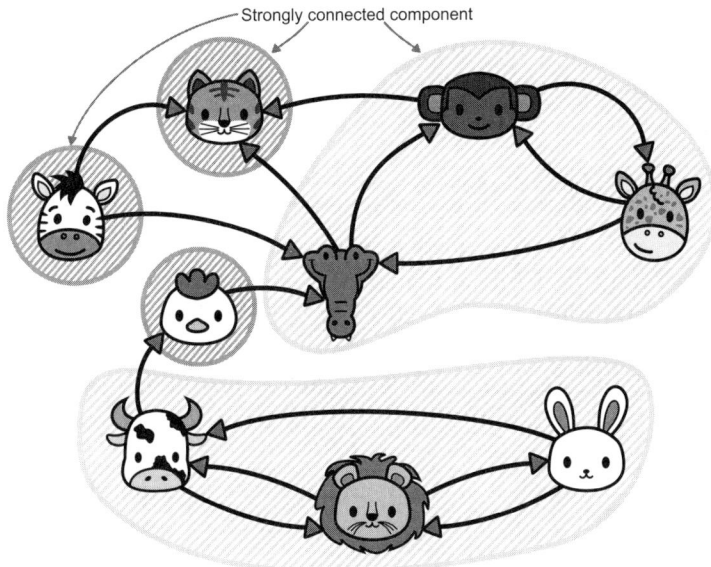

Note that if a vertex has all outgoing edges (like the Zebra) or all ingoing edges (like the Tiger), it will certainly be a degenerate strongly connected component with the vertex itself. Those, however, are not the only cases where this can happen (see the Chicken).

Connected and strongly connected components are especially important for large graphs because they allow us to break a large graph into smaller pieces that can be processed separately.

Trees as graphs

Now that we know all these definitions, we can go back to the difference between trees and graphs and provide a more formal definition of a tree. A tree is, in fact, a simple, undirected, connected, and acyclic graph. As such, a tree with n vertices (*nodes*, in tree terms) must have exactly $n-1$ edges.

A simple undirected acyclic graph that is not connected is called a *forest*. Here, each connected component is a tree of the forest.

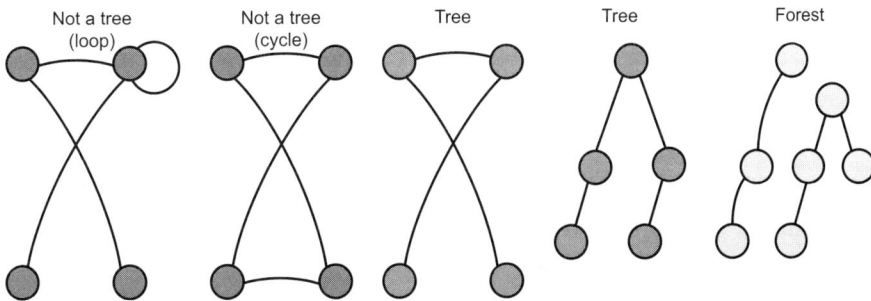

One might argue that edges in trees go from parent to child and thus should be modeled as directed edges. But, in a tree, identifying the root node eliminates any ambiguity between parents and children, and there is no need to make the direction of the edges explicit.

Implementing graphs

Like trees, graphs are better described as a class of data structures than as an abstract data type. But we can still define an API, and there are some common operations that most graphs support, such as adding vertices and edges. There are also many more operations that go beyond this basic API.

When we move to the data structure level, the key is to find a way to store a graph's vertices and edges in such a way that the graph can be easily and conveniently traversed and searched.

In this section, we will look at two ways to implement a graph: the *adjacency list* and the *adjacency matrix*. These are not the only ways, but they are the most common.

Adjacency list

In the adjacency list representation, we group edges by their source vertex. Given a vertex v, the list of all edges with v as their source is the adjacency list for v. We then build a dictionary in which we associate each vertex in the graph with its adjacency list.

In a Python implementation, the adjacency lists can be actual linked lists, but they can also be Python lists or sets—any container that provides search and traversal, really.

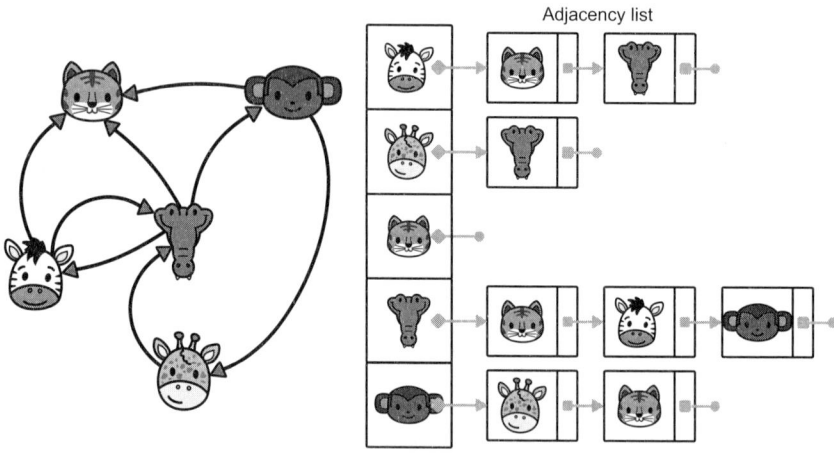

Let's take a closer look at a possible Python implementation. There are so many methods to implement that it's impossible to show them all here, but you can check out the full code on the book's GitHub repo: https://mng.bz/8wgw.

For the dictionary, I used a Python dictionary for clarity and simplicity. To store the adjacency lists, I'll instead use the singly linked lists we defined in chapter 6. Each edge could be stored using a custom `Edge` object, as a pair `(source, destination)` or a tuple `(source, destination, weight)`. But if the graph consists only of unweighted and unlabeled edges, we can just store the destination vertices in the adjacency list because we already know its source vertex.

I'll start by defining an internal class for the vertices. Each vertex will be a wrapper, uniquely identified by its key. It will also store its own adjacency list. This way, we can add all sorts of methods dealing with outgoing edges to the `Vertex` object itself, which will be solely responsible for keeping things in order:

```python
class Vertex:
    def __init__(self, key):
        self.id = key
        self._adj_list = SinglyLinkedList()
    def has_edge_to(self, destination_vertex):
        return self._adj_list._search(destination_vertex) is not None
    def add_edge_to(self, destination_vertex):
        if self.has_edge_to(destination_vertex):
            raise ValueError(f'Edge already exists: {self} -> {
destination_vertex}')
        self._adj_list.insert_in_front(destination_vertex)
```

To keep things simple, I implemented an unweighted graph, and we only store the destination vertex in the adjacency lists. Thus, searching for an edge in an adjacency list means finding a vertex in a linked list, and it can then be delegated to the linked list API. Similarly, to insert a new edge, we can use the method provided by linked lists—after making sure that such an edge doesn't already exist.

We can now define our outer Graph class, with a simple constructor—we just create an empty dictionary for the adjacency list:

```python
class Graph:
    def __init__(self):
        self._adj = {}
```

As I said, vertices will be identified by their keys, and the `Vertex` object should only be used internally by `Graph`. For example, if a client asks to insert a vertex with key `"v"`, they will never get a reference to the instance `Vertex("v")` that is created internally. When they need to perform some action on that vertex, they can only identify it by the ID, `"v"`—for example, a client will call something like `graph.add_edge("v", "u")`. Therefore, we need a way to retrieve the `Vertex` object associated with a given vertex ID. We implement `_get_vertex` as a private method because we don't need to let the client get a reference to these objects (however, the method will be very useful for us). Here is where the `_adj` attribute comes in. It's a dictionary whose keys are the vertex identifiers and whose values are the corresponding `Vertex` objects:

```
def _get_vertex(self, key):
    if key not in self._adj:
        raise ValueError(f'Vertex {key} does not exist!')
    return self._adj[key]
```

Adding a new vertex to the graph simply requires setting a value in the dictionary, plus a check to make sure the vertex isn't already in the graph:

```
def insert_vertex(self, key):
    if key in self._adj:
        raise ValueError(f'Vertex {key} already exists!')
    self._adj[key] = Graph.Vertex(key)
```

Finally, let's see how to add a new edge. We need to get the `Vertex` objects for the source and destination and then we can delegate the operation to the source vertex, which will also check if the edge already exists:

```
def insert_edge(self, key1, key2):
    v1 = self._get_vertex(key1)
    v2 = self._get_vertex(key2)
    v1.add_edge_to(v2)
```

Removing an edge is just as easy: we can follow the same flow, delegating to the source vertex and letting it check for errors. I omit the method here for space reasons, but you can check it on the GitHub repo.

Removing a vertex instead is something we need to think through. Removing the entry for a vertex v in the adjacency list is not enough: that way we would certainly remove v's outgoing edges, but if v also has ingoing edges, those would not be affected. Unfortunately, the only way to do this is to go through all the adjacency lists and remove every edge whose destination is v. As you can imagine, this is an expensive operation that takes $O(n+m)$ steps for a graph with n vertices and m edges:

```
def delete_vertex(self, key):
    v = self._get_vertex(key)
    for u in self._adj.values():
        if u != v and u.has_edge_to(v):
            u.remove_edge_to(v)
    del self._adj[key]
```

Adjacency matrix

In the adjacency matrix representation, we store the edges in a large matrix whose rows and columns are the vertices of the graph. A cell of the matrix with coordinates (u,v) can store a binary value (0 if there is no edge; 1 if there is an edge from u to v), the weight of the edge (or a special value such as None if there is no edge), or an object that models an edge.

Adjacency matrices can be faster than adjacency lists when we need to check whether there is an edge between two vertices: it takes only a single lookup in a 2D array, which is $O(1)$. Thus, adjacency matrices give us an advantage for algorithms that require intensive connectivity checking.

In contrast, an adjacency matrix requires memory proportional to the square of the number of vertices (that is, the maximum number of edges in a simple graph), even if the graph is sparse. Therefore, they are rarely used, and usually only when we are sure that we are dealing with dense graphs. Also, for this reason, we won't dive into the code for the adjacency matrix implementation.

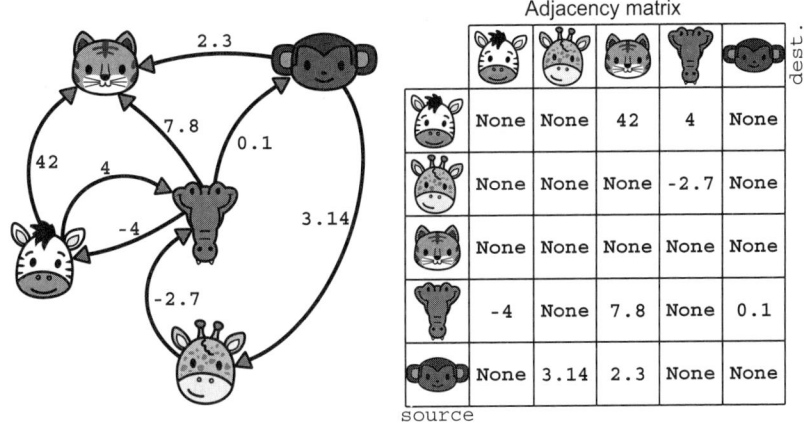

Graph search

Searching in a graph has a different meaning than what we have seen so far. Sure, we can also search whether a vertex or an edge is in the graph by looking at the adjacency list or the adjacency matrix. But that would underestimate the potential of a graph. Remember, a graph is more than just a container: it stores how entities (the vertices) are related to each other.

This section provides some examples of how to extract this kind of information from graphs.

Exploring friends

For this and the next section, we will be working with an undirected graph. However, the same considerations can apply to directed graphs.

There is a flurry of activity at the Tiger campaign headquarters: the IT team is now building a Facebook friendship graph. As we discussed, this is a symmetric relationship that is best modeled with undirected edges. This is a larger graph than we have seen before, and it takes some effort to analyze it. The idea Croc and the team have is to find all the direct friends of the Tiger and compare them to the direct friends of the Lion.

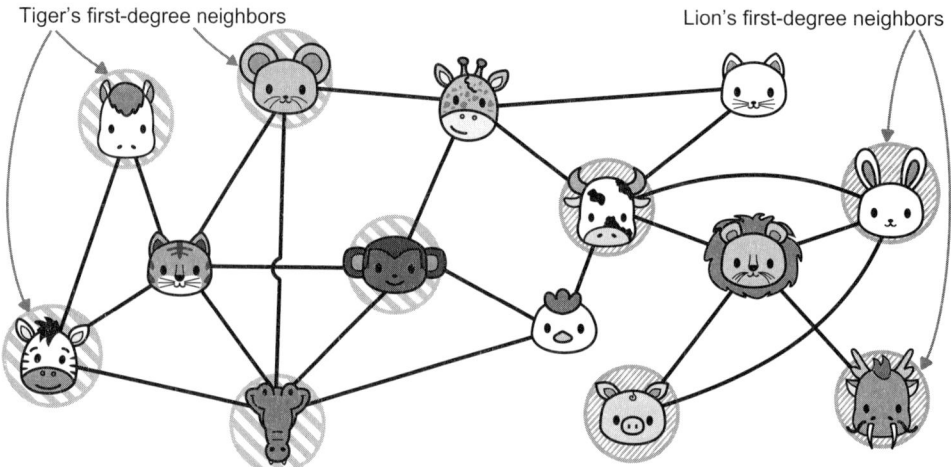

So, the Tiger has five friends, and the Lion has just four of them—that's good news! But, is it all we can learn from this graph?

The next step for the IT team is to study the "friend of a friend" sets. The sets of friends for the Tiger and the Lion don't intersect, so we can suppose these nine animals will vote for their closest friend. And a reasonable guess is that there are undecided voters among the second-degree connections whose preferences can be influenced by their friends. So, it's important to swing those votes.

Here the situation is not as bright. The illustration, for clarity, only shows the Tiger's perspective. The second-degree neighbors for the Tiger are just the Giraffe and the Chicken. The Lion has three second-degree friends: he shares the Giraffe and the Chicken with the Tiger, plus the Cat.

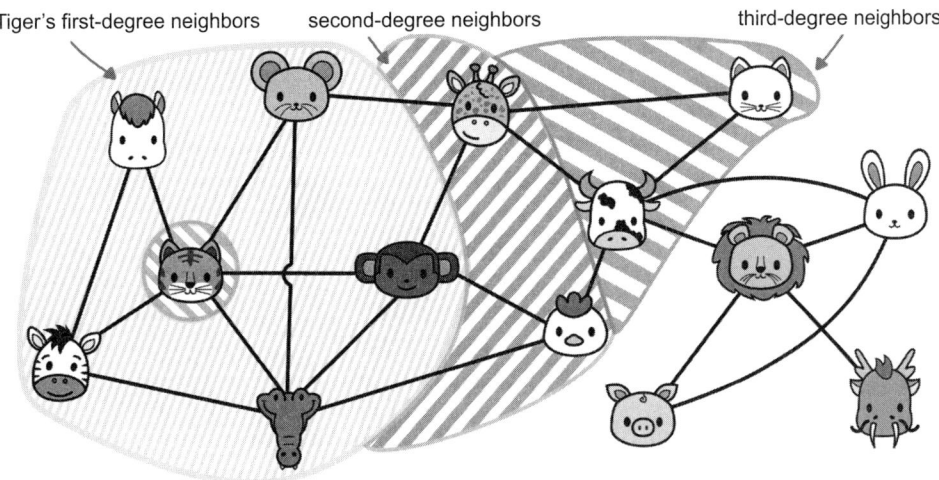

Tiger's first-degree neighbors   second-degree neighbors   third-degree neighbors

What if we get to the third-degree friends? Or the fourth-degree and so on?

Breadth-first search

There is a search algorithm that works exactly this way, exploring the vertices of a graph in concentric rings until it finds what it is looking for.

According to the info gathered by the campaign manager, the Rabbit is the star of the social networks, and winning the Rabbit's support can swing the election. At the Tiger HQ, they want to understand how far the rabbit is in the chain of friends. Also, what's the shortest path between the Tiger and the Rabbit? The plan involves starting with a friend of the Tiger, having that friend introduce the Tiger to one of her friends, who then introduces the Tiger to one of his friends, and so on until she gets to the Rabbit. So, the shorter the path, the fewer people involved.

The *breadth-first search* (BFS) algorithm does exactly this: it explores the graph starting from a start vertex s, the Tiger, by expanding a frontier of vertices connected (directly or indirectly) to s until we reach the target vertex (the Rabbit). More importantly, BFS explores vertices in a specific order, starting with the start vertex's neighbors, then expanding the frontier to the second-degree neighbors, and so on.

In detail, this expansion is not done level by level, but vertex by vertex. To make sure that we explore the closest vertices before the others, we can use a queue: first, we add all of the Tiger's neighbors to the queue.

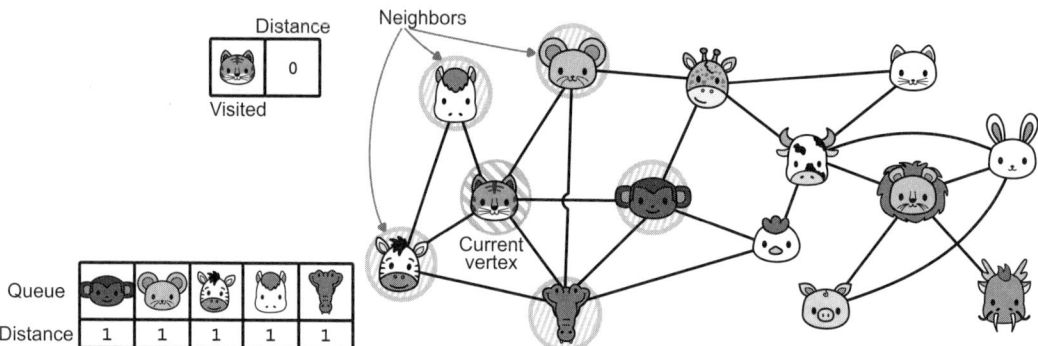

Then, we extract the first vertex in the queue (the Monkey), we go through all its outgoing edges, and add all their destinations to the rear of the queue. These vertices (if not already explored) will be two edges away from the Tiger.

If we add all neighbors to the queue without checking, we may get some duplicates in the queue. These duplicates represent alternative paths to the vertex from the start, but none of these duplicated paths will have a shorter distance to the start vertex! So, we can just ignore the neighbors that have already been added to the queue and avoid adding them a second time.

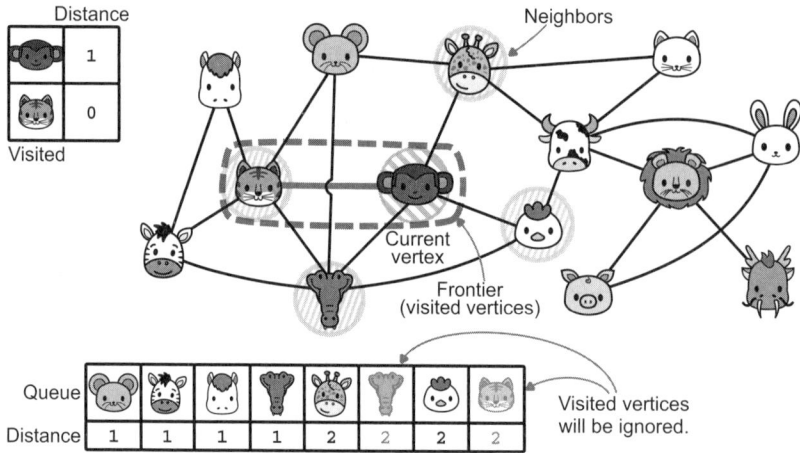

We continue to explore the graph, expanding the frontier of vertices connected to the start vertex, until we finally reach our target (or run out of vertices in the queue).

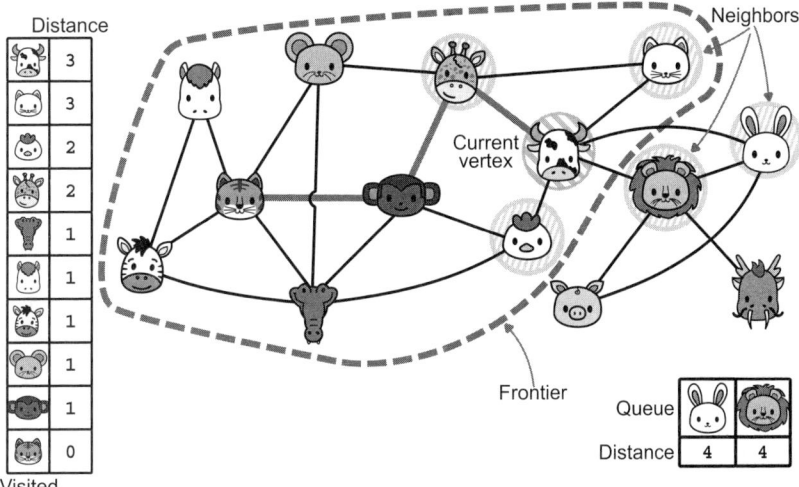

If we keep track of the distance of a vertex v when we add it to the queue, by setting `distance[v]` to 1 plus the distance of the source of the currently traversed edge, we can prove that when we explore a vertex, this value is the minimum distance (in terms of edges to be traversed) between the start vertex and v.

And if we also keep track of which edge we traversed to reach v, at the end of the method, we can reconstruct the shortest path from the start vertex to each vertex (highlighted in the illustrations). In our example, there are multiple shortest paths of length 4 from the Tiger to the Rabbit, so which one we actually choose depends on the order in which vertices were added to the queue.

Now it's time to look at some code for this beautiful method:

```
def bfs(self, start_vertex, target_vertex):
    distance = {v: float('inf') for v in self._adj}
    predecessor = {v: None for v in self._adj}
    queue = Queue(self.vertex_count())
    queue.enqueue(start_vertex)
    distance[start_vertex] = 0
    while not queue.is_empty():
        u = queue.dequeue()
        if u == target_vertex:
            return reconstruct_path(predecessor, target_vertex)
        for (_, v) in self._get_vertex(u).outgoing_edges():
            if distance[v] == float('inf'):
                distance[v] = distance[u] + 1
                predecessor[v] = u
                queue.enqueue(v)
    return None
```

Initially, we add the start vertex to the queue.

At this point, we know there is no path from the start to the target vertex.

Note that, because of how the vertices are explored, when we reach a vertex for the first time, we have already found its minimum distance from the start vertex. So, we don't need to explicitly keep track of visited vertices—we rather make sure to add them to the queue only once.

We still miss the last piece of the puzzle—the helper method that takes a dictionary with the predecessors of each vertex v and reconstructs the shortest path from s to v:

```
def reconstruct_path(pred, target):
    path = []
    while target:
        path.append(target)
        target = pred[target]
    return path[::-1]
```

The list goes from target to start: we need to reverse it.

Overall, in the worst case, the `bfs` method has to go through all m edges and n vertices, so its running time is O(n+m).

This method works perfectly when we are only interested in the distance in terms of the number of edges. If edges are weighted, and we define the distance between two vertices u and v as the sum of the edges' weights on a path from u to v, we need a refined version of the BFS algorithm—Dijkstra's algorithm. If you'd like to learn more about this, you can check chapter 15 of *Advanced Algorithms and Data Structures* (La Rocca, 2021, Manning).

Depth-first search

Is BFS the only way to explore a graph? Of course, it's not. BFS explores the graph in concentric rings of increasing distance from the start vertex. Thus, it expands the frontier of visited vertices like a wave, in all directions. The opposite choice would be to go as deep into the graph as possible, and that's what *depth-first search* (DFS) does. We must choose a start vertex s, and then the algorithm follows one path from s to its end. When the end of a path is reached, it goes back until it finds a vertex where we could have chosen a different edge and again follows that path to the end.

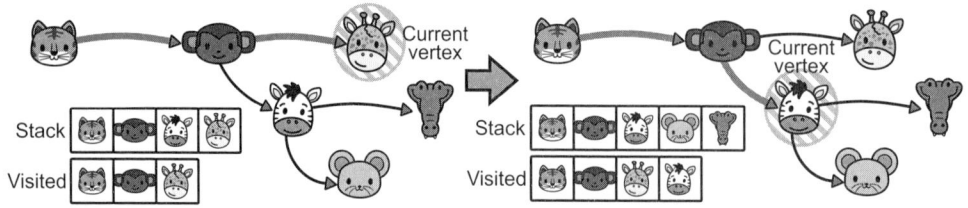

This algorithm can't be used to find the shortest path between vertices. In contrast, it can help us find connected and strongly connected components, understand if a directed graph is acyclic, and find a topological sorting for DAGs (*directed acyclic graphs*).

In this section, we'll look at how to find out if a graph is acyclic; for the other applications, see *Advanced Algorithms and Data Structures* (La Rocca, 2021, Manning).

To use DFS to check for the presence of cycles in the graph, we need to perform some additional actions while traversing the vertices—specifically, we mark the vertices with colors. Initially, all vertices are *white*, then we mark a vertex as *gray* when we visit it, and finally, we mark it as *black* when we leave it, that is, when we remove its first occurrence on the stack after traversing all its outgoing edges.

But what order should we follow when exploring vertices? In BFS, we use a queue to traverse edges in the order we discover them. For DFS, again in a symmetric fashion, we use a stack so that we traverse edges as they are discovered, following paths as far as we can.

Now, what does it mean when we pop a vertex from the stack and discover what color it was marked with?

- If we find a *white* vertex, it's a vertex we haven't explored yet, so we don't learn anything, but we have a lot of work to do: we add its neighbors to the stack and then explore them.

- With a *black* vertex v, we know that we have already fully explored it. Now we have found another vertex u that has an edge to v: thus, we learn that it's not possible to reach u from v.

- If, however, we find a *gray* vertex w, that's a vertex that is not fully explored. Therefore, there is a path in the graph that starts at w and ends at w: we have found a cycle.

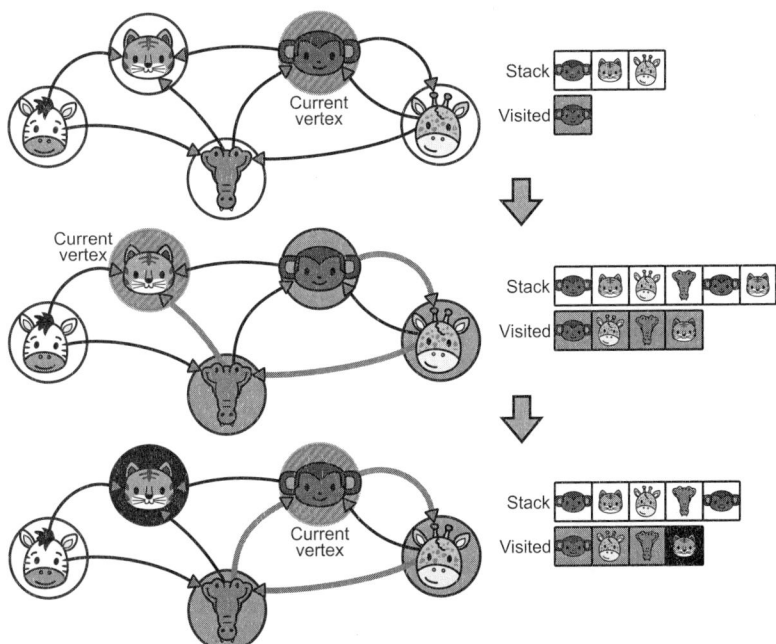

There is a lot more to say about DFS, but now for us, it's time to wrap up and see some code. I have implemented an iterative version of the `dfs` method that uses an explicit stack (as opposed to the queue used by BFS). You should know, however, that it is common to use recursion to implement DFS, implicitly using a call stack to decide the order of the vertices.

With an explicit stack, we need a little trick to know when we are done exploring a vertex. The first time we visit a vertex v, we can push v back on the stack, but that alone is not enough because we could add it again as a neighbor of some other vertex. So, we also need a flag telling us that this is the last occurrence of v on the stack. For this reason, I push a tuple on the stack. The first value in the tuple tells us if we are ready to mark the vertex as black:

```python
def dfs(self, start_vertex, color=None):
    if color is None:
        color = {v: 'white' for v in self._adj}
    acyclic = True
    stack = Stack()
    stack.push((False, start_vertex))
    while not stack.is_empty():
        (mark_as_black, v) = stack.pop()
        col = color.get(v, 'white')
        if mark_as_black:
            color[v] = 'black'
        elif col == 'grey':
            acyclic = False
        elif col == 'white':
            color[v] = 'grey'
            stack.push((True, v))
            for (_, w) in self._get_vertex(v).outgoing_edges():
                stack.push((False, w))
    return acyclic, color
```

This method can be called multiple times with a different start vertex. If a graph isn't strongly connected, it's unlikely we will visit the whole graph with a single call. That's why we return the `color` dictionary along with a Boolean flag that tells us whether DFS found a cycle. We can use the previously marked colors to find out which vertices can be reached from the start vertex and the connected components of the graph (see the tests for this method on GitHub: https://mng.bz/EZ6O).

DFS can traverse all edges and visit all vertices of a graph, so its running time is $O(n+m)$, like for BFS.

What's next

The section on DFS concludes our discussion on graphs, this chapter, and the whole book. If you'd like to learn more about graphs and the algorithms that run on graphs, I recommend the following books:

- *Advanced Algorithms and Data Structures* (M. La Rocca, 2021, Manning)
- *Introduction to Algorithms* (Cormen, Leiserson, Rivest, Stein, 2022, MIT Press)
- *Graph-Powered Machine Learning* (A. Negro, 2021, Manning)
- *Graph Databases in Action* (D. Bechberger, J. Perryman, 2020, Manning)

This is the end of our tour of data structures, and I hope you enjoyed it and are motivated to learn more. Your journey with data structures has just begun, and the wonderful news is that you have many great books to read to learn more about data structures. In addition to classic textbooks such as *Introduction to Algorithms* or *The Algorithms Design Manual*, here are some great Manning books to check out:

- *Grokking Algorithms (Second Edition)* by A. Bhargava is somewhat complementary to this book. It focuses more on algorithms you can run on data structures, such as sorting or searching.
- *Optimization Algorithms* by A. Khamis: Learn about advanced search algorithms, evolutionary algorithms, and machine learning.
- *Advanced Algorithms and Data Structures*: Along with a deeper discussion of graphs, it introduces advanced data structures such as randomized heaps, tries, k-d trees and Ss+Trees, and more.

Recap

- Graphs are much more than containers: they can model relationships between entities (called vertices) connected by edges.
- Graphs are a generalization of trees. Specifically, trees are simple, connected, and acyclic graphs.
- A graph is *simple* if it has at most one edge between any pair of vertices and no loops (that is, an edge from a vertex to itself).
- A graph is *connected* if, given any pair of vertices, it's possible to find a sequence of edges going from one vertex to the other. If a graph is not connected, we can decompose it into its connected components.
- A graph is *cyclic* if it has at least one path that starts and ends at the same vertex; otherwise, the graph is said to be *acyclic*.

- In a *directed* graph, edges can only be traversed in one direction—from their source to their destination. Twitter follows are best modeled using a directed graph. In an *undirected* graph, all edges can be traversed in both directions. An example would be Facebook friendship.

- Graphs are usually implemented using either an *adjacency list* or an *adjacency matrix*. The latter is only used in niche contexts.

- *Breadth-first search* (*BFS*) is an algorithm for traversing graphs and finding paths with the minimum number of edges between a start vertex and the rest of the graph.

- *Depth-first search* (*DFS*) searches the graph by following paths to their end. It can be used to check many properties of the graph, such as whether the graph is connected and has cycles.

index

RELATED MANNING TITLES

Grokking Algorithms, Second Edition
by Aditya Y. Bhargava
Foreword by Daniel Zingaro

ISBN 9781633438538
320 pages, $49.99
February 2024

The Quick Python Book, Fourth Edition
by Naomi Ceder

ISBN 9781633436336
550 pages (estimated), $59.99
Fall 2024 (estimated)

Learn AI-Assisted Python Programming
by Leo Porter and Daniel Zingaro
Foreword by Beth Simon, Ph.D.

ISBN 9781633437784
296 pages, $49.99
September 2023

Advanced Algorithms and Data Structures
by Marcello La Rocca
Foreword by Luis Serrano

ISBN 9781617295485
768 pages, $59.99
May 2021

For ordering information, go to www.manning.com

A new online reading experience

liveBook, our online reading platform, adds a new dimension to your Manning books, with features that make reading, learning, and sharing easier than ever. A liveBook version of your book is included FREE with every Manning book.

This next generation book platform is more than an online reader. It's packed with unique features to upgrade and enhance your learning experience.

- Add your own notes and bookmarks
- One-click code copy
- Learn from other readers in the discussion forum
- Audio recordings and interactive exercises
- Read all your purchased Manning content in any browser, anytime, anywhere

As an added bonus, you can search every Manning book and video in liveBook—even ones you don't yet own. Open any liveBook, and you'll be able to browse the content and read anything you like.*

Find out more at www.manning.com/livebook-program.

*Open reading is limited to 10 minutes per book daily